ORPHAN EAGLES

POLISH ARMIES OF THE NAPOLEONIC WARS

BY

VINCENT W. ROSPOND

WINGED HUSSAR PUBLISHING, LLC

Orphan Eagles: Polish Armies of the Napoleonic Wars

Vincent W. Rospond

ISBN 978-0-9903649-0-0
LCN 2015906233

For more information on Winged Hussar Publishing, LLC, visit us at:

https://www.WingedHussarPublishing.com

Cover art by Peter Dennis (courtesy of Warlord Games)

This book is dedicated to those teachers who encouraged my love of history and endulged my interest in Poland from junior high school through graduate - Mr. Vanderhof, Mr. Kirk, Prof. Futch, Prof. Poter, Prof Jenks, Prof. Hitchens, Prof. Fisher

TABLE OF CONTENTS

Introduction **5**

Origins of the Polish Legions 1795-1807 .... **6**

The Army in Poland **33**

The Coming War – 1812 .... **87**

The 1813 Campaign and the End **93**

Appendix I – Select Biographies **100**

Appendix II – Battles of the Legions in Italy **112**

Appendix III – Battles of the Duchy of Warsaw **120**

Chronology of the Polish Legions **163**

Chronology of Military Operations for the
       Polish-Austrian War of 1809 .... **165**

Chronology of 1812 .... **166**

List of Illustrations **167**

Bibliography **170**

INTRODUCTION

Orphan Eagles is the history of the soldiers who spoke Polish, Lithuanian, Ukrainian, and Belrusian; but acknowledged themselves as citizens of the Commonweath of Two Nations (Poland-Lithuania). They fought for the French Republic and Napoleon from the years 1795 – 1815. For simplicity, I have referred to these soldiers as "Polish," as that was the common name use of that time. The Poles and Imperial France both used "eagles" as symbols for their military, but the Poles never really re-estblished their former frontiers. Despite veiled assurances from Republican and Imperial France, the Poles fought miles away from their homes with a dream of independence that was never achieved. Even in 1814, when most of France's allies had deserted them and it might have been easier to make a deal with the Allies, the Poles fought for Napoleon up to the gates of Paris. They fought under the eagles of Poland and for the eagles of France for over twenty years. Except for five of those years, most were spent without a homeland.

Gembarzewski's excellent work on Polish regiments 1717-1831 served as the framework for this book, along with several of his illustrations, but it has been a subject I have been working on for many years - collecting information and illustrations. It was not the objective of this work to recount all the information on all the battles fought during the Napoleonic era, but just to focus on the Polish contribution to those efforts across several oceans. I have tried to use the Polish spelling where possible, so words that include "ą" would be pronounced "om". I have tried to provide translations of terms where possible; please excuse errors of omission.

-VWR

ORIGINS OF THE POLISH LEGIONS
1795 - 1807

Jan Henryk Dąbrowski – Commander of the Polish Legion in Italy (Julian Kossak, author's collection)

ORIGINS

The death of the Commonwealth, following the Kosciuszko Uprising in 1794 and the subsequent third partition, did not end the armed conflict for many of the officers and soldiers. According to Adam Skałkowski, an estimated 30,000 soldiers of the former Commonwealth of Two Nations were incorporated into the armies of the partitioning countries. As the insurrection was ending, soldiers were finding ways to keep up the fight. According to Pachoński, the first Polish troops used during the revolution arrived in Paris in 1792 – ex-soldiers of the Bar Confederation.[1] An officer of the Commonwealth, Wojciech Turski, tried to solicit help for Poland from Revolutionary France, but his efforts were met without success. In the interim, events in Poland helped to save France as troops from Prussia and Russia were diverted to deal with the Polish uprisings.

According to Knötel, Prince Lubomirski agreed to raise a 1,000 man ułan regiment in 1793, complete with a British version of the lancer uniform, but it did not attract many Poles. In the end it was filled with deserters and mercenaries. It was used for a short time in the Netherlands until it was disbanded.[2]

By the end of 1794, there was a concentration of ex-soldiers in Moldavia and Wallachia, hoping to use Turkey as a base of operations against Russia. The Central Committee of Lwow was founded in January 1796 in Krakow on the heels of the third partition of Poland and the Kosciuszko Insurrection. Soon afterwards, the Committee moved its operations to Lwow. It was composed of mostly rich landowners from Austrian and Russian occupied parts of Poland, with the bulk of them living in Galicia. The Central Committee also had members in Volhynia and former Grand Duchy of Lithuania: its target was a general insurrection, with support of Turkey and revolutionary France.

The first Polish military units were organized in Podolia, Bucovina, and Wallachia in 1795. Polish patriots hoped for an armed conflict between Russia and Turkey, in which they supported the Ottomans for the re-establishment of a Polish nation. Eventually they managed to recruit about 1,700 soldiers in the northern borders of the Ottoman Empire, where they were encouraged by French and English officers to take up arms.

In early March 1797, a group of Polish officers created ZwiazekWojskowy (Military Association), commanded by Joachim Denisko. An "Act of Insurrection" was published, which promised the abolition of social divisions and serfdom. Walerian Dzieduszycki was named military leader of the rebellion, while Karol Kniaziewicz became its civilian leader and speaker of the National Assembly.

In May 1797, after an internal conflict, Denisko was forced to give up his position. As a result of Russian counterintelligence, several members of Central Committee of Lwow were arrested, including Dzieduszycki. Despite these setbacks, on 26 June , Denisko crossed the Austrian-Turkish border near Zaleszczyki with 200 soldiers. Four days later, on 30 June, Austrian forces destroyed the Polish detachment. Some Poles managed to return to Turkey, but those captured were hanged on 11 July near Czerniowce. By the end of July, all Polish military camps were destroyed. Eight prisoners were hung, including a former Guardsman and hero of the Warsaw Insurrection of 1794 – Frederic Mellfort. Revolutionary France encouraged and supported these actions on the border, but after the battles around Bukovina, Francis I issued a special decree in which he announced that insurgents would be sentenced and hanged within twenty-four hours. This sent some soldiers to seek a "pardon" from Austria or Russia; others sought legitimate service with the Porte. Denisko himself fled to Turkey. In 1798 he returned to Volhynia, after the Russian government declared an amnesty. He died in 1812 in Saint Petersburg.

In revolutionary France, the Polish revolutionaries promoted the idea of a Polish legion using Polish prisoners of war in Austrian and Prussian service. While the Third Committee of Public Safety was interested in diverting attention from France in the form of a Polish Insurrection in Turkey, the Constitution of 1795 forbid the employment of foreign troops in the service of the Republic.

---

[1] Jan Pachoński. *Legiony Polskie: Prawda i Legenda.* (WydawnictwoMinisterstwa Obrony Narodowej: Warszawa. 1969), p. 43
[2] Col. John R Elting. Napoleonic Uniforms Vol I. (Macmillan Publishing Co: New York. 1993), p. 36

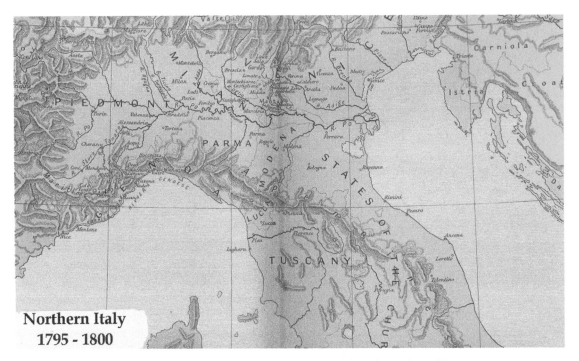

Fig. 1 Northern Italy during the initial operations of the Polish Legions 1797 – 1800

THE POLISH LEGIONS

DĄMBROWSKI'S LEGION

Despite the fact that the Directory forbade foreign troops serving in the French army, this was first ignored in April 1795. Nafziger cites Belhomme as a source for a Polish battalion raised by Gen. Kellerman as part of the 21st Demi-brigade consisting of eight fusiliers and one grenadier company.[1] Records are unclear as to what happened to this battalion, with some authors citing it as the nucleus of the Polish legions in Italy.[2] In the autumn of 1796, however, Napoleon's Armies needed reinforcements in Northern Italy to take advantage of the victories in that area. At the same time, Lt. Gen. Jan Henryk Dąbrowski had been able to make his way to Paris after refusing service in the Russian and Prussian armies. Because Dąbrowski had earned a strong reputation for his campaign against Prussia in 1794, he was the right man in the right place to take advantage of Napoleon's needs. He was allowed to raise detachments of Polish units in the service of the Lombard Republic. This gave the French experienced soldiers who would be more reliable than local troops.

Although there was some hesitation on the part of Napoleon toward Dąbrowski when he arrived in Milan in December 1796, by 20 January 1797, the Convention of San Marco was signed by Napoleon between the government of Lombardy and Dąbrowski for the creation of an auxiliary unit of Polish Legions for the Cisalpine Republic. This set the stage for all the re-constituted Polish troops of the Revolutionary and Napoleonic Wars.

A proclamation was issued from Milan in Polish, German, French, and Italian for distribution around the occupied terrirtories and where the Austrian army was bivouacked:

Fig. 2 Gen. Dąbrowski's Polish Legion uniform (Polish Army Museum)

Poles!
Faithful to my country to the last moment, I fought for her
Freedom under the immortal Kosciuszko; she was oppressed and we
Have nothing but the consoling memory of shedding our blood
For the country of our Forefathers, and seeing our triumphant
Banners at Dubienka, Raclawice, Warsaw and Vilna.
Poles!
Our hope unites us. France is triumphant; she is fighting for the
Cause of the nations; let's try and enfeeble her enemies: she is
Granting us asylum, let us wait for a more favorable moment for
Our Country. Let us gather under her banners, over which preside
Honor and victory.

May Polish Legions be formed in Italy, where already once the
Sanctuary of Freedom shown! The officers and soldiers who
Were companions in troubles and in valor are already here,
The battalions are already being organized.
Come citizens!
Cast away those arms that you were compelled to carry.
Let us fight for the common cause of the nations, for Freedom
Under the valiant Bonaparte, victor in Italy.
The trophies of the French Republic are our only hope,
Thanks to her and to her allies, we will perhaps see again
Those native walls that we so greviously abandoned.

From the Headquarters in Milan, January 20th 1797

---

[1]George Nafziger, *Poles and Saxons of the Napoleonic Wars.* (Chicago:Emperor's Press, 1991), p.61
[2]While some of the members of the legions might have been part of the 21st Demi-brigade, the legions were formed around two companies of Poles aready in Lombard service.

Lieutenant General DABROWSKI

The first Polish Legions resembled the old Polish Army uniforms in design, but with certain local twists. The Poles were regarded as brothers in arms and citizens who would return to Poland when needed, differing them from mercenaries. General Dąmbrowski issued a manifesto calling for Poles to come to Lombardy, "for the common cause of all nations – freedom…when in joy you will again see your families and victoriously restore your own country."

The initial cadre of troops came from former officers living in Poland or exile as well as Poles who were in Austrian service, and then prisoners of the French, as well as deserters. Finally, there were volunteers who travelled across Europe to join the embryonic ranks. It took some time to arm and organize these men, so that they missed the 1797 campaign. By the time of the Peace of Leoben in April 1797, the ranks of the Polish Legions had swelled to 6,000 men.[3] Later that summer, they were organized into two legions of infantry (similar to a French Demi-Brigade), each of three battalions and one battalion of artillery.

In October 1797, the Treaty of Campo Formio confirmed the conditions of the Peace of Leoben, which amounted to an end of hostilities in Northern Italy. By this time, the ranks of the Polish recruits had reached 7,600. The frist legion was placed under the command of Gen. Kniazewicz, the second under the command of Gen. Wielhorski, and the artillery under Gen. Axamitowski. Without the potential for war against Austria, the officers and politicians used the ideology of Revolutionary France combined with the rhetoric of 1794 to hold the troops there and not accept an Austrian "pardon". As advocated by Kosciuszko and others, the soldiers were schooled to become citizens of a "new Poland".

A new "Convention" was agreed upon between the Cisalpine Directory and Dąbrowski in November of 1797, confirming their earlier agreement, but expanding the unique place of the Polish troops in the political and military structure of the Republic, which included the ability to return to Poland if it was restored. In the end, however, this was not ratified by the legislative body as the Legionnaires were increasingly viewed as a tool of the French Revolutionaries over a sister republic.

In December 1797, the Legions were sent into the Papal States under the direction of Generals Dąbrowski and Kniaziewicz. In April 1798, the Legions were designated the first and second demi-brigades, each of 3,201 men. Though they stayed in garrison duty for most of 1798, the Legions took part in the Neapolitan Campaign in December 1798; fighting at Magliano, Falari, Cavi, Gaëta, and Capua. The rewards from the campaign included thirty captured banners that were presented to the Directory in Paris by Gen. Kniaziewicz and enough horses to form a cavalry brigade composed of four squadrons with companies of 116 men each – totalling to 946 men.[4] After the Seige of Gaeta ended on 31 December 1798, the thoroughbreds on the estate of the King of Naples allowed Dąbrowski to organize a second cavalry regiment 400 strong under Maj. Alexander Rozniecki. By this time, the Poles had earned a reputation in Italy for ferocious attacks with their ancient warcry, "God is with Poland!"[5]

Gen Kosciuszko returned to France in 1798, in part because of the formation of the legions. At one point, Talleyrand was going to use him to help raise additional Legions for service in Helvetia and Batavia, but that idea was abandoned, and Kosciuszko believed the French Republic or Napoleon would only use the Poles for their own ends. As a consequence, the former leader of the 1794 insurrection sat out the Revolutionary and Napoleonic wars as an observer, working behind the scenes to help his compatriots.

When Napoleon went to Eygpt, he took part of the Polish Corps with him, including Joseph Grabinski. The Legions suffered their first major setbacks in March 1799. The Second Legion lost two-thirds of its soldiers and its commander, Gen. Rymkiewicz, at the battles on the Adige. The remnants were placed under the command of Gen. Wielhorski and used in the garrison defending Mantua. When the fort surrendered, the secret clause accepted by Gen. Foissac-Latour allowed the Austrians to beat and seize legionnaires as deserters. Many were sent to regiments in chains or deported back to occupied Poland. The outcome of this was the extinction of the Second Legion.

The remainder of the Legion arrived in Naples under the command of Dąbrowski as part of MacDonald's

---

[3]Reddaway quotes 6,000 W.F.Reddaway, et al, *The Cambridge History of Poland: From Augustus II to Pilsudski (1697 – 1935)*. (London: Cambridge University Press 1941) p.221 and Previato quotes 5,000. *Luciano Previato. Le Legioni Polacche in Italia 1797 – 1806*. Magliavacca: Pavia. 1980. p. 4
[4]Previato, p.8
[5]Previato, p. 21

Army of Naples at the battle of Trebbia (17-19 June). As it happened, they primarily faced Russian troops under Suvorov. Of the five remaining battalions, only two were able to survive. The Legion began to face additional loses through the neglect and disorganization of the French Army that was bivouacked in Liguria. Through the summer and fall of 1799, the French forces were pushed into Northern Italy. What was left of the legion regrouped at Massa Carrara and then back to Genoa, where they were joined by other elements of Polish troops under Gen. Karwoski. Maj. Kazimirz Konopka brought 500 newly enlisted recruits from Milan, as well as a detachment of artillery. This allowed Dąbrowski, headquartered in Torriglia, to bring his numbers up to 2,500 men in late July.

It was decided to take both these units into French service, which, although they retained their uniforms, were not accorded the same political concessions they had in Cisalpine service. In 1800, the two legions comprised eleven battalions of infantry, one cavalry regiment, one battalion of foot artillery, and one company of horse artillery amounting to 13,000 troops.[6]

---

[6] W.F.Reddaway, p. 225

Fig 3 Grenadier in the Polish Legion in Italy 1796 (New York Public Library)

Fig 4 Fusilier in the Polish Legion in Italy 1796 (New York Public Library)

THE DANUBE LEGION

By late 1799, Paris decided to organize a new legion under Gen. Kniaziewicz to make up for the men the Second Legion lost at Mantua. This new unit was known as the "Danube Legion". The Danube Legion was considered a light force, though it was organized similar to the Legions in Italy. The artillery company consisted of 73 men, two 8-pounders, two 4-pounders and two 6-inch motars.[7]

In May 1800, the Danube legion was depoyed in Germany, taking part in several actions including operations around Frankfurt. On 3 December, the unit took part in the battle of Hohenlinden, making a flanking movement that helped seal Moreau's victory. They subsequently took part in the follow-up, fighting at Grosskaiserdorf and Lambach.

[7] Morawski, Ryszard and Dusiewicz, Andrzej. Wojsko Polskie w Służbie Napoleona: Legiony Polskie we Włoszech. (Karabela: Warszawa. 2010) p 348

Fig 5 Danube Legion in 1800 by Knötel. Fusilier, Grenadier, Hussar, Horse Artillery in jacket, Ułan, Horse Artillery in dolman (Author's Collection)

HAITI AND THE FIRST LEGION

The Treaty of Lunéville once again created peace in Italy and Germany, which did not work towards the aims of the legions and its leadership. In December 1801, the ułan regiment was withdrawn from the Danube Legion and the Legion was renamed the 3rd Polish Demi-brigade. In March 1802, all the legions were then placed in Italian service and re-organized as Demi-Brigades along French lines. This did not sit well with the more politically minded of the Legion leadership; they openly grumbled and planned action on their own rather than sit in the status quo. At the same time, Gen. Dąbrowski was appointed Inspector General of the Republic of Italy's cavalry.

Since 1800, the French were waging a back and forth battle with Tousant Lovertoure for control of Sant-Domingo. In 1801, Napoleon sent his brother-in-law, General Leclerc, with 22,000 soldiers, along with Gen. Rochembeau, to reclaim the island. The Peace of Amiens in 1802 gave the French the ability to send ships and troops unopposed to the Carribean. In order to get rid of potential political troublemakers, the French Republic sent two Demi-Brigades (over 6,000 men) under Gen. Jabłonowski against their will to battle the uprising in San Domingo (1802). Only 300 men returned; the rest perished, were captured, or went over to the locals because they felt strongly against the mission they were then expected to carry out.[1]

By the summer of 1802, Gen. Leclerc had convinced Napoleon that without additional troops they could not hope to quell the rebellion. The former elite unit of the Polish legions had become a political burden and had received no pay for months. Among the rank and file there were desertions while the officers harassed the French authorities with petitions. The 3rd Demi-brigade, the old Danube Legion, was then stationed at Livorno, where it had been renamed the 113th Demi-brigade. When they found out about the discussion, the soldiers were on the verge of mutiny; some officers attempted to submit their resignation. Dąbrowski protested the decision, but at the same time would not allow the soldiers to go to Turkey after the failed Kamieniec rebellion.

While some new recruits thought of the trip as a chance for fortune and glory, any thoughts of adventure and glory were quickly dissuaded upon disembarking in September 1802. Shortly after their arrival, Gen. Jabłonowski died of yellow fever. The Poles suffered terribly from the heat, and many got sick from the water or eating unripe fruit. Compounding this were the insects and parasites which decimated many Europeans under normal circumstances. The biggest problem however was that the Poles were completely unfit for guerrilla warfare. Unlike the lines and columns of European warfare, Haiti required dispersed formations and independent actions by small groups. The solid formations of the Polish proved not only to be totally inflexible, but also provided excellent targets for snipers.

The first battalion was first deployed in the north of Cap-Français, where the soldiers marched aimlessly through the mountains, occupied blockhouses and redoubts, only to vacate them a little later. They suffered casualties in ambushes without ever seeing the enemy. The situation changed only when two black generals with their troops changed sides to the rebels and Cap-Français itself was threatened. In the hard fighting for the city, the Poles proved their worth for the first time, fighting bravely to ensure the city could be held.

After the action at Cap-Français, the French high command decided on a counter-offensive. The center was formed by two colonial battalions of former slaves, while a Polish and a French battalion covered the flanks. However, when they encountered the enemy, the two colonial battalions switched sides, forcing the French battalion and part of the Poles to withdraw. The remaining Poles were cut off and had to barricade themselves in a building on a plantation; they were burned to death after their ammunition ran out. Those who managed to escape were so decimated by yellow fever by the time they made their way to Le Cap that by the end of the year there were only about 100 men left.

The second battalion, landed in Mole Saint Nicolas with the strength of 701 people. They took part in the battles to regain control of the more important towns there. Because of the perceived treachery by colonial battalions such as the one led by Gen. Dessalines, combined with the brutal nature of the warfare, the area was ripe for atrocities. The remaining black troops were disarmed and many were killed. The second battalion, which had been moved to Saint Marc, was used to disarm the remaining insurgents. A battalion of 400 blacks was disarmed

---

[1] "A Desperate Struggle for Survival" Neil Smith. Wargames Illustrated. Issue 293. March 2012. Pg. 73

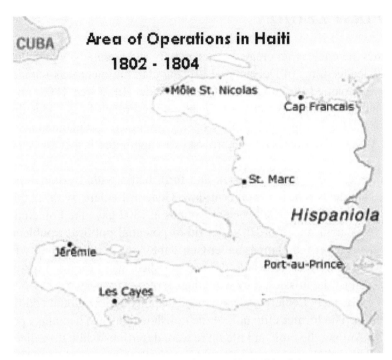

Fig 6 Operations in Haiti 1802-1804 (Wikipedia)

and mustered without weapons; they were then surrounded by French troops and massacred with bayonets. Some begged their white comrades in arms for mercy, others tried to flee into houses; both proved useless, and all were finished off without compassion. The roads must have been littered with corpses for days. Some Polish historians have argued that the Poles were not involved in this massacre, or that they had heroically rejected the command. The sources, however, indicate quite clearly that the Poles played a significant role, even though they weren't the only ones and probably carried out their task with reluctance. After the death of Gen. Leclerc in November 1802, his successor, General Viscount Rochambeau, took the prosecution of the war to a new and more brutal level.

The third battalion, which started out with 634 soldiers, was deployed slightly further west in the region of Plaisance and suffered a similar fate, when in October, the colonial troops under General Dessalines went over to the enemy en masse, many small groups of the third Battalion were totally isolated in the countryside. Few were able to fend for themselves and a good number surrendered to the enemy. The Poles were included in the pacification of the northern mountains and to secure the pathways. On 14 October, they defended the town of Limbe through in house-to-house fighting with numerous counterattacks. However, this did not stop the attacks by the rebels. Through continuous fighting, the battalion suffered significant casualties. On 9 November, they evacuated Cap Francais with 178 soldiers. On 1 December 1802, the remains were incorporated into the French 31st Demi-brigade.

By January 1803, the Poles had been reduced to a few hundred men that were transferred to other units. These remaining troops developed a bad reputation because they were not used to jungle warfare and tended to surrender in perilous situations. The rebels encouraged non-French troops to defect and spared them as prisoners. On hearing the history of Poland, the former slaves saw certain parallels between the miserable fate of the foreign mercenaries to their own. Their hatred was directed against the French, especially the white militias, who were the most racist. Most mercenaries by contrast lacked both the racial arrogance of the native whites and their desire for revenge.

At Rochambeau's insistence, another auxiliary corps of 12,000 men, including the 2nd Polish Demi-brigade was sent to Haiti. By this stage, enough was known about the situation in Haiti for there to be no doubt that most soldiers were being sent to certain death. Consequently, the mood among the troops was bleak and desertions became more frequent. After a promise to pay arrears and better conditions, 2,500 men were finally mustered in Genoa. The officers looked on this as an opportunity, which underscored the differences between them and the rank and file.

Fig 7. Poles in San Domingo (January Suchodolski)

Many volunteered because they had been put on half-pay or were entirely without money. As emigrants they were leading a miserable life, and had often accumulated significant debts. Only two took their leave, and were replaced without a problem.

Rochambeau had a high opinion of the Poles, being familiar with their actions in Italy and Germany. Unfortunately, the experience of European battles did not come in handy on the island, where the enemy used different tactics – particularly guerrilla warfare. In addition, the Poles did not fight as a whole unit; the battalions were assigned to different areas and were often used as smaller units in isolated areas for specific purposes. There was no communication between local colonial forces and the Republican forces, which resulted in heavy losses. The initial strength of the Wodziński battalion was 984 men. Subjected to ambushes and lack of support, the battalion only had 150 men left a year later.

The 2nd Demi-brigade arrived in time for Rochambeau's spring offensive in the south, which was to be conducted by three columns against enemy bases on the southwestern peninsula. The newcomers were totally unable to adapt to their new circumstances and suffered the same fate as the 3rd Demi-brigade. When, for example, a column marched through a narrow valley which was blocked by a barricade of felled trees, the Polish infantry attacked in solid formation with fixed bayonets, and received heavy fire not only from the front, but both flanks. To penetrate the jungle on the flanks, they would have needed machetes which they didn't have, and furthermore they weren't used to such maneuvers. In the end, they were forced to retreat after suffering heavy losses. Since nobody thought of moving the troops by sea, they dragged their guns under unspeakable hardships over mountain paths, fell into ambushes, and were ultimately decimated.

Soon the shattered remnants of the columns had to withdraw. Emboldened by these successes, the rebels, now with a strong army, launched an attack on the city of Les Cayes. In this open warfare, the Poles were able to show once again that they could fight. They bravely defended the crumbling ramparts and when the enemy entered the city, a counterattack by the Polish infantry gave the gunners the necessary time to adjust their guns, with which the attack was finally repelled. But this victory did nothing to halt the yellow fever claiming so many men. The French were now no longer capable of offensives and tried only to keep the cities. If this was not possible, they had to withdraw with heavy losses to the next base.

The situation worsened dramatically in spring of 1803, when war with Great Britain broke out again. That meant new weapons for the rebels and a blockade of the sea by British ships. The French retreated to the three biggest cities in the south: Jérémie, Les Cayes, and Port-au-Prince. By this stage, everyone was simply holding out for the end. The Poles and other foreign mercenaries began to defect at a higher rate. The first attack by the rebels started in July on Jérémie, but they no longer made the same mistake as they had with their attack on Les Cayes.

They enclosed the city from the land side while the British ships blocked supplies from sea. The garrison of the city consisted mostly of mulattoes from the National Guard, many of whom went over to the enemy, along with several hundred Poles and Frenchmen. Although some ships succeeded in slipping through the blockade at night, supply was increasingly becoming a problem.

With the arrival of the 114th Demi-brigade, Gen. Rochambeau wanted to take the offensive. They took part in the operations around Cayes, where the Poles helped to defend the city, thanks to high morale. The attackers took great losses, but this joy was overshadowed by the fever that caused greater losses from enemy bullets. Further fighting to defend the fortified points in May and June 1803 caused increasing losses.

The main rebel effort was directed at the French defences from November onward. Guerrilla attacks whittled the size of the armed forces, and without reinforcements from Europe, it was impossible to take offensive action. Poles fought as a component of mixed fighting formations. Similar incidents of atrocities occurred in February on the island of Tortuga, as occurred elsewhere on the island. Losses increased, especially through fever. The 113th Demi-brigade losses were so severe that at the end of March there was a discussion about removing them from the register of active units.

The renewal of war with England accelerated an already hopeless situation . When the supplies finally ran out, the commander of Jérémie decided to abscond at night to Cuba in the remaining ships with the soldiers. This withdrawal was to remain secret at all costs. They decided to sacrifice the 140 Poles who were stationed in the citadel and 40 French who were defending a river crossing in front of the city. Ignominiously, the Polish officers were also informed of the plan, and used the opportunity to make off with the French; leaving their men to their fates. The British intercepted the greater part of the ships and brought the prisoners to Jamaica, but three ships with 250 men managed to reach Cuba. There, the commanding general and the other officers became primarily concerned with writing their memoirs to justify their "heroic" deeds while blaming each other. Meanwhile, when the rebels entered Jérémie on the next day, the Poles in the citadel were allowed to surrender honourably. The rebel general Ferrou explained the treachery of their superiors, showing them the mutilated bodies of the 40 Frenchmen, but was willing to give them mercy if they were forced to fight. During the siege of Jérémie, Polish and German deserters in the army of Rebel General Ferrou discussed the role of the Poles. There were many rumors about Polish deserters fighting for Dessalines, most probably greatly exaggerated, though it was not unusual for prisoners to take that route in order to save their own lives. Without doubt there were some genuine defectors who were sick of receiving only empty promises instead of pay while watching their officers enrich themselves at their expense. Rumours even circulated that Dessalines himself kept a bodyguard of 30 Poles. In any case, foreign deserters were appreciated by the rebels since they could provide needed roles as artillerymen, as instructors, and also repairing weapons. German and Swiss mercenaries are mentioned as well, but the Poles apparently enjoyed special esteem. In the opinion of Dessalines, they were "the white slaves of Europe". This point of view might not have been entirely wrong and is illustrated by another event; of the prisoners which the British kept in Jamaica, a British captain bought 120 men for $74 per head and sold them later to the British army as soldiers for a sizeable profit.

After the fall of Jérémie, the rebels started laying siege to Les Cayes. When food ran out there, the French commander negotiated with the British. To save their own skins the French abandoned the mulattoes and the sick to the vengeance of the victors, who massacred thousands. The British and their prisoners watched the bloody carnage safely from aboard the ships. Refugees who tried to reach the ships were slaughtered in the water directly in front of them. This also provided material for the justification documents and memoirs which the officers for the French would write later in the prisoner camps. In Port-au-Prince a large part of the garrison were successful in secretly escaping by night to Cuba. About a month later, the last two French bases in Haiti - Le Cap-Francais and Môle-Saint-Nicolas - fell in the north. The garrison from Môle-Saint-Nicolas managed to slip through the British blockade and escaped to Cuba, while those at Le Cap-Francais fell into British captivity.

Those who survived the fighting and made it to captivity were not done with their troubles. About 7,000 prisoners in English captivity were transported to Jamaica. They were treated worse than most prisoners of the day. Breaches of the capitulation agreements were committed such as personal belongings being taken away, uniforms stolen, and abysmal housing and food. The rank was often forcibly conscripted into the English regiments. Officers placed in Spanishtown and Kingston, where in time with the means to travel, were released on parole. Privates, having no chance of release found themselves in a difficult situation. They were divided and the seriously wounded and sick returned to the United States under the protection of the French consul in Charleston. A total of 36 then returned to France. Lightly wounded and sick were in captivity in the hospital, where they died, or were able to return to good health. The third group was a capable military service and sent back to England. The lack of proper POW camps kept the prisoners in floating prisons of receiving ships. Horrible living conditions caused high mortality. While recruiters offered a chance of survival, when this did work by free will, recruiting parties might resort to beatings and special treatment. It is estimated that approximately 1,000 former legionnaires entered British service in this manner, mainly to the 60th Regiment, who was later involved in the fighting in Spain. The other prisoners were in different places of the British Isles, of which there were still 6 officers and 72 Polish soldiers in 1814.

Approximately 40 Poles were able to evacuate to Havana from Jeremie and Port au Prince in October 1803. The Poles were kept in camps at the expense of France with limited movement. In December they were joined by an additional 80 who left with Gen. Noailles. By this time, the camp held about 200 former legionnaires under the command of Capt. Berensdorff. A third group of soldiers were in the eastern part of San Domingo, near the capital under Gen. Ferrand. In December 1803 there were still 800 soldiers fighting, including 75 Poles. While they sought help from Cuba, there was none coming, so they began to use bases in that part of the island for "pirate" like actions against isolated settlements and shipping. These insurgents attacked Santa Domingo on 6 March 1805. Despite some initial successes, disease took its toll. The last of these troops surrendered on 8 July 1809 almost seven years after they first arrived and more than five years after the island effectively fell. There were still approximately 40 Poles in their ranks. In 1807, some officers managed to return to Europe under parole and began serving in the army of the Duchy of Warsaw.

Most of those who went with the Polish Demi-brigades to the Caribbean didn't make it back to France. At the end of 1803, only 12 of the officers from the 113th Demi-brigade had survived. About 300 rankers survived the return to France in addition to the 150 serving with the 60th regiment in Spain. There were still some serving in the English ranks at the Battle of New Orleans in 1815, where they managed to desert to the American lines. Many stayed in Santa Domingo where they made new lives among the islanders.

One Demi-Brigade and one cavalry regiment remained in Italy, fighting at Castel Franco (24 November 1805) and Maiella (Santa Euphemia, 3 July 1806). Supernumerary officers were gradually pressed into French service in 1805 and 1806. By this time, Dąbrowski commanded as a General de Division in Italian service in Abruzzi. On 4 August 1806, Napoleon ordered all the Polish regiments in the Italian army into service with the Kingdom of Naples. When war broke out with Prussia, Dąbrowksi was ordered to encourage insurrection against Prussia, reminiscent of his last campaign of 1794.

Fig 8 Dąbrowski in Italy 1800 (Walski, Brown University Collection)

THE LEGION OF THE NORTH AND THE WIELKOPOSKA UPRISING

When war broke out between France and Prussia in 1806, Napoleon once again sought to make use of Polish soldiers in Prussian service as well as prisoners of war. On 20 September 1806, he issued a decree creating the Legion of the North under Gen. Zajączek. Napoleon hedged his bet about angering the Prussians, by not calling upon the Poles, but calling for the "children of the north, the fearless warriors".[1] Napoleon brought Dąbrowski to his HQ at Potsdam after Jena where they began negotiations on a 40,000 man Polish Army. For his part, Dąbrowski demanded that Napoleon issue a manifesto to the Polish nation and Polish administration into any new lands conquered by the French. He only approved of a proclamation written by Wybicki and signed by Dąbrowski (4 November 1806) which he said he would, "...see whether the Poles are worthy to be a nation."

The 1806 Greater Poland Uprising was organized by General Dąbrowski to help advance French forces under Napoleon in liberating Poland from Prussian occupation. The Wielkopolska Uprising was a decisive factor in the formation of the Duchy of Warsaw (1806) and the inclusion of Wielkopolska in that state.

Prussia gained vast areas of Polish territory during the partitions of Poland, and the War of the Fourth Coalition against Prussia gave hope to the Polish inhabitants of Wielkopolska for recovering their independence. There were so many recruits, that two days later Napoleon decided to form a second Legion of the North. Because of the potential of conflict, Prussia could only maintain a small number of garrison troops in Wielkopolska and a large portion of those soldiers were Polish nationals. This caused a great deal of trouble for Prussian commanders; between 1 November and 20 December, 3,000 Polish troops deserted from the Toruń Corps. The legions were organized like light infantry units in the French army. Each legion was to have four battalions composed of seven chausser companies, one carabiner, and one voltiguer compny. By October, recruitment for the second legion did not accumulate many troops and it was thus incorporated into the first legion.

Dąbrowski and Wybicki entered the Poznań on 3 November 1806, leading the first units of the French army. Their arrival became a large Polish patriotic demonstration. On this same day, Dąbrowski called Poles to stand with arms on Napoleon's side and fight against Prussian occupation. Dąbrowski and Wybicki created Voivodship Commissions (Komisja wojewódzka) whose tasks were to take administrative control and keep the area quiet, preventing infighting.

By the time Dąmbrowski arrived at Poznań on 6 November, an insurrection had already broken out. Officers from the legions and veterans from the time of the Partitions organized units. This insurrection took Kalisz, along with the garrison, money, and stores. By 18 November, they attacked the fortress at Częstochowa and forced its garrison to capitulate. As it liberated territories, the Polish insurrection authorities established armed units.

Large groups of insurrectionists were formed in Kalisz and Konin. On 10 November, Polish fighters engaged in battles against Prussian troops near Ostrzeszów and Kepno. By 13 November, the uprising spread to the area around Sieradz. The most difficult fighting took place in the Bydgoszcz Department where Gen. Amilikar Kosiński faced the largest concentration of Prussian soldiers left in the interior, an uncooperative French commander and raw recruits.

Dąbrowski consolidated his position by decreeing every ten houses should produce one fully equipped foot soldier and every tenth horse, which would have amounted to 36,000 soldiers. At the time of the rising, politicians, including Napoleon, looked to Kościuszko to take lend support to the new regime, but he would not come unless Napoleon guaranteed the restoration of the Commonwealth. Prince Jozef Poniatowski had stayed in Warsaw away from politics, but realising that the French were going to create some sort of rump Polish state, decided to return to active service.

On 1 January 1807, Dąbrowski received the hetman's bulawa [2] of the great leader Stefan Czarnicki, but while Dąbrowski was popular with the troops Poniatowski had political support. There was a problem in that Dąbrowski had control of the military, while Poniatowski had a military and political authority from his uncle and the 1792 war against Russia. The two men did not get along, and many had ill-will against the Prince because of his

[1] Reddaway, p. 226

[2] The was a war mace signifying command of field armies from the old Commonwealth

connection to the former King and the belief that he favored Austria. In Napoleon's decree of 14 January 1807, he established a Governing Commission of five ministers and gave Poniatowski the position of Minister of War.

On 3 January, the existing units of planned divisions from the Poznań and Kalisz Departments were ordered to form one brigade from each Department. The Commander of the Poznań Brigade was Gen. Wincenty Axamitowski and the Kalisz Brigade was commanded by Gen. Stanisław Fiszer. Both brigades of infantry formed a division commanded by Gen. Dąbrowski. Brigades were strengthened by 300 cavalry, in addition to the unit from the Warsaw Department under the command of Lt. Col. Jan Michał Dąbrowski. This group was designated to meet in Bydgoszcz. On 16 January, the Legion consisted of 4,966 soldiers.

At the same time, Amilkar Kosiński, who had been continuously fighting since December, won the battle of Koronow and marched to Świecie. Soldiers of the Poznań Division staying near Bydgoszcz advanced on Gniezno and Tczew. Poniatowski ordered a part of the Pospolite Ruszenie (general levy of the szlatcha) organized in this area which weakened the Poznań Division and caused it to disband. After that, only the troops of Gen. Kosiński were fighting in this area.

After reorganization, the Poznań Division was composed of 6 battalions of infantry, 3 squadrons of cavalry, and 2,000 pospolite ruszenie commanded by Gen. Michał Sokolnicki. On 15 February, cavalry again captured Dirschau (Tczew), but was once again forced to retreat. On 23 February, the whole division attacked the town which was defended by a strong Prussian garrison. After 7 hours of battle, Poles captured Tczew, but Gen. Dąbrowski was wounded, forcing him to leave his division for a while, and his son was badly injured as well. Therefore, Col. Dąbrowski was promoted to the rank of General de Brigade and moved to the Invalide Corps. After the battle, Gen. Kosiński became the new division commander.[3]

Earlier, in January 1807, Dąbrowski had formed a division group commanded by Col. Garczyński from the Poznań troops. In February 1807, Garczyński's group was subordinated to Gen. Kosiński and later, with some troops of pospolite ruszenie,[4] was sent to fight near Neustettin. At this time, the troops of Sokolnicki captured Stolp and later took part in the siege of Gdansk, which surrendered in May. After the capture of Danzig, Polish troops fought in Napoleon's campaign in Poland, including Freidland. At the beginning of 1808 this unit became the 5th and 6th Infantry regiments of the Duchy of Warsaw.

[3]Dezydery Chlapowski. Memoirs of a Polish Lancer. Emperor's Press: Chicago. 1992. pp 8-31
[4]Noble levy – any noble was required to come with his retainers

Fig 9 The Siege of Danzig 1807 (Lorenz, Brown University Collection)

UNIFORMS

POLISH LEGIONS IN ITALY

As Dąmbrowski had requested, the initial uniforms of the Polish troops of 1797 were based on the styles worn by the troops of the Polish-Lithuanian Commonwealth in the 1792-94's. The jacket was based on the kurtka, a short skirted, closed lapel jacket worn by infantry and cavalry units in 1792. Grenadier uniforms were modeled after the Polish cavalry national. They consisted of dark blue pants and jacket with crimson lapels, collar, cuffs and rear turnbacks. The light infantry wore a similar uniform with green destinctions. This uniform was modelled after the 3rd Infantry regiment of the Duchy of Lithuania – The Grand Hetman's regiment. The fusiliers had light blue distinctions. Shoes were black leather that came to mid-calf. The trouser had a stripe down the outside in the facing color; the pant leg was inserted into the shoe. A red-white-and-green kontrepolet in the colors of Lombardy with the inscription "Gli uomini sono liberi fratelli," was worn on the right shoulder. The fusiliers and grenadiers both wore four-cornered hats similar to the czapka worn by the ułan cavalry, while the light infantry wore broad brimmed hats, similar to those worn by the Republic's light infantry. All the hats had red and white cords. All troops soon wore the czapka with black lamb's wool around the lower base without a visor. The top half of officer hats was red, while the infantrymans' was blue.

In May 1797, the two legions were proposed to be uniformed as follows: the jackets and pants continued to be navy blue. The distinctions and turnbacks were organized in the colors of Lombardy. The First Legion had to have white lapels, red collars, and red and green flaps and turnbacks. The Second Legion had green lapels and white collars with red flaps and turnbacks. This proposal was not accepted by Dabrowski. Eventually, the basic color of the uniform remained navy blue. The czapka remained dark blue, with a crimson band about three inches wide, surmounted by a thin white band. Battalion colors were based on the regiments of the Commonwealth. The uniforms were organized accordingly as I Battalion 1st Legion - crimson turnbacks, silver epaulettes, and buttons based on the national cavalry; II / 1 – turnbacks were green and gold buttons modeled on the 3rd Infantry regiment of the Grand Hetman; III / 1 was based on the 10th regiment that had yellow distinctions and silver buttons. The piping for the first legion was white.

Fig 10 Polish infantry of the Lombard Legion 1796 (Walski, Brown University Collection)

Fig 11 The 1st Legion – I, II, III Battalions 1797 (Walski, Brown University Collection)

For the 2nd Legion: I / 2nd Battalion - black lapels and silver buttons based on the 8th Radziwill Infantry regiment of the grand Duchy; II / 2 used the 16th Crown Infantry regiment which had blue lapels, edged in red and silver buttons. The III / 2 were based on the 2nd Wodzicki Crown Infantry regiment or 3rd Crown Infantry with red distinctions and silver buttons. For economic reasons the soldiers used their "current uniforms" until they wore out. Only III / 2 Legion received their regulated color. The second legion was piped crimson.

In the autumn of 1798, the uniforms were reorganized again. The legions retained dark blue as the basic color, but the 1st Legion wore crimson facings, while the 2nd wore "poppy"facings. The czapkas were blue with red-white piping. Plumes for the 1st battalions were blue-red-white for fusiliers, red over white for grenadiers, and green over white for light infantry. For the 2nd battalions, it was red-white-blue for fusiliers, red over red for grenadiers, and green over red for light infantry. For the third battalions, the plumes were white/blue/red for fusiliers, red over blue for grenadiers, and green over blue for light infantry.[1] The battalions were differentiated by the felt (baize) cap bands. For the 1st Legion: 1st battalion – crimson, 2nd battalion – green and 3rd battalion – yellow. For the 2nd Legion: 1st battalion – black, 2nd battalion – blue and the 3rd battalion – poppy.

In 1800, the Polish Legion continued the uniform of dark blue with crimson distinctions. The czapka was made taller, similar to the height of the cavalry czapka. These had a dark blue top, a black band with a leather visors. Officers wore a fringed sash of red and white.

In 1801, when the Legions were turned into Demi-brigades, they were given yellow distinctions. When the 2nd emi-brigade was made the 114th Line Demi-brigade, some were given French tropical uniforms, but many kept their czapkas.

In 1806, those units that remained in Italy were given yellow distinctions. They had round, rather than pointed cuffs on the kurtkas, and the shoulder straps of the fusiliers were piped yellow. The trousers had a yellow stripe down the side. Drummers seem to have the same uniform, but with wide white lace on the edges and yellow swallow-tails on the shoulders also with white lace. By this time, the czapkas had acquired a sunburst plate. They wore a French cockade on the left side under the pompom of the company and red cords for grenadiers, green for voltiguers, and white for fusiliers.

The cavalry that was formed in 1798 were uniformed similar to Polish Towarzycz cavalry. They were given dark blue kurtkas with crimson facings. The trousers were also dark blue with crimson side stripes. Their czapkas were a little taller than those of the infantry, also without visors. The band was crimson with a thin white band above that. The top of the czapka was also dark blue. They were armed with lances, sabers, pistols, and carbines. The saddle cloth was dark blue edged red-white-red.

By 1799, the czapkas were worn with or without black leather visors. The czapka is trimmed in white, with white cords. The plumes followed the same rules as the infantry. The lance was striped white, red and blue, or black. The initial lance pennants were swallow-tailed blue/white/red.

Knötel shows a lancer from 1799 in dark blue czapka with a black base and visor. The cords were red with a red plume over a red/white/blue cockade. The uniform was dark blue with crimson collar and cuffs piped white. The lapels were dark blue, piped crimson, as were the trousers. The girdle was dark blue piped crimson with a tricolor front. The jacket had red epaulettes and the lance penant was red/white/blue.[2]

In 1800, the lower part of the czapka was crimson. The plumes were in the squadron colors. The saddle cloth was white sheepskin edged in red. The lance penants were swallow-tailed with a triangle in the middle, while the top and bottom were different colors. For the first squad it was blue/white/red. The second squad was red/white/blue.

Trumpeters had red jackets with ochre distinctions, edged in white. The cuffs were pointed. There were white antiguettes on the left side. The bugle cords were red. The Hungarian trousers were also ochre with red side stripes and Hungarian knots. The czapka was ochre with a black fur lower half, white cords, and red over white plume. The saddle cloth was white lambswool edged red.

In 1803, the uniform was dark blue. The turnbacks, collar, and lapels were edged in yellow. The cuffs were yellow, pointed. The breeches had yellow side piping and Hungarian knors. The czapka was blue with a white wool bottom, edged in yellow. The plume was worn on the left – red topped with white. The lance penant was top red,

[1] Morawski, p. 346
[2] Elting, Vol I, p. 220

bottom green and white fly. The lance was striped white, red, and green.

In 1805, the czapka had a dark blue top, a black felt bottom, with a white leather strip separating them. It was edged in white with white cords. The black leather visor was edged in brass and brass chinscales. A French cockade was worn on the left with a red plume, topped with white. The distinctions remained yellow for the jacket and trousers. White metal shoulder boards were worn on both shoulders. The lance was black lacquered. The swallow tailed pennant had three equal horizontal stripes of red-white-blue. The saddle cloth was dark blue edged with a broad yellow. In the back corner was an imperial "N" under a crown. The pistol holders were covered by white lambswool edged yellow.

In 1797 the uniform of the three companies of legion artillery incorporated elements of the Cisalpine army with traditional elements of the Polish-Lithuanian artillery. This consisted of a green kurtka with black lapels, collar, and cuffs with red piping, epaulettes, and skirts. The rest of the uniform consisted of white vest, green trousers with black side stripes, and black gaiters. According to Morawski, the headgear was a dark blue czapka with a visor, a black wool band surmounted by a white band. The czapka had a French cockade. The cords were gold and the plume was red. In 1798, some units used the habit-vest with the white vest showing through. The turnbacks were red and the collar, lapels, cuffs, and cuff flaps were edged in red.[3]

In 1799, the czapka was dark green felt with a black fur band for enlisted men. For officers, the black fur had a white felt band on top of that. A French cockade was worn on the left side of the czapka with a red plume. The kurtka and trousers were dark green. The collar, lapels, turnbacks, and pointed cuffs were black and the buttons were black. The officers had all this edged in silver. The belting was white.

Sappers also wore a dark green uniform with light green lapes, turnbacks, collars, and round collars. The epaulettes were medium green edged in red. They wore a black, broad brimmed hat edged in red/white cords. A French cockade was worn in the front and a light green plume was worn on the left side.

In 1798, the adjutants were dressed in a kutka and trousers like the cavalry, but their distinctions were light blue. They wore a traditional Polish sash around their waists of red and silver with fringed ends. The czapka was light blue with a black wool band. It was edged in white cords. A French cockade was worn on the left side with a white plume. The saddle cloth was dark blue edged red/white/red.

In 1803, adjutants wore a czapka that was crimson on top, a white felt middle band, and a black fur band on the bottom. The French cockade was on the left with a white plume. The jacket was dark blue with crimson col-

---

[3] Morawski, Ryszard and Dusiewicz, Andrzej. Wojsko Polskie w Służbie Napoleona: Legiony Polskie we Włoszech. Karabela: Warszawa. 2010. Pp. 168-169

Fig 12 Legion Cavalry Officer 1799 (JOB, Author's Collection)

Fig 13 Polish Infantry 1799 (Maciej Szcezpamczyk, Wikipedia)

lars, lapels, turnbacks, and cuffs. A white metal fringed shoulder board was worn on the right side. The trousers were dark blue with a crimson stipe down the side.

DANUBE LEGION

The cavalry had a dark blue czapka with a black fur band, black leather visor, and red plume. They wore a dark blue kurtka and trousers. The kurtka had crimson distinctions with white piping and yellow buttons. They had a golden aiguiltte on the right shoulder and a contre-epaulette on the left. The saddle cloth was white sheepskin, edged red or black edged white and crimson. The lance pennant had three horizontal lines of red, white, and blue.

In 1801, the basic unform remained the same, but the cuffs, collar, and lapels were edged in white. The trousers had silver buttons down the leg in the crimson stripe. The czakpa was light blue with a black leather base and black visor. The cords and plume were red. The French cockade was on the left side. Black girdle edged crimson was worn around the waist. For the first squadron, the lance penant was blue/white/red. The second squadron was white/red/blue. The third squadron was red/white/blue. By 1801, the lance was striped white/red/blue. The trumpeters wore red plesses with blue collars and cuffs piped white with white lace. They had black shakos with white cords and red plumes. By 1802, they had ułan style uniforms, but the coat was red, faced yellow; the czapka was yellow. The breeches were yellow trimmed red.

The horse artillery had a lace dolman similar to French chasseurs with crimson piping, cuffs, and aiguillettes. Gunners wore both the mirlitron and the czapka. The trumpeters wore a red dolman trimmed in white. The collar and cuffs were medium blue, edged white. The Hungarian trousers had a white stripe down the side and Hungarian knots in the front. The cap was a black mirlitron with a French coackade on the left side along with a red plume and white cords.

Early in 1800, the infantry was uniformed in French coats – dark blue with crimson collars, cuffs, flaps, and shoulder straps all edged in crimson. The lapels were white edged in crimson. Trousers were white with blue horizontal stripes. Their headgear was a black bicornes with a French cockade. Morawski shows a drummer for

Fig 14 Danube Legion Chasseur (Gembarzewski author collection)

Fig 15 Danube Legion Grenadier (Gembarzewski author Collection)

the legion in a blue kurtka with crimson cuffs and collar piped white. The coat had red epaulettes. The trousers were yellow with a red stripe down the side. The headgear was a light blue czapka with a black band and visor. The czapka was piped white with a red plume and cords.[4] Later the infantry wore dark blue kurtka and trousers. The kurtka had crimson distinctions piped white. Grenadiers had red epaulettes and the light infantry had green epaulettes. All the belting was black leather. The czapka was light blue with a black band around the base and a black leather visor. The cords were in the color of the company with a French cockade.

The pontonniers wore green jackets with red collars, cuffs, and turnbacks. The jacket was not closed and showed a grey vest underneath. They had tan britches with black gaiters. They had black leather belting. The hats were broad brimmed with the right side turned up with red cords and plume, like the artillery.

HAITI

Initially the troops of the 2nd and 3rd Demi-brigades wore thier proscribed uniforms. For the 3rd Demi-brigade, it was dark blue kurtkas with dark blue trousers and black gaiters. Cuffs, collars, and lapels were crimson with no piping. The czapkas were dark blue with black felt bases and leather visors. The czapkas were piped white with white cords and a French cockade on the left.

For the 2nd Demi-brigade, the uniform was the same as the 3rd, but with yellow distinctions, and the seams also piped yellow. The shoulder straps of the fusiliers were also piped in yellow. The leatherwork was white.

[4]IBID, p. 191

Fig 16 Polish Legionnaire in summer dress in Haiti

Fig 17 Officer of the 114 demi-brigade in San Domingo by an English officer

Eventually, the jackets were cut to waistcoats, worn open to the shirt beneath. White linen trousers were also worn in addition to the standard blue.

THE POLISH-ITALIAN LEGION

The infantry continued to wear a dark blue kurtka and trousers. The distinctions are yellow for the collar, lapels, and turnbacks. For the first and second regiments, the cuffs were yellow. For the third regiment, the cuffs were blue with yellow piping. The czapka was black felt with the lower part leather with leather visor. The czapka had brass chinscales. Enlisted men did not have cords on their czapkas. The French cockade was worn in the front or left side. In some cases the regimental number is shown on the front of the lower czapka. [5] Officers wore the French habite-vest using the same coloring for distinctions.

Sappers wore the same uniform, but had a white leather apron over it with white work gloves. They carried axes and wore a bearskin hat with red cords and plumes. The bearskin had a brass sunplate with the regimental number in the middle.

The cavalry wore the same uniform as the infantry – dark blue with yellow distinctions. The czapka had a dark blue felt top with a black leather base. There was a white felt band between the top and bottom halves. The czapka had a brass sunburst plate in the front with an imperial eagle in the center. The cords were white.

In 1807, the kurtka was dark blue. The cuffs, lapels, collar, and turnbacks were yellow. The troopers had blue shoulder straps edged yellow; the elite company had red fabric epaulettes. The trousers were blue with a yellow side strip and silver buttons. The czapka had a yellow top and black leather bottom with a visor. The cords were white, as well as the plume. The French cockade was worn on the left. The lance pennant had three hotizontal srtipes – blue/white/red.

Trumpeters wore reserved colors on the kurtka; yellow jackets with blue distinctions. The czapka had a yellow top, edged in blue. The plume was white with a red top. The cockade was on the left side.

THE LEGION OF THE NORTH

The unifom was the same dark blue kurtka with crimson facings and piping, similar to the Italian legions with dark blue trousers and black knee high gaiters. They had silver buttons with the inscription, "Legion du Nord". The headgear was a black felt czapka with a black felt base and leather visor. They had a brass faceplate of a rising sun and a French cockade. The plumes, pompom, and cords depended on the company. The carabiners wore red, the voltiguers yellow, and the chassuers light blue (Knötel calls them fusiliers).

---

[5] IBID, p. 287

ORGANIZATION AND UNITS

LOMBARD LEGION

Each legion consisted of two "demi-légions", each of three battalions and one artillery company. In February 1797, 1,128 men were divided into two, five company battalions. Initially, the first battalion was called a "grenadier", the second called a "chasseur". By June, the six battalions were reorganized into eight fusilier, one grenadier, and one chasseur companies, each company consisting of 178 soldiers.

By July 1797, there were two legions, each composed of three battalions with an artillery company equipped with 4-lbs. There was also squadron of chasseurs. Each battalion had ten companies organized like a Polish battalion from 1792. Each battalion had a staff of one battalion chief, one major, one captain adjutant major, one quartermaster, one chief surgeon, one adjutant NCO, one drum major, one sergeant, and twenty sappers. Each company had three company officers (captain, lieutenant, and 2nd lieutenant), eight NCO's (one staff sergeant, four sergeants, one fourrier-captain,[1] and eight corporals) and one hundred six soldiers (including two drummers)[2].

In September 1798, the legions were reorganized again. Still consisting of ten companies, it now had one grenadier and one chasseur company. Each company was one hundred twenty men. The artillery battalion had three companies, each of one hundred one men. The ulans consisted of two companies of one hundred sixteen cavalrymen. Each company maintained Polish cavalry terms: three officers (captain, lieutenant, and 2nd lieutenant), eleven NCO's (sergeant-major, four sergeants, fourrier, eight brigadiers (corporals)), two trumpeters, and ninety-six ulans.

DANUBE LEGION

Initially this formation had four battalions, each of 10 companies of 120 men. There were also four cavalry squadrons, made up of 2 companies consisting of 116 troopers per squadron. Finally, there was a horse artillery company of 76 artillerymen. The horse artillery company had two 8-lb, two 4-lb and two 6-inch howitzers.

THE LEGION REORGANIZED

In early 1800, the three legions were organized into four battalions of ten companies (one grenadier, one chasseur, and eight fusiliers), each of 123 men. The artillery battalion had five companies.

DEMI-BRIGADES

In January 1802, the legions were re-organized into Demi-brigades. The first and second demi-brigades had three battalions and the third had four. Each battalion at this point had nine companies of one grenadier and eight fusiliers. The grenadier company consisted of 84 soldiers and the fusilier companies had 123 soldiers.

In April 1802, the battalions were reduced to eight companies, consisting of six fusiliers, one grenadier, and one chasseur companies.[3] The cavalry was organized as a regiment of 946 troopers.

THE ITALIAN-POLISH LEGION

In April 1807, the legions in Italy were organized into one lancer regiment (4 squadrons of 300 men) and an infantry legion of three regiments. Each regiment had two battalions of 9 companies each. Each company consisted of 150 soldiers. The legion staff consisted of 100 men.

---

[1] Essentially a company level quartermaster responsible for feeding or supplying the troops

[2] Jan Pachonski, Legiony Polskie, Vol I, p 278

[3] IBID, p.260

Fig 18 Legion Cavalry, Grenadier and Artillery 1800 (Walski, Brown University Collection)

Fig 19 Legion Cavalry of the Lombard Cavalry (Gembarzewski, Author Collection)

POLISH LEGION – LOMBARD AUXILARIES

Under the command of Jan Henryk Dąbrowski, organized 9 Jan 1797, reorganized 2 June 1797.

1st BATTALION GRENADIERS.

Formed 9 Feb. 1797 in Milan.
Commander: Strałkowski from March 1797, leading the 2nd Battalion of the 1st Legion, 2 June 1797.

2nd BATTALION LIGHT INFANTRY

Formed 9 Feb. 1797 in Milan.
Commander: Kosiński, leading the 2nd Battalion of the 2nd Legion, 2 June 1797.
Battles and Skirmishes: **1797**: Rimini.

3rd BATTALION FUSILIERS

Formed 13 March 1797 in Mantua.
Commander: Ludwik Dembowski, commander 1st Battalion of the 2nd Legion, 2 June 1797.
Battles and Skirmishes: **1797**: Verona.

　　　　The Lombard Legions consisted of three battalions of ten companies; each company consisting of 100 men.

Each battalion also had a 120 man artillery company consisting of 2 or 3 lb guns.

In October 1798, the legion was reorganized so that each company consisted of 120 men. There was now an artillery battalion of 313 men in three companies of 101 men each plus command. The cavalry regiment formed in December had two squads, made up of two companies. Each company consisted of 116 men.

In May 1799, the 1st Legion formed two elite battalions each of three 150 men companies – one grenadier and one chasseur.

POLISH LEGION – LOMBARDY AUXILIARIES
Commanded by Gen. Jan Henryk Dąbrowski, reorganized from 2 June 1797 until 27 May 1800.

1st LEGION
Maj. Gen. Józef Wielhorski; Brig. Gen. Franciszek, 1 September 1797; Brig. Gen. Kniaziewicz; Brig. Jan 1799; Col. Chamand, 5 February 1799 until his death 14 May; Col. Forestier, 14 May 1799.

1st BATALLION
Formed 2 June 1797 in Milan.
Commander: Białowiejski, 2 June 1797.
Battles and Skirmishes: **1797**: San Leo; **1798**: Ferentino; Frosinone, Terracina; Magliano; Nepi or Civita Castellana; Calvi; Gaeta; **1799**: Terracina styca, Borghetto; Cento-Croci; Busano; Cervarecca and Campo Forte; near Trebbią; Novi; Pozzolo; Bosco; Novi; Ronciglione.

2nd BATTALION
Formed 2 June 1797 in Ferrara.
Commander: Forestier, Chief of the Legion 14 May 1799; Maj. Józef Chłopicki, 14 May 1799.
Battles and Skirmishes: **1797**: San Leo; **1798**: Magliano, around Cita Castellana, Calvi, Gaeta; **1799**: Sezza, Cascano, Castiglione-Fiorentino, Sillano, Ospedaletto, near Trebbia, Novi, Pozzolo, Bosco, siege of Serravalli; **1800**: Casa Bianca.

3rd BATTALION
Formed 2 June 1797 in Bologna.
Commanders: Col. Zabłocki; Maj. Grabiński, went to Eygpt; Seydlitz, Świderski 1799.
Battles and Skirmishes: **1797**: San Leo; **1798**: Magliano, around Civita Castellana, Gaeta, **1799**: Terracina, Cortona, near Trebbia, Novi, Pozzolo, Bosco, Novi, Ronciglione.

GRENADIER BATTALION
This unit was organised in March 1799 and broken up in early 1800.
Commander: Maj. Kazimirsz Małachowski, until transfer 18 June. 1799; Maj. Downarowicz.
Battles and Skirmishes: **1799**: Aulla, San Terenzo, near Trebia, Novi, Pozzolo, Bosco, Novi.

RIFLE BATTALION
Formed in March 1799, disbanded in early 1800.
Commanders: Maj. Jasiński, until transferred; 17.VI .1799, Maj. Borowski.
Battles and Skirmishes: **1799**: Aulla, Novi, Pozzolo, Bosco, siege of Serravalli.

2ND LEGION
Commander: Maj. Gen Rymkiewicz until killed; Brig. Gen. Józef Wielhorski; Brig. Gen. Amilkar Kosiński 17 June 1799; Ludwig Dembowski, 5 April 1799.

1st BATTALION
Formed in Mantua.

Commander: Ludwig Dembowski; Maj. Królikiewicz 5 April 1799.
Battles and Skirmishes: **1799** Vaganza, Vigo and Legnano, Magnano, around Mantua.

2nd BATTALION

Formed in Tartoni.
Commander: Lipczyński, killed 26 March 1799; Maj. Mosiecki; Maj. Zawadzki.
Battles and Skirmishes: 1797 Reggio; **1799** Legnano, Magnano, around Mantua.

3rd BATTLATION

Formed in Milan.
Commanders: Niemojewski, Zagórski, Maj. Woliński.
Battles and Skirmishes: **1799** Legnano, Magnano, around Mantui.

CAVALRY REGIMENT

Formed in early January 1799, it was transferred to the Danube Legion in December 1799.
Commander: Gen. Aleksander Karwowski.
Battles and Skirmishes: **1799** Cortona, Castiglione-Fiorentino, Aulla, San Terenzo, around Trebbia, Novi, , Pozzolo, Bosco , Novi.

ARTILLERY BATTALION

Commander: Wincenty Aksamitowski.
Battles and Skirmishes: **1799** around Mantua 12 April – 28 July.

Fig 20 Artilleryman of the Legion 1800 (Walski, Brown University Collection)

Fig 21 Flag of the Legion Artillery 1800 (Polish Army Museum, Author's Collection)

POLISH LEGION

Under the command of General of Division Jan Dąbrowski. Reorganized from 27 April 1800 until 21 December 1801.

Flag: 1800 The French tricolor. In the center is a naturaloak wreath. The top is closed by a gold ribbon. On the left in blue lettering "LEGION POLSKI", on the right "AUXLIARNY LOMBARDYI". In the center of the wreath was a red/white/blue phygrian cap. Undeneath this in blue was written, "WSZYSCI LUDZIE/WOLNI SĄ BRACIA" (All Free Men are Brothers). Underneath this was a plumb level. On the lower interior was a white block, inside was written in blue "FISYLIERY", the lower right was the same block, but "I,ZY BATALLION" was also written in blue.

1801 was a square flag with a blue background. The center was a white square set on its edge. In the center of the white square was a gold cock with a red plume. In its left claw (facing the flag) was an olive branch, in it right were gold thunderbolts. On top was a light blue ribbon with dark blue letters "REPUBLIQUE FRANCAISE". On the bottom was also a light blue ribbon with dark blue letters, "2ND BAT LEGION POLONAISE". In the corners were white darts, inside of them were red flechettes. It seems all the battalions had similar flags, but with the battalion number in it.

The arillery battalion had a similar design to the above. The bottom ribbon said, "BATAILLON D'ARTILLERIE". In the center was a cock on crossed cannons.

1st BATTALION
Commander: Białowiejski.
Battles and Skirmishes: **1800** Malaussene, near Var, Utelle, blockade Ventimiglia, seige of Peschiera and 1801.

2nd BATTALION
Commander: Józef Chłopicki.
Battles and Skirmishes: **1800** Malaussene, near Var, Utelle, blokada Ventimiglia, seige of Peschiera and 1801.

3rd BATTALION
Commander: Świderski.
Battles and Skirmishes: **1800** Malaussene, near Var, Utelle, blokada Ventimiglia, seige of Peschiera and 1801.

4th BATTALION
Commander: Małachowski.
Battles and Skirmishes: **1800** the siege of Peschiera.

5th BATTALION
Commander: Jasiński.

6th BATTALION
Commander: Zagórski.

7th BATTALION
Commander: Zawadzki.
Battles and Skirmishes: **1800** Guastalia, siege of Peschiera and 1801.

ARTILLERY BATTALION
Commander: Jakóbowski.
Battles and Skirmishes: **1800** seige of Peschiera and 1801.

DANUBE LEGION
Organized 8 September 1799, disbanded in March 1802.
Cavalry and artillery were incorporated in the Cisapline Republican Army, 31 December 1801.

Commander: Gen. Karol Kniaziewicz, until dismissed 22 April1801, Gen. Władysław Jabłonowski.
Commander of the Infantry: Stanisław Fiszer, until replaced June 1800, Michał Sokolnicki.
Commander of the Cavalry: Aleksander Rożniecki.
Battles and Skirmishes: **1800** Erbach, Ulm, Hochstaedt, Offenbach, Frankfurt, Hohenlinden, Bergheim, Salzburg, Lambach.

The cavalry regiment of the Danube Legion had four squadrons, each of two companies, each company consisting of 115 men. The horse artillery company was equipped with two 8-lbs., two 4-lbs., two 6-inch howitzers, eight cassons, one wagon, and one field forge.

1st POLISH DEMI-BRIGADE
Formed 21 December 1801 as the Italian-Polish Legion in French service, 5 February 1802 transfered to Italian service.
Commander: Brigade Chief Józef Grabiński.
Battles and Skirmishes: **1805** Castel-Franco.

2nd POLISH DEMI-BRIGADE (114th)
Formed 21 December 1801 as the Italian-Polish Legion, 10 December 1802 transfered to French service under the designation 114th Demi-Brigade.
Commander: Brigade Chief Wincenty Aksamitowski.
Battles and Skirmishes: Sent to Santo Domingo 1803.

3rd POLISH DEMI-BRIGADE (113TH)
Formed in March 1802 from the Danube Legion, 2 August 1802, given the designation 113th Demi-Brigade.
Commander: Chief Władisław Jabłonowski.
Battles and Skirmishes: Sent to Santo Domingo 1803.

Fig 22 114th Demi-brigade 1802 (Walski, Brown University Collection)

Fig 23 Banner of the Legion Infantry 1801 (Polish Army Museum)

THE POLISH-ITALIAN LEGION

This unit was formed from the 1st Polish Demi-Brigade, on 5 August 1806 transfered service to the Kingdom of Naples, on 2 February 1807 to French service under the command of Col. Grabiński.

1st Regiment, commanded by Col. Józef Chłopicki.
2nd Regiment, commanded by Col. Białowiejski.
3rd Regiment, commanded by Col. Świderski.

On 11 November 1807 the cavalry regiment was transferred to Westphalian service. On 20 March 1808 it was transferred to French service.
Commander: Col. Aleksander Rożniecki, from 13 July 1807 Col. Jan Knopka.
Battles and Skirmishes: **1807** The siege of Kładzka.

THE 1st POLISH LEGION

Formed on 20 September 1806 in Landau and Hagenau and converted into the 5th Regiment of the Duchy of Warsaw on 13 February 1808.
Commander: Division Gen. Józef Zajączek, from January 1807, Col. Michael Radziwiłł.
Battles and Skirmishes: **1807** Tczew; the siege of Gdańsk.

2nd POLISH LEGION

Formed on 23 September 1806 in Nuremberg; in March 1807 it was incorporated into the 1st Legion.
Commander: Gen. Henryk Wołodkowicz.

THE ARMY IN POLAND

THE ARMY IN POLAND

The initial forces raised after the campaign in Poland were three large divisions which were called legions. Each legion was organized with four infantry and two cavalry regiments, three companies of foot artillery, and one company of auxiliary troops. The legion formed in Warsaw was designated number one and under the command of Poniatowski, the second was organized in Kalisz under Zajączek, and the third in Poznań was Dąbrowski. Of the three, only the third was actually operational. Napoleon then invoked the mass levy which had the gentry gather with their retainers and substitutes. In the end this did not result in substantial forces, but did provide 3,000 to 4,000 cavalry available for use. At this time, a Polish light-horse regiment of the Guard was organized from noble volunteers.

The old Dąbrowski Legions were brought from Italy and organized in Silesia under the name of the "Polish-Italian Legion". This legion was composed of three infantry and one cavalry regiments, numbering 8,000 men. The total military effort of Polish troops at this point amounted to 50,000 men.

The Legion of the North went into action around Gdansk (Danzig) along with elements of the 2nd and 3rd Legions under Zajączek headquartered near Neidenburg. Dąmbrowski took elements of the 2nd, 3rd, and mass levy into West Prussia, East Prussia, and the Friedland Campaign in June 1807. Individual regiments took part in the battles at Kołobrzeg (Kolberg) and Grudziądz (Graudenz).

In 1806-7 each of the three legions (divisions) had a single company of light infantry. These companies were formed into 400-men battalions of Chasseurs (light infantry/riflemen). In March 1807, this unit was combined into a line infantry unit and absorbed into the 11th Infantry Regiment. The chasseurs were armed with muskets and rifled carbines.

Fig 24 Flag of the Kingdom supposedly sewn by the wife of Gen Dąbrowski in 1807 (Polish Army Museum)

The Duchy of Warsaw was created by the Treaty of Tisit in July 1807 with an army of 30,000. Poniatowski kept the title as Minister of War and succeeded in incorporating some of the independent units such as the Legion of the North into the Duchy of Warsaw as the 5th Regiment. The Polish-Italian Legion, however, was kept in French service against their wishes and renamed, "The Vistula Legion". When it became apparent that the truncated Duchy of Warsaw could not maintain 30,000 soldiers at peacetime, three regiments (the 4rd, 7th, and 9th) totalling 8,000 men were taken into French service with the promise that he would give them back to the Duchy when needed. All the troops in French service would make their way to Spain from 1808-1812.

The Treaty of Tilsit outlined the following terms which established the Duchy of Warsaw.

Art. 5. The provinces which were part of the Kingdom of Poland as of the first of January 1772, and which have passed on since then at various periods to Prussia shall, with the exception of the countries named in the preceeding article and those specified in Article 9 of this Treaty, be possessed in full sovereignty by His Majesty, the King of Saxony. These possessions shall be given the name of Grand Duchy of Warsaw and be governed by constitutions which shall assure the people privileges and liberties in conformance to their neighbours' tranquillity and welfare.
Art 7. In order to communicate between the Kingdom of Saxony and the Duchy of Warsaw, the King of Saxony shall have free use of military roads crossing the possession of his Majesty, the King of Prussia. The particular road, number of troops permitted to travel it, and bivouac areas shall be determined at a special meeting between their Majesties under the mediation of France.

The area of the Duchy comprised about one quarter of the land of the old Commonwealth, made out of sections of lands seized by Prussia, Austria, and Russia. It was an odd shape without much of the prime farm or industrial areas. While Warsaw was initially included in the Duchy, the Royal City of Krakow, as well as much of the southern areas of the Commonwealth was not. At this stage, the majority of the ethnic population was Polish, with areas of Lithuanian, Belorus, and Ukrainian populations, but the vast majority of the old Commonwealth lay outside the Duchy's borders. Despite the fact that Prince Poniatowski was the nephew of the last king – Stanisław Augustus, the terms of the old 3rd of May Constitution were adhered to and the King of Saxony, Frederick Augustus, was brought in as the hereditary Duke of Warsaw.

The army of the Duchy of Warsaw was organized along French lines, with French military law and regulations translated into Polish. The army of the late Commonwealth was based on the Prussian model, with a regiment comprised of ten companies – one of which was light or "rifle" company. Under the French model, regiments were two to three battalions, each of six companies, of which one was a light and the other a grenadier company. Some, historians such as Kukiel, have suggested that the introduction of the French model brought a more nationalistic nature to the army.[1] Poniatowski introduced conscription along the French model which was more uniform across all classes rather than just as the landowners thought expedient.

Marshal Davoût was charged with reorganizing and training the Duchy's army according to French tactics and standards. Prince Poniatowski attached himself to the Marshal in order to learn all he could. Gen. Pelletier was placed in charge of training the artillery. The Polish cavalry, however, had their own tactics, developed in the last years of the Commonwealth and in Italy; many of these troops being armed with lances.

---

[1] Reddaway, p. 229

Fig 25 The Coat of Arms of the Duchy of Warsaw (Steifer, Wikipedia)

1809 – The Makings of an Army

The importance of the Polish-Austrian War was that it established the ability of the Poles to defend their lands, which provided a secure flank for Napoleon during the battles of the Fifth Coalition. Though theoretically supported by Saxony and Russia, the Saxons were only available for the opening phases of the battle of Raszyn and the Russians helped the enemy more than their nominal ally. Internally, this firmly shifted the leadership from Dąbrowski to Prince Józef Poniatowski.

Even though Russia was allied with France during the 1809 campaign, she did not assist the Polish in their defence of the Duchy, but seemed to act in a way to make sure the Polish troops did not move into the former parts of the Commonwealth in eastern Galicia between Lwow and Tarnopol. In one case, the Rusians tried to occupy Krakow for the Austrians, which almost resulted in combat.

The Duchy's army was not fully prepared or strengthened for the war that broke out in 1809. Napoleon had underestimated the Austrians capacity to mount an offensive and overestimated the enthusiasm the Russians would show to support him. The Emperor had counted on the Russians to counter any Austrian push into the Duchy or Germany through the then Austrian provinces of Galicia and Lodomeria, with the Polish troops advancing on Krakow as a feint. Because of this strategy, the Duchy's reserves were relocated into Prussian areas.

When war did break out in April, Archduke Ferdinand d'Este crossed the Pilica River with 32,000 troops against 14,000 Poles on 14 April. With no options or support in the immediate future, Poniatowski decided to make a stand near Warsaw. Assisted by a contingent from the Saxon Army, the Prince fought the Austrians to a draw at Raszyn on 19 April, but concerned about his position and the enemy's size, he withdrew from Warsaw. A 48 hour truce was arranged for the Duchy's troops to evacuate the city and Poniatowski moved his headquarters to Zegrze on 23 April.

Because the Austrians needed to leave troops to garrison the city, once they tried to resume the offensive, they lost some of their numerical superiority. The Austrians tried to attack, back across the Vistula where they were defeated at Grochow on 25 April, Radzymin on 27 April, and Ostrówki on 2-3 May. Gen. Sokolnicki deserved much of the credit at Grochow and Ostrówki, capturing 1,000 prisoners in the process.

In the hope of bringing Prussia into the war, Archduke Ferdinand moved part of his force north towards Plock and Torun. Torun was important because it guarded the way into Wielkopolska and a potential escape route into Saxony. The city was not prepared for the attack, but Gen. Woyczyński put together a defense which thwarted the Austrians who laid siege to the fortress from 15-19 May. They eventually were forced to give up the siege and retreat back to Warsaw.

Fig 26 Infantry of the Duchy 1807 Voltigeur and Fusilier (Author's Collection)

Fig 27 General de Brigade 1809 (Bronisław Gembarzewski, Brown University Collection)

At this point, the Polish forces got behind the Austrian line and advanced quickly into Malopolska (Galicia). In quick succession they took Lublin, Sandomierz (18-19 May), and Zamość (20 May). At the fortresses of Sandomierz and Zamość they acquired prisoners and war material. By the end of May the Duchy's troops had captured Lwow on 27 May and a revolt broke out against the Austrians in eastern parts of the Galicia under the command of Piotr Strzyżewski. In turn, this allowed the Poles to raise new troops which amounted to six infantry regiments and seven cavalry regiments.

The Austrians decided to recapture Sandomierz and left Warsaw on the 2nd of June. The Archduke drove Poniatowski over the San River on 12 June and recaptured Sandomierz on the 18th. In theory, Russia was an ally of the Poles and French, but while in the area of these operations, sat aside. Prince Golitsyn had an auxiliary corps of 32,000 men, but according to a secret agreement between Alexander I of Russia and the Austrian special deputy, Prince Schwartzenberg, on 18 April Russian troops would avoid combat.

Poniatowski regrouped his forces around Puławy by the end of June, reinforced by Zajączek and Dąbrowski's divisions. He launched an offensive to capture Krakow and fought several actions against the rearguard of the Hapsburg troops. On 15 July, the Duchy's troops entered the ancient Polish capital of Krakow. At this time, the Austrians had been convinced the Russians to move towards Krakow as well. Although the Russian and Duchy troops were allied on paper through France, there was a potential flashpoint for battle over control of the city. In the end, the Polish and Russian troops occupied the city jointly. The Galician insurgents captured Tarnopol on 17 July.

Following the Battle of Wagram in July, France and Austria agreed to an armistice which eventually resulted in the Treaty of Schönbrunn in early October. The lands recaptured against Austria in western Galicia were awarded to the Duchy, although Tarnopol was granted to Russia.

As a result of the war and the insurrection in Galicia, additional units were raised for the insurrection army that was known as the "French-Galician" army. Combined with the "Warsaw Army" and various legions, the Duchy had contributed over 60,000 men by the end of the year, of which Prince Poniatowski had close to 50,000 at his disposal in the country. The Prince had also learned his lessons of war during this time and he was considered a hero in some circles. Napoleon was so happy with his conduct of the war that he gave him a ceremonial saber.

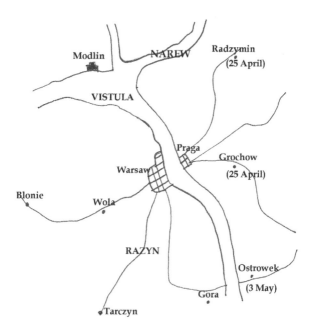

Operations around Warsaw April 1809

Fig 28 Operations around Warsaw 1809

ARMY OF THE DUCHY OF WARSAW 1806 – 1814

1ˢᵗ INFANTRY REGIMENT
Formed in Warsaw, 1806.

Commanders: Col. Michał Grabowski, 4 January 1807; Col. Kazimirz Małachowski, 8 April 1808; Col. Stefan Koszarski, 21 October 1812; Col. Tadeusz Piotrowski, 18 January 1813.

Garrisoned: Warsaw, Kalisz – Częstochowa.

Battles and Skirmishes: **1807:** Wały, Ruda; **1809:** Raszyn, Praga, defense of the Wisła, Ruda, Sandomierz, Wrzawy; **1812:** Kazimierzówka, Horbaszewice, Pankratowice and Borysów, on the Berezyna; **1813:** Ebersdorf, Penig, Lunzenau, Chemnitz, Leipzig.

Flag: Prior to 1812 the unit standard was a white flag 95cm wide by 80 cm deep. It had a gold polish eagle with gold fringe. The cords and tassles from the pole were also silver. The above was captured by the Russians in 1812 and replaced by a crimson flag, 55cm square. The center was a silver Polish eagle, while underneath was gold lettering "PUŁK PIERWSZY / PIECHOTY" (First Regiment of Infantry)

2ⁿᵈ INFANTRY REGIMENT
Formed in Warsaw, 1806.

Commanders: Col. Stanisław Potocki, 9 December 1806; Col. Jan Krukowiecki, 20 March 1810.

Battles and Skirmishes: **1807:** at Narwa, the siege of Grudziądz; **1809:** Grzybów, Zamość, Jankowice, Wrzawy, Sandomierz; **1812:** Smoleńsk, Możajsk, Czeryków, Woronowo, Medyna, Wiaźma, at the Berezyna; **1813:** Tyniec, Wittenberg, Raguhn, Rosslau, Kosswig, Düben, Jüterbog and Dennewitz, Skenditz, Liepzig.

Flag: The flag was crimson with silver fringe, 48cm high by 50cm wide. Both sides were the same, though closer to the fly of a white metal Poish eagle with the inscription in white above the eagle, "LEGIA. 1." (Legion 1) and below "PUŁK 2YC PIEHOTY" (2ⁿᵈ Infantry Regiment)

3ʳᵈ INFANTRY REGIMENT
Formed in 1806.

Commanders: Col. Edward Żółtowski, 2 March 1807; Col. Kalikst Zakrzewski, 27 December 1811; when he was wounded Col. Ignacy Blumer, 19 August 1812.

Battles and Skirmishes: **1807:** Nibork, Dobremiasto, Wały; **1809:** Raszyn, Zamość, Sandomierz, Jankowice, Sadomierz; **1812:** Smoleńsk, Mazhaysk, Czeryków, Czeczerynka, Studzianka, Wachau and Leipzig, the siege of Modlin and Zamośc.

4ᵗʰ INFANTY REGIMENT
Formed in Płock in 1806.

Commanders: Col. Feliks Potocki, 1 January 1807; Col. Maciej Wierzbinski, 16 October 1809; Col. Tadeusz Woliński, 21 July 1809

Battles and Skirmishes: **1807:** the siege of Grudziądz; **1808:** Almazaz; **1809:** Consuegra, Ciudad Real, New and Old Castile, Asturja, The Kingdom of Leon, Talavera, Almonacid; **1810:** Ocana, Fuengirola, Coien, Monbella; **1811:** Ximenes de a Frontera; **1812:** Czaszniki, Krasnoje; **1813:** the Seige of Spandau, Belzig, Jüterborg, Wittenberg, Düben and Leipzig, Leipzig.

Flag: The first flag was square, crimson with a white (silver) Polish eagle in the center with silver fringe. Above the eagle in silver, "Gdy sie chie bronic nie in nych ciemiezyc" and below, "haslem Polaka zginac, lub zwyciezyc" (To defend ourselves, and not to oppress others, the slogan of the Polish is to die or vanquish). The second flag was 42cm high by 51cm wide with silver fringe. The flag was crimson on the left side with a white metal eagle with its beak and claws in gold. "PUŁK 4" was written below this in gold. The opposite side seems to have been a light blue background with the same design, but the inside fly had a small inscription, "Svte reka Zofia Potocki Zony Pierwszego Połkownika Regimenta" (Sewn by the hand of Sofia Potocki, wife of the first Colonel of the Regiment)

5th INFANTRY REGIMENT

This unit was formed in Płock in 1806 as a battalion of light infantry from the foresters around Płock.

Commanders: Col. Ignacy Zieliński, Prince Michał Radziwiłł, 19 January 1807; Col. Stefan Oskierko, 27 December 1811; Col. Cyprjan Zdzitowiecki, 18 January 1813.

Battles and Skirmishes: **1809:** around Cżętochowa, Grzybów, Żarnowiec; **1812:** Tylża, Dynaburg, skirmish in September, Gansenburg, skirmishes in October, Neugat, Walkow, skirmishes in November, December, Tylża, skirmish in December; **1813:** the defense of Gdańsk and important skirmishes.

Flag: The flag was 54cm wide by 50cm high with a crimson background with silver fringe. There was a white eagle in the center. Above the eagle in silver was written "Pułk 5"

6th INFANTRY REGIMENT

Formed in Dobrcze near Kalisz in 1806.

Commanders: Col. Maciej Sobolewski; Col. Ignacy Zieliński; Col. Juljan Sierawski, 19 January 1809.

Battles and Skirmishes: The **1807** campaign; **1809:** Razyn, Radzymim, Góra, Sandomierz, Zamość, Góra, Wrzawy, the defense of Sandomierz; **1812:** Borysów; **1813:** Hrubieszów the defense of Zamośc.

Flag: 54cm wide by 50cm high in crimson. The eagle was white (silver) with the orb, scepter, and crown in gold. Above the eagle was written, "WOYSKO POLSKIE", below the eagle was "PULK SZUSTY".

7th INFANTRY REGIMENT

The regiment was organized in Kalisz in 1807.

Commanders: Col. Walenty Skórzewski, 10 March 1807; Col. Maciej Sobolewski, 1808, killed 11 August 1809; Col. Stanisław Jakubowski, 12 October 1809; Col. Paweł Tremo, 24 October 1810.

Battles and Skirmishes: **1807:** Grudziądz, Nibork, Koła; **1809:** Ciudad Real, Talavera, Toledo, Almonacid, Ocana; **1810:** Venta Nueva, Sierra Morena, Ronda, Malaga, Baza, Vera; **1812:** Salinas, Smoleńsk, Czaszniki.

Flag: Von Pivka shows the 7th infantry flag, fourth battalion, in a French design. It was square 85cm. Based on Westphalian examples it was crimson, with a white diamond center. The eagle would have been gold with thunderbolts in its claws. Underneath the eagle, also in gold letters, it said, "Number" then the battalion number "B". In the corners of the flag were voltiguer horns angled with the regimental number in the horn.

8th INFANTRY REGIMENT

The regiment was organized in Kalisz in 1807.

Commanders: Col. Cyprjan Godebski, 8 March 1807, killed 19 April 1809; Col. Kajetan Stuart, 5 May 1809.

Battles and Skirmishes: 1809 Raszyn, Sandomierz, Baranów, Jankowice, Wrzawy; **1812:** Smoleńsk, Mazhaysk, Woronowo.

Flag: The flag was 42cm square in crimson. The fringe was silver. On both sides were silver laurel wreaths that were joined at the base by a blue ribbon, similar to designs from the old Commonwealth. On one side, in the center of the wreath was "PUŁK 8SZY" while on the other side was "BATALION Ie". The lettering was in black thread.

9th INFANTRY REGIMENT

The regiment was formed in Gniezno in 1806.

Commanders: Col. Prince Anton Sułkowski, 29 November 1806; Col. Michał Cichocki, 20 March 1810.

Battles and Skirmishes: **1807:** Tczew, Gniew, the siege of Gdańsk, the siege of Kołobrzeg; **1809:** Herencia, the defense of Toledo, Almonacid, Ocana; 1810 La Carolina, Malaga; 1811 in the mountains of Ronda, Lubrin, Baza, Moro; Ronda Mts, Utera, Lanjaron, Montril; 1812 Czaszniki, Smolany; the siege of Spandau.

10th INFANTRY REGIMENT

The regiment was formed at Rogożna in Poznań in 1806.

Commanders: Col. Anton Downarowicz, 4 September 1807; Col. Bazyli Wierzbicki; Col. Henryk Kamieński, 27 December 1811.

Battles and Skirmishes: **1807** the siege of Gdańska and Kołobrzeg, Friedland; **1809:** Torun; Żarnowiec; **1812:** Tylża, Dyneburg, skirmish in September, Skirmishes in October, Neugat, Walkow, skirmishes in November and December, Tylża; **1813:** Labiau, Stublau, the defense of Gdańsk.

Flag: According to Over, there is no known flag for the 10th, but the Eagle is known to be silver with a gold crown. The base was also silver with gold lettering in the front, "PUŁK 10ty" and the reverse "WOYSKO POLSKIE". It was known to have a long white cravat – 53cm long, 14cm wide - attached to the staff. The cravat had a design of gold oak leaves at the ends, which had gold fringe. It was not unusual for some units, especially 2nd battalions to use these "cravats" as a standard.[2]

11th INFANTRY REGIMENT

The regiment was formed in Poznań during 1806.

Commanders: Col. Stanisław Mielżyński, 24 November 1806; Col. Aleksander Chlebowski, 10 June 1810.

Battles and Skirmishes: **1807:** Tczew, Gdańsk, Friedland, Pomorze; **1809:** Torun; **1813:** Gdańsk.

Flag: The flag for this regiment is also unknown, but it was reported to have a white cravat similar to the 10th, but without the oak leaf embroidery.

12th INFANTRY REGIMENT

The regiment was formed Kościan in Poznań during 1806.

Commanders: Col. Stanisław Poniński; Col. Ignacy Zieliński, 1 June 1807; Col. Jan Wyssenhoff, 29 July 1808; Col. Maciej Wierzbiński, 25 May 1812.

Battles and Skirmishes: **1807:** Tczew, Gdańsk and Friedland; **1809:** Grochów, Góra, Zamość and Sandomierz, Torun; Jedlińsk; **1812:** Smoleńsk, Mazhaysk, Czeryków, Woronów, on the Berezyna; **1813:** Wachau, Leipzig.

Flag: A crimson square with silver fringe. The eagle in the center was white (silver) with gold crown. "PUŁK SZUSTY" was embroidered below the eagle; on the reverse was "WOYSKO POLSKIE".

1st REGIMENT OF CHASSEUR CAVALRY

The majority of the regiment was created during the uprising at Łęczycka in 1806.

Commanders: Col. Michał Dąbrowski, 1 December 1806; Col. Konstantine Przebendowski, 9 November 1808; Col. Józef Sokolnicki, 18 January 1813.

Battles and Skirmishes: **1806:** Pułtusk; **1807:** Tczew, the siege of Gdańsk; **1809:** Gaszyn, Radzymin, Góra, Roźki, Sandomierz, Wrzawy; **1812:** Grodno, Romanów; **1813:** Rumberg, Kirschenstein, Seidenberg, Haesslich, Altenburg, Penig, Wachau.

Flag: The standard for this unit was crimson, 61cm square with silver fringe. Above the eagle in silver was written, "LEGIA I" and below was written, "I PUŁK LEKKI IAZDV".

2nd REGIMENT OF UŁANS

This was formed in 1806 as a cavalry regiment – the 2nd Light Cavalry of Legion I.

Commanders: Col. Walenty Kwaśniewski, 26 December 1806; Col. Tadeusz Tyszkiewicz, 14 December 1808; Col. Ludwuik Pac, 28 June 1812; Col. Józef Rzodkiewicz, 18 January 1813.

Battles and Skirmishes: **1807:** Zatory; **1809:** Nadarzyn, Praga, Grochów, Sandomierz, Rożki, Baranów, Wrzawy, Przedborz; **1812:** Mir; **1813:** Gera, Dennewitz.

3rd REGIMENT OF UŁANS

This unit was formed in 1806.

Commanders: Col. Wojciech Męciński, 11 April 1807; Col. Tyszkiewicz; Col. Augustyn Trzecieski, 19 April 1812; Col. Aleksander Radzimiński, killed 7 September 1812; Col. Aleksander Oborski, 18 January 1813.

Battles and Skirmishes: **1807:** Szczytno, Passenheim, Ortelsburg; **1809:** defense of Częstochowa, Nadarzyn, Grójec, Raszyn, Grochów, Radzymin, Grochów, Słupca, Wielatów, the siege of Zamość, Zawady, Zaleszczyki, Horo-

---

[2] Keith Over, *Flags and Standards of the Napoleonic Wars.* (Bivouac Books Ltd: London. 1976) p. 104

denka, Tarnopol, Chorostków, Wieniawka; **1812**: Mir, Mazhaysk; **1813**: Gross-Schweidnitz, Altenburg, Penig, Wachau, Leipzig, the defense of Zamośc.

4th REGIMENT OF CHASSEUR CAVALRY
The regiment was organized in 1806.
Commanders: Col. Wojciech Męciński, 11 Aril 1807; Col. Tadeusz Tyszkiewicz; Col. Walenty Kwaśniewski, 14 December 1808; Col. Stanisłwa Dulfus, 20 March 1810.
Battles and Skirmishes: The **1806/7** campaign; **1809**: The 1809 campaig in Swedish Pommerania, northern Germany and the Westphalian campaign against Schiller; **1812**: Smoleńsk, Mozhaysk, Czeryków, Medyna, at the Berezyna.

5th REGIMENT OF CHASSEUR CAVALRY
The regiment was created in 1806 and known as the 1st Regiment of Light Cavalry.
Commanders: Col. Kazimerz Turno, 30 December 1806; Col. Zygmund Kurnatowski, 20 March 1810.
Battles and Skirmishes: **1807**: Tczew, siege of Gdańsk, Dobremiasto (Gutstadt), Lidzbark (Heilsberg), Frydląd nad Łyną (Friedland); **1809**: Grzybów, Wiązownia, Góra, Kock, Sandomierz, Rożki, Baranów, Nowe Miasto, Wrzawy; **1812**: Smoleńsk, Mazhaysk, Czeryków, Woronowo.

6th REGIMENT OF UŁANS
The regiment was formed in 1806 in Bydgoszczy.
Commanders: Col. Wincenty Krasiński, 27 December 1806; Col. Dominick Dziewanowski, 3 January1807; Col. Michał Pągowski, 20 March 1810; Col. Tadeusz Suchorzewski, 11 October 1812.
Battles and Skirmishes: **1807**: Tczew, Gdańsk, Frydląd nad Łyną (Friedland); **1809**: Włodawa, Zamość, Sandomierz, Sobota, Skierniewice, Sandomierz, Pińczów; 1812 Ostrowno, Jelnia, Mazhaysk, Winkowo; **1813**: Neustadt, Lauterbach, Zehma, Wachau.

1st BATTALION OF FOOT ARTILLERY
This unit was formed in January 1807 as the artillery company of Legion I.
Commander: Col. Ludwig Dobrski; Lt. Col. Anton Redel, 16 September 1808, Col. 20 March 1810.
Campaigns: **1809, 1812, 1813**.

2nd BATTALION OF FOOT ARTILLERY
This unit was formed in December 1806 as the artillery company of Legion II by Gen. Zajączka in Częstochowa.
Commander: Col. Józef Hurtig, 20 December 1806.
Battles and Skirmishes: **1807** the siege of Gdańsk in February, Friedland 14 June, The campaigns of **1809, 1812** and **1813**.

THE HORSE ARTILLERY
This unit was formed by decress in the Duchy of Warsaw on 1 December 1808 as a horse artillery battery at the expense of Prince Włodzimierz Potocki; the 2nd battery was formed in 1809 by Roman Sołtyk. By decree on 30 March 1810, a horse artillery regiment was authorized with two squadrons.
Commanders: Capt. Prince Włodzimierz Potocki, Chief of the Squadron 1809, Col. 24 October 1810, Col. Józef Hurtig, 30 March 1810.
Battles and Skirmishes: **1809**: Raszyn, Grochów, Kock, Zamość, Sandomierz, Wrzawy; The Campaigns of **1812** and **1813**.

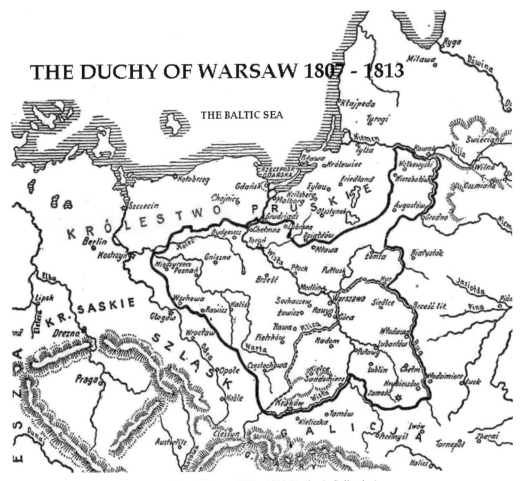

Fig 29 Duchy of Warsaw 1807 – 1813 (Author's Collection)

THE FRANCO-GALICIAN UNITS

1st FRANCO-GALACIAN/13th INFANTRY REGIMENT

This regiment was raised in 1809 at the expense of the gentry from around Lublin, Siedlce, and Bialski. Until 26 December it was the 1st Infantry of the Franco-Galician army.

Commanders: Col. August Szneyder, August 5 July 1809; Col. Jakób Kęszycki, 20 March1810; Col. Francuszek Żymirski, 17 April 1811.

Battles and Skirmishes: The defense of Zamość during the years 1812 and 1813.

Flag: The regiment had two eagles, but the second was without a crown. The first flew a white cravat 62cm long with a silver border of stars and the end fringed. The regiment had two known standards. The first battalion, according to Knötel, was square crimson with silver fringe and an eagle with a silver crown. The lettering above the eagle was also silver, "WOYSKO POLSKIE" and below, "13 PUŁK PIECHOTY". [3] The standard for the second battalion was white with painted devices in a Roman motif. It had a silver border and above this was a gold wreath of laurel leaves that was joined at the bottom and open at the top, following the square of the standard. In the center of the wreath was a gold frame and within the frame was a female seated in blue and white robes. Her face and arms were flesh color and hair was brown. Cradled in her right arm was a Roman septre – an eagle abve a laurel wreath. In her other hand she cradled a round silver shield with the initials "S.P.Q.R." in gold in each corner. At her feet on the right was an anchor. At her feet on the left was Romulus and Remus suckeling at a she wolf. Above the frame was a scroll with just the words, "PUŁK", but no number.

[3]Col. John R. Elting. Napoleonic Uniforms Vol IV. Emperor's Press: Rosemont. 2000 pg. 353

2ⁿᵈ FRANCO-GALICIAN/14ᵗʰ INFANTRY REGIMENT

This regiment was formed in 1809 at the expense of the citizens of Łomza and Płock. Until 28 December it was the 2nd Infantry of the Franco-Galician army.

Commanders: Col. Euzebusz Siemianowski, 25 April 1809; Col. Cyprian Zdzitowiecki, 18 January 1813; Col. Feliks Grotowski.

Battles and Skirmishes: **1809**: Kępy, Ośnicka, Tokarska and Zawadzka, Góra, Jankowice; **1812:** Borysów and Usza, on the Berezyna; **1813:** Düben, Leipzig.

Flag: The flag was 56cm wide and 77cm high. One side was blue with a white eagle. Above the eagle was written, "PUŁK 14sty" and below the eagle, "BATTALION 1szy". The reverse was crimson with white lettering "PUŁK 17", then "PIECHOTY LINIONEY", then "BATTon 1szy"

3ʳᵈ FRANCO-GALACIAN/15ᵗʰ INFANTRY REGIMENT

This regiment was formed in 1809 at the expense of the citizens of Wielkopolski. Until 28 December it was known as the 3rd Infantry of the Franco-Galician army.

Commanders: Col. Kacper Miaskowski, 9 July 1809; Col. Maciej Straszewski, 18 January 1813.

Battles and Skirmishes: **1812:** Smoleńsk, Jelnia, Mazhaysk, Czeryków, Medyna, Wiaźma, on the Berezyna, Wilno; **1813:** Ebersdorf, Neustadt, Eschfeld, Leipzig.

4ᵗʰ FRANCO-GALICIAN INFANTRY REGIMENT

Formed in Galicia in July 1809, in April 1810 it was dissolved and the men distributed throughout the various regiments of the Duchy of Warsaw.

Commander: Col. Jakób Kęszycki 10 July 1809.

Fig 30 Poniatowski's Guides 1809 (Chełminski, Author's Collection)

Fig 31 13th Regiment Grenadier (Gembarzewski, Author's Collection)

Fig 32 Aide to General du Division (Gembarzewski, Brown University Collection)

Fig 33 Grenadiers of the Gdańsk Free State (Knötel, Author's Collection)

5th FRANCO-GALACIAN/16th INFANTRY REGIMENT

This unit was formed in 1809 from Poles captured in the Austrian Army. It was paid for by Prince Konstantine Czartoryski. It was known as the 5th Infantry of the Franco-Galician army.

Commanders: Prince Konstantine Czartoryski, 22 May 1809; Maj. Ignacy Bolesta, 1813.

Battles and Skirmishes: **1812:** Smoleńsk, Mazhaysk, Czeryków, on the Berezyna; **1813:** Chemnitz.

6th FRANCO-GALACIAN/17th INFANTRY REGIMENT

The regiment was formed in Zamość in 1809, paid for by the Zamość Community.

Commanders: Col. Horonowski, 20 June1809; Col. Stefan Koszarski, 8 October 1812. Col. Feliks Grotowski, 18 January 1813.

Battles and Skirmishes: **1812:** Mohylow, Berezyna; **1813:** the defense of Modlin and Zamość.

Flag: Crimson 52cm wide by 46 cm high. On the right side was a white eagle; on the reverse was a white circle with the words, "PUŁK 17", "IMIENIA", and "ZAMOYSKICH" in crimson. At an angle on each corner was a white grenade.

BANNER (Company) OF HORSE GUIDES

Organized by Poniatowski on 8 May 1809 in Lublin, dissolved 27 Novmber.

Commander: Capt. Stanisław Miączyński.

1st FRANCO-GALACIAN CAVALRY/7th UŁAN REGIMENT

The regiment was formed in 1809 at the expense of the Łomza and Płock departments. It was designated the 1st Cavalry of the Franco-Galician Army.

Commander: Col. Augustyn Zawadzki, 26 April 1809 (see notes).

Battles and Skirmishes: **1809:** Góra-Piaseczno, Kozienice, Kobylin, Konary, Grabowo, Sulejów; **1812:** Mir, around Bobrujska, Kojdanow.

2ⁿᵈ FRANCO-GALICIAN CAVALRY/8ᵗʰ UŁAN REGIMENT

The regiment was raised in Podolia and Galicia in 1809. Until 28 December 1809 it was known as the 2nd Cavalry of the Franco-Galacian Army.

Commanders: Col. Stanisław Dulfus, 21 July 1809; Col. Kazimirsz Rozwadowski, 3 August 1809; Col. Prince Dominik Radziwiłł, 1 April 1811; Col. Józef Sokolnicki, 18 January1813; Col. Anton Potocki, 11 February 1813.

Battles and Skirmishes: **1809:** Rożniszewo, Jedlińsk, Chorostków, Grzymałowo, Zaleszczyki, Tarnopol, Wieniawka; **1812:** Ostrowno, Witebsk, Smoleńsk, Walutina Gora, Mazhaysk, Woronowo, Tarutina; **1813:** Neustadt, Wachau.

3ʳᵈ FRANCO-GALICIAN CAVALRY/9ᵗʰ UŁAN REGIMENT

The regiment was formed in Wielkoposka in 1809. Until September it was considered a mounted chasseur unit. Until 28 December it was designated as the 3rd Cavalry of the Franco-Galacian Army.

Commanders: Col. Feliks Przyszychowski, 8 August 1809; Col. Makymiljan Fredo, 18 January 1813.

Battles and Skirmishes: The **1809** Campaign; **1812:** Oszmiana, Wilejka, Ljady, Krasne, Smoleńsk, Wiaźma, Jelnia, Mazhaysk, Czeryków, Tarutina, Małojarosławiec, Berezyna; **1813:** the defense of Gdańsk.

Fig 34 Poniatowski at Raszyn (Juliusz Kossack, Author's Collection)

Fig 35 Stanisław Mielżyński battles the Austrians at Torun (Wojcieck Kossack, Author's Collection)

10ᵗʰ HUSSAR REGIMENT

The regiment was formed in 1809 in Wielkopolska.

Commander: Col. Jan Nepom Umiński, 21 July 1809.

Battles and Skirmishes: **1809:** Jankowice; **1812:** Mazhaysk, at the Dźwina, the Druja, Woronowo.

4ᵗʰ FRANCO-GALICIAN CAVALRY/11ᵗʰ UŁAN REGIMENT

The regiment was formed in Lwow at the end of May at the expense of Adam Potocki and others. Until 28 December this unit was known as the 4th Cavalry regiment of the Franco-Galician Army.

Commanders: Col. Adam Potocki, 1 July 1809; Aloysius Oborski, 18 January 1813.

Battles and Skirmishes: **1812:** Mir, Mazhaysk.

5th FRANCO-GALACIAN CAVALRY/12th UŁAN REGIMENT

The regiment was formed in 1809 in Podlaise at the expense of the of the Rzyszczewskis and the residents of Russian and Austrian Podlaise. Up until 28 December it was known as the 5th Cavalry regiment of the Franco-Galician Army.

Commander: Col. Gabriel Rzyszczewski, 1 July 1809.

Battles and Skirmishes: **1812** Grodno, Romanowo, Mazhaysk, Czeryków, Medyna.

1st HUSSARS OF THE FRANCO-GALACIAN ARMY/13th HUSSAR REGIMENT

The regiment was formed in Lublin in 1809. Prior to 28 December they were known as the 1st Hussars of the Franco-Galician Army.

Commanders: Col. Józef Toliński, 18 June 1809; Col. Józef Sokołnicki, February 1813.

Battles and Skirmishes: **1812**: Mir, Romanówo, Smoleńsk, Mazhaysk, Czeryków, Woronow, Małojarosławiec, Borysów, at the Berezyna, Hellensdorf, Peterswalde, Sere, Pirna, Drezno, Pirna.

1st CUIRASSIERS OF THE FRANCO-GALACIAN CAVALRY/14th CUIRASSIERS

The regiment was originally known as the 1st Cuirassiers at the expense of Stanisław Małachowski.

Commanders: Col. Stanisław Małachowski, 1 November 1809; Col. Kazimirsz Dziekoński, 18 January 1813.

Battles and Skirmishes: **1812**: Mazhaysk; **1813**: Friedland; Pitterbach, Krakaw, Strohweide, Weida, Leipzig.

6th FRANCO-GALACIAN CAVALRY/15th UŁAN REGIMENT

The regiment was formed in 1809 in Galician Podlaise and up to 28 December it was known as the 6th Cavalry Regiment of the Franco-Galician Army.

Commanders: Col. Augustyn Trzecieski, 5 June 1809; Col. Ludwik Pac, 14 April 1812.

Battles and Skirmishes: **1812**: Zaleszczyki, Tłuste, Dyczkowo, Tarnopol, Wieniawka, Podhajce, Mir, Bobrujsk, Rohaczew, at the Berezyna; **1813**: Kalisz.

Flag: The standard was crimson 57cm wide by 55cm high with silver fringe. The eagle was silver on both sides with the number "XV" in gold in the lower fly.

7th FRANCO-GALACIAN CAVALRY/16th UŁAN REGIMENT

The regiment was rasied in Podlaise in 1809 and up to 28 December it was known as the 7th Cavalry Regiment of the Franco-Galacia Army

Commander: Col. Marcin Tarnowski, 1 October 1809

Battles and Skirmishes: **1809**: Tarnopol, Grzymałów, Chorostków; **1812**: Zaleszczyki, Marjampol, at the Dniestre, Mir, Rohaczew, Smoleńsk, Dubrowno, Mazhaysk, Kaługa, Borysów; **1813**: Hellensdorf, Peterswalde, Sere, near Dresden, Pirna, near Dresden.

Fig 36 Polish Ułan attacks an Austrian Cheval Leger
in 1809 (Marinet, Brown University Collection)

FLAGS AND STANDARDS

All units received a Polish Eagle as a main standard. This was usually silver metal with a gold crown and lettering. Most had the phrase on the front that said, "PULK / PIECHOTY" (infantry regiment – often with the number) with the reverse saying "WOYSKO / POLSKIE" (Polish Army). The pole was usually black between 7.4 ft and 9.5 ft long. Second or third battalions would have a pole with a cravat of white cloth that could be seen over a distance. In some ways this might be similar to the "bunczuk" carried by the Krakus cavalry and Cossack troops.

Fig 37 An example of an eagle used with Polish regimental standards (Polish Army Museum)

Fig 38 Official version of the czapka plate – 1st regiment infantry

THE NATIONAL GUARD

The National Guard was organized along the lines of the French National Guard for internal protection. It was organized with two battalions. For the most part these were organized around major cities and guardsman had to purchase thier own uniforms and equipment. All property owners were drafted into the guard. While Jewish men and public school students were exempt, they often enrolled. Guardsmen were unpaid unless they did service more than two miles from their garrison.

According to Nafzinger, Poniatowski thought the Guard was a drain on the economy and manpower. Nonetheless, it was reorganized and expanded in 1811. [4] It was divided into the Sedentary Guard, Mobile Guard, and permanent Paid Guard. The Sedentary Guard acted as a police force for towns and villages in case of direct attack. The Mobile Guard was organized into small units and combined into larger units or companies and battalions that could be used anywhere in the duchy. The Paid Guard consisted of volunteers, preferably veterans, formed into permanent formations that relieved the regular army. The following areas organized National Guard Units – The City of Warsaw, Department of Kalisz, Department of Radom, Department of Krakow, Department of Lomza, Department of Posen, Department of Bromberg and the Department of Płock.

The Mobile Guard was deployed on the Russian Frontier, but only the Krakow force had any military potential. The majority of the Mobile Guard seemed to have been used as fortress garrisions. The total Mobile Guard activated in 1812 was 3,900. In 1813, most of these were absorbed into regular army units. Of these units, the Krakow Guard was the most heavily engaged of any units.

[4] George Nafziger, Poles and Saxons of the Napoleonic Wars. (Chicago: Emperor's Press, 1991) pp. 38-39

ORGANIZATION

INFANTRY

Dąbrowski initally intended to organize the infantry into a similar three-battalion, nine-company structure that the legions followed. By December 1807, he settled on a two-battalion, six-company structure along the lines of French regiments. Each company would have a compliment of 95 men. In 1808, the company size was increased to 140 men per company. In 1810, the number of battalions was increased from two to three. The 4th, 7th, and 9th regiments were organized in two-battalions of eight or nine companies of 140 men. In 1812, they reduced thier companies to six to be in line with the rest of the Polish regiments.

CAVALRY

The Polish cavalry regiment consisted of a command staff and usually three (from 1806-1809) or four squadrons composed of two companies. The four squadron regiment was commanded by a colonel, major, two chefs d'escadron, and two adjutant-majors. There was also a standard-bearer and trumpet-major.

In 1810 the organization of a company was: four officers (captain, lieutenant, and two second lieutenants), fourteen NCO's (sergeant-major, four sergeants, fourrier, and eight corporals), one blacksmith, two trumpeters, and 79 troopers.

ARTILLERY

Starting in 1808, the artillery battalions were organized into three companies, each company with three platoons and each platoon with three sections. Two of the sections were gunners and the third was made up of drivers. Each company had six guns – 4 6-lbs and 2 6-inch howitzers. In 1810, the foot regiment consisted of 12 field companies and 4 static companies.

The Poles never formed so-called grand batteries as there were not enough guns. In 1809, at Raszyn, Poniatowski deployed 16-gun batteries against the Austrians; and in 1812, at Smolensk, he set up 16-gun batteries. French officer Pelletier, who commanded all Polish batteries, took 42 guns and joined the grand French battery pounding the Russians in the Smolensk. Firing at ranges of 2,000 paces and more was considered as waste of ammunition. Prince Poniatowski sometimes used guns in an aggressive way; for example in 1813, several guns participated in the actions of advancing skirmishers.

When firing from a fixed position it was recommended to make a shallow ditch in front of the battery. This ditch served as a "trap" for enemy's rolling cannonballs. The gunners also liked to place their cannons behind obstacles; fences, cultivated fields, etc. This was especially important if the enemy had a strong and aggressive cavalry. It was unlikely that the Polish gunners would use grenades (shells) if during battle the enemy stood on a soft or muddy ground.

In 1813, the artillery consisted of six-gun horse artillery battery, six foot companies, and an artillery train. In April 1813, a second horse artillery battery was organized.

The Polish 6-lb cannon had a crew of ten men, the 12-lb required thirteen men, and 3-lb had eight men. The company (battery) usually had six-guns formed in three sections of two guns each, or two half-batteries of three –guns each. Artillery doctrine recommended deploying batteries on a hard and slightly elevated area. For communication and passing orders, the foot artillery had drummers and the horse artillery had trumpeters.

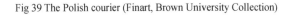

Fig 39 The Polish courier (Finart, Brown University Collection)

UNIFORMS

LINE INFANTRY

Even though Polish units were put together quickly in 1806, they were able to approximate some uniformity. The basic color remained a dark blue kurtka with either dark blue or grey trousers. The czapka was either dark blue, black, or dark grey. The czapkas had gold (brass) trim, the front plate had the regimental number. There was a French cockade in the front corner, surmounted by a six inch pompom – gold for fusiliers, red for grenadiers, and green for voltiguers. They wore white vests with blue collars. They had grey overcoats with collar and shoulder straps in the unit color.

In March 1807, supply problems forced Dąbrowski to modify the regulations for uniforms so that Warsaw (1st Division) had yellow cuffs and lapels, poppy collars, and yellow buttons. The Kalisz (2nd Division) had crimson cuffs, lapels, and collars with white metal buttons. The Poznan (3rd Division) wore white distinctions with yellow buttons. The piping on the uniform matched colors. Under the new regulations, pompoms for officers were white, poppy red for grenadiers, light green for voltiguers, and black for fusiliers. The French cockade was replaced by a white cockade for the Commonwealth. According to Nafziger, grenadiers were supposed to wear bearskins, but it seems some wore shakos or czapkas with a brass grenadier badge.[5]

As always, there were variations to regulations. In August 1808, the 4th, 7th, and 9th regiments were sent to Spain, where they were outfitted in French cut uniforms with the old regimental distinctions. In many cases, they were issued shakos with French cockades. In February 1812, these troops were issued French habite-vest coats and shakos with tricolor cockades, but the 4th evidently continued to wear thier old division dress until 1813 – albeit with some updates like green coats for drummers per the French regulations. The 7th regiment had crimson lapels and collars piped white. The cuffs and cuff-flap was blue piped white. The 9th had white lapels piped red; the collar and cuffs red, piped white. Knötel shows the musician of the 9th with a white coat, red lapels and cuffs, yellow collar, and cuff-flaps. All the lace was red and white. The shako was yellow with green destinctions.

After 1809, a large number of Austrian uniforms fell into the hands of the Duchy. The 13th regiment therefore was uniformed in white with light blue distinctions. Their grenadiers had poppy red pompoms, cords, and epaulettes. The voltiguers had dark green pompoms, cords, and epaulettes. According to a drawing in the National Army Museum, this unit did not seem to wear the czapka, but rather a shako. For volitguers, it was a brass horn with the regimental number, but not the eagle.

In September 1810, all units were to have a uniform of a dark blue kurtka with white lapels, cuff–flaps, and turnbacks. The collar and cuffs were crimson, though the 1st, 2nd, 3rd, and the voltiguers of the 5th regiments wore yellow cuffs wih white piping. The 4th, 5th, and 9th regiments had dark blue cuff flaps with white piping. Pants were white in the summer and dark blue in the winter. They were worn with and without gaiters. Grenadiers generally had full moustaches.

In 1813, the uniform for all units was dark blue with white lapels and cuffs. The collar was red, piped white. The czapka featured a white cockade.

The grenadiers' bearskin was supposed to have a leather visor with a brass frontplate showing a Polish eagle and the number between two grenades. The back patch of the bearskin had a red patch with a white cross; also popy red cords and a red plume. If the grenadiers wore a czapka it might have been edged in red or have a red body.

Voltiguers who wore a czapka had white cords with a yellow over green plume. They had green epaulettes, with yellow collars, and short moustaches.

Fusiliers supposedly had a white metal eagle over the cooper plate on the czapka. The edges of the czapka were also trimmed in red. They had black pompoms on their czapka with white cords. NCOs had crimson and white tassles. Shoulder straps were generally blue edged in white or crimson.

Sappers were dressed similar to grenadiers, but included a long white leather apron and gloves. They also had a black bearskin with a crimson plume and white cords. They wore red epaulettes and full beards.

[5] George Nafziger, Poles and Saxons of the Napoleonic Wars. (Chicago: Emperor's Press, 1991) pg 35

Other variations included:

1st Regiment drummers had white uniforms with red lapels and turnbacks piped white. The collars and cuffs were light blue, piped red. The epaulettes were light blue with red fringe. The czapka was light blue, piped red. The visor was black leather with a brass edge. The plate was brass with the number cut out surmounted by a white metal Polish eagle with a white cockade. The plume was red over light blue surmounted a white pompom.

The 8th infantry in 1812 still wore a blue uniform with crimson lapels and cuffs. There were white cuff-flaps, piped crimson. The turnbacks were also dark blue and the seams were piped crimson. The 17th infantry's sappers had white jackets with red collars, cuffs, and epaulettes.

According to a print by Józef Kosiński in the Polish Army museum the infantry regiments had the following distinctions in 1810:

| REG. | GRENADIERS | | | | | VOLTIGUERS | | | | |
	Collar	Cuffs	Headgear	Plume	Cords	Collar	Cuffs	Headgear	Plume	Cords
1st	Blue	Yellow	Bearskin	None	None	White	Yellow	Czapka	None	White
2nd	Blue	Yellow	Bearskin	None	White	White	Yellow	Czapka	Lt. Blue/ White tip	White
3rd	Blue	Yellow	Bearskin	None	White	Yellow	Yellow	Czapka	None	Yellow
4th	Red	Red	Bearskin	Red	None	White	Red	Czapka	White tip/ Green	White
5th	Red	Red	Bearskin	Red	Red	Yellow	Yellow	Czapka	White tip/ Green	Green
6th	Blue	Red	Bearskin	None	White	Yellow	Yellow	Czapka	None	White
7th	Red	Red	Bearskin	None	Red	Yellow	Yellow	Shako	Yellow tip / Green	Green
8th	Red	Red	Bearskin	None	White	White	Yellow	Czapka	None	Green
9th	Yellow	Yellow	Bearskin	None	White	Yellow	Yelow	Shako	None	Green
10th	Yellow	Yellow	Bearskin	None	White	Yellow	Yellow	Shako	None	White
11th	Blue	Red	Bearskin	None	White	Yellow	Red	Czapka	None	Green
12th	Blue	Red	Bearskin	None	White	Yellow	Red	Czapka	None	Green
13th	Lt. Blue	Lt. Blue	Shako	None	Red	Lt. Blue	Lt. Blue	Shako	None	Green
14th	Blue	Red	Bearskin	Red	White	Yellow	Red	Czapka	None	Yellow
15th	Red	Red	Bearskin	None	White	Yellow	Yellow	Czapka	None	Yellow
16th	Red	Red	Bearskin	Red	White	Yellow	Yellow	Shako	None	Green
17th	Red	Red	Bearskin	Red	White	White	White	Shako	Yellow tip / Green	White

The 1st, 2nd, 4th, and 15th Grenadier bearskins had a front plate. The 5th had a white metal "grenade" badge.

Fig 40 2nd Infantry NCO's czapka of a fusilier company (Polish Army Museum)

Fig 41 3rd Infantry czapka for a drummer (Polish Army Museum)

Fig 42 An officer's Uniform from 1810 (Polish Army Museum)

Fig 43 Fusiliers and NCO's of the 2nd Infantry (Chełminski, Author's Collection)

Fig 44 Drum Major and Drummer of the 2nd Infantry / Grenadier and Officer of the 5th Infantry in 1808 (Knötel, Author's Collection)

Fig 45 Czapka of the 4th Infantry voltigeurs 1807-1808 (Polish Army Museum)

Fig 46 Drummer of the 4th Infantry (Author's Collection)

Fig 47 Voltigeur 4th Infantry / Grenadier 17th Infantry 1809 (Knötel, Author's Collection)

Fig 48 5th Infantry Fusilier 1812 (Author's Collection)

Fig 49 5th Infantry Grenadiers (Chełminski, Author's Collection)

Fig 50 Drummer 13th, Drum Major 1st, National Guard Drummer, 4th Drummer Infantry (Chełminski, Author's Collection)

Fig 51 Infantry officers – Voltigeurs, Grenadiers and Fusiliers 1812 (Gembarzewski, Author's Collection)

Fig 52 8th Infantry in attack (Chełminski, Author's Collection)

Fig 53 10th Infantry, voltigeurs (Brown University Collection)

Fig 54 11th Infantry NCO czapka 1808-1814 (Polish Army Museum)

Fig 55 Infantry colorguard (Gembarzewski, Author's Collection)

Fig 56 Voltigeur trumpeter (Gembarzewski, Author's Collection)

Fig 57 Voltigeurs and grenadiers (Gembarzewski, Author's collection)

FOOT ARTILLERY

Up to 1810, the foot artillery wore dark green kurtkas with black collars; cuffs, cuff-flaps, and turnbacks piped red. The epaulettes were red. Their trousers were black with red side stripes and black gaiters. The shako was black with red pompoms and cords. Officers had gold epaulettes, pompoms, and silver cords. The bands around the top and bottom of the shako were also gold.

After 1810, the artillery retained the dark green coats with black facings and red piping. In the summer they wore white breeches with white gaiters or dark green breeches with black gaiters. The shako had red pompoms, plumes, and cords. They had brass cannon plates surmounted by a white metal Polish eagle. The buttons were yellow metal.

Fig 58 Foot artillery in action (Chełminski, Author's Collection)

Fig 59 Officer and cannonier in 1807 (Gembarzewski)

Fig 60 Field artillery in action 1812 (Gembarzewski)

Fig 61 Field artillery in summer dress 1812 (Gembarzewski)

ENGINEERS AND SAPPERS

The engineers and sappers wore uniforms similar to the foot artillery. In this case, however, the kurtka had no cuff-flaps. The trousers were dark grey with double drak green sidestripes. The shako was black with a white metal Polish eagle and white cockade. The cord and pompom was red. The officers had gold bands around the top of their shakos and silver cords.

Fig 62 Sappers (Gembarzewski)

Fig 63 Engineer and officer (Chełminski, Author's Collection)

NATIONAL GUARD

Warsaw Guard - The guard wore dark blue kurtkas with white lapels piped light blue. Grenadiers had red collars and voltiguers had yellow. The cuffs were dark blue, piped light blue as were the turnbacks. The collar was light blue piped white. The shoulder straps were dark blue, piped light blue. Grenadiers had red epaulettes and voltiguers green. Belting and trousers were white. The shako was black with a diamond plate that included a white Polish eagle, white cockade and light blue pompom.

Krakow Guard – the kurtka was dark blue with light blue collars and poppy red cuffs piped with white; the voltiguers had yellow cuffs. The facings were white, piped with red. The turnbacks were piped in white. The epaulettes and shoulder straps were the same as for the Warsaw Guards. The ranks wore black czapkas with light green pompoms. The cords were white for fusiliers and green for voltiguers. They had a yellow brass sunburst plate with the Krakow coat-of-arms. The grenadiers wore black bearskins with red cords and a red plume with a white tip.

The Vilna Guard had the same uniform as the Polish Guard.

Fig 64 Jewish National Guard of Warsaw (Brown University Collection)

Fig 65 Officer's uniform Lublin National Guard (Polish Army Museum)

Fig 66 National Guard of Warsaw (Chełminski)

Fig 67 Wilno National Guard cap plate

CORPS OF VETERANS AND INVALIDS

Veterans and invalids generally manned fortresses and installations. Their uniforms were identical to the line infantry, but they generally wore a light blue uniform with piping of crimson. They wore a black felt czapka with a light blue turban and a brass plate that said, "Weterany". Their pants were light blue or white. Officers had bicornes with red pompoms.

Fig 68 Line voltigeurs, Veteran and Krakow National Guard in 1812 (Knötel, Author's Collection)

Fig 69 Veteran (Gembarzewski, Author's Collection)

CAVALRY

The initial regulation did not show a distinction between types of cavalry except that uhlans carried lances. Like the infantry, they were organized by division. The basic uniform remained the dark blue kurtka and dark blue or grey trousers.

The first division had poppy red collars and cuffs piped white. The facings were yellow, also piped white. The trousers had double yellow side stripes with yellow buttons. They wore shakos, although uhlans had czapkas with black plumes and white cords. The elite companies either had black lambswool sown around their headgear or wore bearskin colpaks. The elites had a poppy red bag, plume and cords. Senior officers had white plumes and silver cords.

The second division had crimson collars, cuffs, and facing edged in white. The stripes on the pants were also crimson; the buttons were white and all else the same as the first divison.

For the third division, white was the distinctive color, as well as the trouser stripes. The buttons were yellow. All the rest of the details were the same as for the first division.

Fig 70 1st Legion cavalry in 1807 – NCO, Horse Artillery, Trooper and Trumpeter (Knötel, Author's Collection)

GUIDES

According to Knötel, the guides wore a mounted chasseur uniform with a green jacket that had pointed cuffs in crimson, along with a crimson collar and piping on the seams. On the left shoulder was a white aiguillette. They had yellow metal epaulettes. The vest was red, piped orange. The pants were red with an orange seam stripe and orange Hungarian knots. The black Hungarian boots had gold tassles on the top. They wore a black or brown colpak with a red bag with orange piping. The colback had a white metal Polish eagle in the front, gold cords, and a white plume. The schabraque was green with a crimson and orange stripe along the edge. A white Polish eagle was in the back corners. The trumpeters wore reversed colors with a crimson schabraque. Their colback was either white with a crimson bag or brown with a green bag.

CUIRASSIERS

The cuirassiers were part of the Franco-Galician units raised in 1809. Their original uniform was a white single breasted kinski with with poppy-red distinctions. The collar and cuffs were piped white. The steel helmet was the same as the French pattern – it had a black bearskin turban; brass crest, chinscales, and edging on the visor. The houpette was white horsehair, the crest was black horsehair, and there was a red plume on the left side of the helmet. The breeches were white leather with high black boots. The cuirass was steel for the front and back with scaled cooper straps on the shoulder. The arm holes were trimmed with red cloth. In late 1809, they wore a blue habit-veste lined red. The collar and cuffs were poppy-red piped in dark blue. The officers had brass epaulettes, the NCOs' were red with yellow, and the troopers had red ones. In the 1813 campaign they did not have their cuirasses.

The trumpeters wore a white spencer coat with a white vest. The chest lace was yellow and red. The collar and cuffs were red with gold lace. The epaulettes were yellow metal with red and white fringe. The helmet had a white turban with red horsehair and houpette. In the 1813 campaign, the trumpeters wore red coats with white horsetail plumes.

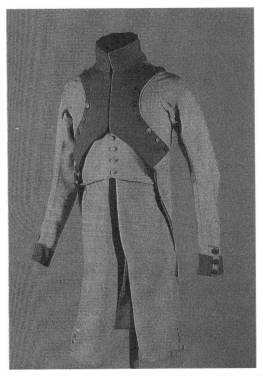

Fig 71 Cuirassier uniform 1809 – 1812 (Polish Army Museum)

Fig 73 14th Cuirassier in 1812 (Gembarzewski, Author's Collection)

Fig 72 14th Cuirassier in 1812 (Author's Collection)

Fig 74 Cuirassier trumpeter (Chełminski, Author's Collection)

CHASSEURS Á CHEVAL

In 1808, the chasseurs were given green kurtkas, however, the 5th chasseurs continued to wear their blue uniforms until 1810. The collar, cuffs, piping, and turnbacks were in the regimental colors. For the 1st regiment the color was poppy red, the 4th regiment was crimson, and the 5th was orange. The buttons were yellow and their breeches were green.

The elite companies wore a colpack of black bearskin with the bag in the regimental color. Some companies, like those of the 5th chasseurs, wore a "shako à poil", which was a shako covered with bearskin that included a bag in the regimental color and a gold Ploish eagle plate. The cords and plumes were red. The center companies wore a black shako with white cords. The plume was in the regimental color tipped green. After 1810, the bags on the colpack went away. In 1813, the 1st chassuers carried lances and the 4th were converted into an ułan regiment. During the 1809 camaign, they also carried lances.

Regimental staff officers wore white plumes. Elite troops wore a carrot shapped pompom – golden for officers and poppy red for troopers. Officer cords were silver.

Fig 75 1st Chasseurs (Gembarzewski, Author's Collection)

Fig 76 1st Chasseurs Elite Company 1812 (Author's Collection)

Fig 77 1st Chasseurs 1810-1812 – Trumpeter, Officer, Trooper and Elite (Gabrys, Author's Collection)

Fig 78 4th Chasseurs 1810-1812 – Officer, Trumpeter, Elite and Trooprt (Gabrys, Author's Collection)

Fig 79 4th Chasseurs 1809-1814 Officer's jacket (Polish Army Museum)

Fig 80 5th Chasseurs 1810-1814 Officer's jacket (Polish Army Museum)

Fig 81 4th Chasseurs (Chełminski, Author's Collection)

Fig 82 5th Chasseurs (Chełminski, Author's Collection)

Fig 83 5th Chasseurs 1810-1812 – Elite, Trooper, Trumpeter, Officer (Gabrys, Author's Collection)

Fig 84 5th Chasseurs – Trumpeter, Officer, Trooper (Knötel, Author's Collection)

HUSSARS

The hussars wore a dark blue pelisse. For the 10th regiment, the pelisse was trimmed with black fur and gold lace. For the 13th, it was trimmed with white fur and lace. They had dark blue breeches with gold side stripes for the 10th and silver side stripes for the 13th. For undress they wore gray Hungarian breeches with crimson side stripes. The shakos were black, but the 13th later wore a light blue shako with white cords. They had white metal chinsclaes with a black plume. The officers and elite companies wore black or brown colpaks with light blue tops, poppy red cords and plumes. Officers wore either gold or silver cords.

The 10th hussars trumpeter had white pelisse with brown fur and gold lace around the collar and cuffs. The lace braiding was red/white. The dolman was dark blue for the 10th and red for the 13th, the cuffs and collars were red with gold trim. The girdle was gold and red vertical stripes. The chest lace was red/white. The trousers were red with gold side stripes and Hungarian knots. The busby was brown fur with a red bag, red/white cords, and white/red feathers.

Fig 85 10th Hussars – Elite, Trooper, Trumpeter, Officer (Gabrys, Author's Collection)

Fig 86 10th Hussars (Gembarzewski, Author's Collection)

Fig 87 Trumpeter 13th Hussars (Chełminski, Author's Collection)

UŁANS

The ułans were based on the main Polish-Lithuanian cavalry of the old republic called "Towarzycz". They wore a kurtka that differentiated the regiments by the cuffs, collars, turnbacks, and piping color. Piping was used around the cuffs, collars, pockets, and in addition to the seams of the backs and sleeves. The kurtka had yellow buttons that featured the regimental number. A white vest was worn under the kurtka. The breeches were dark blue with a side stripe, worn over short boots with screw in spurs.

The czapkas were stiff leather with yellow metal or leather corners with cords that hung from corner to corner. The cords were gold for officers, white for troopers, and red for elite companies. In theory, there was a gold shield in the front of the czapka with a white eagle on top of that. There are several variations of this, however, that include a sunburst, a heraldic shield, and the Lithuanian rider.[1] The officers had a two-inch wide gold band above the turban for officers and a white one for troopers. They wore a plume in front of the czapka that was white for staff officers, black for troopers, and red for elites. Elites wore balck lambskin over their czapka or a colpak with red poppy bags, plumes, and cords. Several units wore a plume against regulation that was known as "à la russe" which was a long horse hair that cascaded down from the top.

The 6th lancers continued to wear its old legion uniform into 1810. In 1813, the 4th lancers were converted from the 4th chasseurs, uniformed in a dark blue kurtka with crimson collars, facings, and cuffs. They had crimson breeches with dark blue double stripes. They wore yellow epaulettes and aguilettes on the right shoulder. The collar was piped yellow. The czapka was crimson with yellow piping and trimmings. They had yellow turbans and cords with white plumes. Some wore black turbans topped with yellow bands and cords with white plumes. The czapka had a sunburst plate.

Reg.	Collar	Piping	Turnbacks	Piping	Cuffs	Piping	Side Stripe	Piping
2nd	Poppy Red	White	Dark Blue	Yellow	Poppy Red	White	Yellow x 2	White
3rd	Crimson	White	Dark Blue	White	Crimson	White	Yellow x 2	White
6th	White	Crimson	Dark Blue	Crimson	Dark Blue	Crimson	Crimson	White
7th	Yellow	Poppy Red	Dark Blue	Poppy Red	Yellow	Poppy Red	Yellow x 2	Poppy Red
8th	Poppy Red	Dark Blue	Dark Blue	Poppy Red	Poppy Red	Dark Blue	Poppy Red	Poppy Red
9th	Poppy Red	Dark Blue	Dark Blue	White	Dark Blue	Poppy Red	Poppy Red	White
11th	Crimson	Dark Blue	Crimson	White	Dark Blue	Crimson	Crimson	White
12th	Crimson	White	Dark Blue	White	Dark Blue	White	Crimson	White
15th	Crimson	White	Crimson	White	Crimson	White	Crimson	White
16th	Crimson	White	Dark Blue	Crimson	Crimson	White	Crimson	White
17th	Crimson	Dark Blue	Dark Blue	Crimson	Crimson	Dark Blue	Crimson	White
18th	Crimson	Dark Blue	Crimson	White	Crimson	Dark Blue	Crimson	White
19th	Yellow	Dark Blue	Dark Blue	Yellow	Yellow	Dark Blue	Yellow x 2	White
20th	Crimson	Dark Blue	Yellow	Dark Blue	Yellow	Dark Blue	Yellow x 2	White
21st	Orange	Dark Blue	Orange	Dark Blue	Orange	Dark Blue	Orange	White

The trumpeters for the 7th ułans wore a white kurtka with red lapels and turnbacks. The collar and cuffs were yellow, piped red. The epaulettes were red with gold crescents on the edges. The trousers were dark blue with a yellow side stripe split with red. The czapka had a white top and black leather bottom piped red. There was a gold amazon shield surmounted by a white metal Polish eagle. The pompom and cords were also red.

The trumpeters for the 9th ułans wore a white kurtka piped red with blue lapels piped white. The turnbacks were blue. The collar and cuffs were red. The collar had a gold "grenade" device. Epaulettes were yellow metal with red fringe. The trousers were dark blue with a red side strip split by a white stripe. The plume was white, with a white metal Polish eagle. The cords and pompoms were also white with the pompom surmounted by a red tuft. The bag was red with a white tassle and zig-zag embroidery down the middle.

[1]Żygulski, Zdzisław and Wielecki, Henryk. Polski Mundur Wojskowy. Krakow: Krajowa Agencja Wydawnicza w Krakowie. 1988. Pp. 184-190

Fig 88 2ⁿᵈ Ułans - Trumpeter, Officer, Trooper and Elite (Gabrys, Author's Collection)

Fig 89 2ⁿᵈ Ułans – Trumpeters (Chełminski, Author's Collection)

Fig 91 3ʳᵈ Ułans – Trooper (Chełminski, Author's Collection)

Fig 92 3rd Ułans - Elite, Trooper, Trumpeter and Officer (Gabrys, Author's Collection)

Fig 93 6th Officer, 7th Trumpeter, 6th Trooper and 7th Trooper Ułans (Gabrys, Author's Collection)

Fig 94 7th Ułan officer with a regimental adjutant (Chełminski, Author's Collection)

Fig 95 8th Ułan (Gembarzewski, Author's Collection)

Fig 96 8th Ułans – Trooper, Elite, Trumpeter and Officer 1810-1812 (Gabrys, Author's Collection)

Fig 97 8th Ułan uniform jacket and czapka (Polish Army Museum)

Fig 98 8th Ułan trooper (Author's Collection)

Fig 99 9t[h] Ułan Elite, Trooper, Trumpeter, Officer 1810-1812 (Gabrys, Author's Collection)

Fig 100 11th Ułan in winter dress (Chełminski, Author's Collection)

Fig 101 17th Ułan jacket and czapka (Polish Army Museum

Fig 102 Elite Ułan company (Gembarzewski, Author's Collection)

HORSE ARTILLERY

From 1807 to 1810, the horse artillery wore a uniform similar to the ułans in dark green. The collar, facings, and cuffs were black velvet with poppy red piping – this was consistant with the uniform of the pre-partition Commonwealth artillery. The seams of the kurtka were also piped red. The trousers were also dark green with a black sidestripe piped red. The epaulettes were also red. The buttons were gold metal and the belting was white. The czapka had a dark green top, a black leather bottom, and red piping with a middle red band. The plate was a sunrise design in brass with a white metal center, along with brass chinscales. The cockade was white with a red pompom.

After 1810, the headgear was changed to a black or brown colpack with a dark green bag. The cords, pompom, and tassels were also red. The breeches were either dark green with double black side stripes, piped red or grey breeches.

The trumpeters were depicted in white kurtkas with black distinctions and red piping. The buttons were brass. They wore dark green trousers with a wide red stripe. The busby was white. The bag was red with a white tassle. The cords and pompom were also red.

Fig 103 The Horse Artillery in action at Raszyn (Wojciech Kossack, 1913)

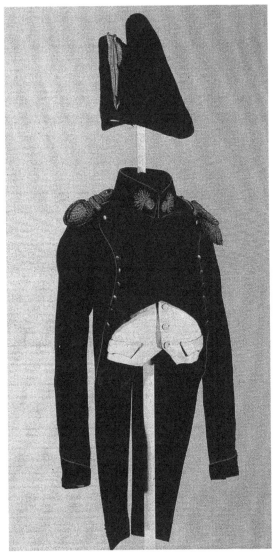

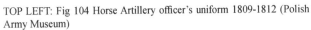

TOP LEFT: Fig 104 Horse Artillery officer's uniform 1809-1812 (Polish Army Museum)

TOP RIGHT: Fig 105 Horse Artillery trumpeter 1809 (Chełminski, Author's Collection)

BOTTOM RIGHT: Fig 106 Horse Artillery in action 1812 (Gembarzewski, Author's Collection)

TRAIN DRIVERS

The train drivers moved the equipment, supplies, and ammunitions of the army. Prior to 1811, this consisted of a single-breasted blue-gray tunic and trousers with yellow metal buttons, yellow cuffs and collars, as well as piping on the outer seam and shoulder straps. The czapka was dark blue with a black lambskin turban and white metal eagle in the front. The cords and pompom were red. Officers had gold edged around top of the czapka and the eagle was yellow metal. After 1811, they wore black shakos with yellow pompoms and white eagles. Drivers wore a brass plate on the left arm with the number of the column. The vehicles also had a plate number.

Fig 107 Gendarmes and Train Drivers (Chełminski, Author's Collection)

THE VISTULA LEGION

The majority of surviving Polish troops from the Italian Legions sought to be gathered into one unit. They were organized as the Polish-Italian Legion on 5 April 1807. They were initially placed in the service of Jérôme Bonaparte in the Kingdom of Westphalia. On 20 March 1808, the Polacco-Italian Legion was renamed the Vistula Regiments and transferred from Italian to French pay. It was organized into three, two battalion regiments in a depot at Sedan in May 1808, and by June, they were serving as part of Grandjean's division of the III Corps. The lancer regiment was supposed to consist of 1,200 men in four squadrons and the infantry of 8,200 soldiers and officers. After inspecting the units in June 1808, their administration was split up. The Legion was then under the command of the Chief of the first regiment with the nominal head being a colonel. The second and third regiments were then commanded by majors. The cavalry regiment became known as the Vistula Lancer Regiment.

According to Leśniewski, when the lancers first went into battle at Mallen, on 13 June 1808, the peasants ran away shouting, los picadors infernales, (the infernal picadors) which was supposedly incorrectly recorded as "los infernos picadors" (the picadors from hell). [1] About this time, the lancers were separated from the infantry and made part of Mashal Lefebvre's IVth Corps.

In 1809, Napoleon attempted to raise another legion from Austrian prisoners, but that fell short of anticipation. Another infantry regiment and lancer regiment were added (a second lancer regiment was added in February 1811) to the existing regiments raising it to the status of a legion. The name "legion" is somewhat of as misnomer, as this was actually only an official "legion" for a short time. In June 1811, the lancer regiments were taken into the French army as the 7th and 8th Chevaux-léger-lanciers.

The legion infantry fought in many of the pitched battles in Spain including Saragossa, where they lost one-third of their men, as well as Tudela, Maria, Belchite, and Sagonte. The majority of their time, however, was spent fighing a guerrilla war against Spanish insurgents. The units were constantly under fire so that Heinrich von Brandt stated by the time they left for Russia in 1812, "not one man in his company had not been wounded".[2]

The 1st and 2nd lancers served with distinction in Spain. The first was famous for their charge at Albuera, where it destroyed Colborne's Brigade. The second served in Spain until 1812 when they were sent to Russia. In preparation for the Russian campaign, a third battalion was added to each of the three infantry regiments, but it never attained the anticipated paper strength of 10,000 men. Because the Emperor wanted to make units self-suffient, as with other French units, a company of artillery was added to the infantry units in March 1812. The 4th regiment remained in Spain until September 1812, when it was moved to Posen, so it was still at an effective strength of 1,800 men in January 1813 when the Grand Armée returned.

On 13 March 1812, the Legion was renamed, "Légion du Grand Duché de Varsovie (The Legion of the Duchy of Warsaw)". The existing regiments were all given another battalion and reinforced with an artillery company. In June 1812, the Legion was attached to Mortier's Young Guard and renamed the Vistula Division. The members of the Legion that went into Russia were assigned to the Young Guard. Because many soldiers were young recruits, the quick advance took its toll on the troops, losing about one-third of their number. Having survived the battles in Russia, the retreat, guarding the Beresina, and marching back into Lithuania, the survivors of all three legions managed to muster only 450 men.

In 1813, all the remaining soldiers from Russia, plus the 4th regiment, were combined into a two-battlaion Vistula Regiment. By July 1813, the regiment numbered 1,400 men and was attached to the 2nd Infantry Division of the Polish VIIIth Corps. Fighting through the 1813 campaign, it was all but destroyed in the rear-guard action of 19 October, but was re-formed in 1814 fighting that campaign and serving as shelter for Napoleon at Arcis-sur-Aube.

On Napoleon's return in 1815, Poles from the original Vistula regiments formed an infantry regiment and provisional 7th lancer regiment. Although they were too late for Waterloo, they did fight at Sèvres Bridge on 3 July.

---

[1] Ryszard Morawski and Sławomir Leśniewski. *Wojsko Polski w Służbie Napoleona: Legia Nadwiślańska , Lansjerzy Nadwiślańscy*. (Karabella: Warszawa. 2008) p 265
[2] Heinrich von Brandt. *In the Legions of Napoleon*. (Stackpole Books: Mechanicsburg. 1999) p. 26

Most of the Poles who fought in these units were transferred to the Bourbon Legion.[3] A battalion of six companies, each of 75 men, was also raised under the name "3e Régiment Étranger", but it was never able to develop into a full regiment.

The Legion initially consisted of 3 two-battalion regiments. Each battalion consisted of six companies – the first being designated a grenadier company and the sixth a light infantry company. The balance was designated as fusiliers. On paper, each company was 148 men. In Russia, the regiments were reinforced by a third and perhaps fourth battalion.

The cavalry regiments were theortically composed of 1,043 men in eight companies. Each company made up of 128 men and 19 officers. Like the infantry, the first and last companies were considered "elite" and wore a special uniform. The first was designated "grenadiers" and the last the "flank" companies.[4]

According to John Elting, in 1806, the fortress of Stettin surrendered to the French cavalry and this was something unusual in the annals of military history; but there was no fighting and the defenders were bullied into surrender. During the siege of Saragossa, the Vistula ułans actually charged the fortified city. Fedup with the Spanish sniping, the Vistula Lancers climbed down from their saddles and stormed en entrenched Spanish camp near Saragossa during the first phase of the siege – they charged a fortified city. They penetrated to the center of the city. Alone and unsupported they then charged back out.

ORGANIZATION

In November 1807, the newly designated Vistula Legion was organized along the lines of French infantry regiments with each company consisting of 140 men. In April 1808, each regiment was to consist of two battalions of six companies (four fusiliers, one grenadier, and one chasseur). Each company numbered 140 men. The battalion staff amounted to 79 men. In 1812, the legion's regiments were ordered to form a third battalion.

In 1813 and 1814, what was left of the legion was organized into a two battalion regiment. Each battalion had six companies consisting of the standard four fusiliers, one grenadier, and one chasseur companies of 140 soldiers.

The lancer regiment was organized into four squadrons, each of two companies. Each company numbered 128 troopers. The regiment's staff amounted to 19 men.

THE VISTULA LEGION

It was originally formed 31 March 1808 as the Polish-Italian Legion, which continued until 18 May 1813.
Commanders: Gen. Józef Grabiński from 7 June, 1808; Col. Józef Chłopicki.

1st REGIMENT OF THE VISTULA LEGION INFANTRY
Formed 31 March 1808 as the 1st Regiment of the Polish-Italian Legion.
Commander: Col. Józef Chłopicki, from January 1812; Col. Pawel Fądzielski, killed 7 January 1813.
Battles and Skirmishes: **1808:** Mallen, Alagon, Siege of Saragossa ; **1809:** Maria, Belchite; **1811:** the siege of Tarragony, the siege of Murviedra (Saguntu); **1812:** Smoleńsk, Mazhaysk, Krymskoje, Czerykow, Woronowo, Tarutina, Krasne, along the Berezyna.

2nd REGIMENT OF THE VISTULA LEGION INFANTRY
Formed 31 March 1808 as the 2nd Regiment of the Polish-Italian Legion.
Commanders: Col. Białowiejski, killed 1808; Col. Kąsinowski, from the half of July 1812; Col. Chłusowicz, 22 August until commanding the 3rd Guard Cavalry; Col. Malczewski 23 August 1812.
Battles and Skirmishes: **1808:** the siege of Saragossa; **1809:** Perdiguera, Santa Fe, Belchite, Aquila, El Frasna, Calatayud, Retascon, Daroca, Ojos Negros, Tremedal; **1810:** Torre la Carcel, Teruel, Villastar, Villel, Lancosa, the siege of Tortosa; **1811:** Operations in Aragon, Catalonia and Valencia; **1812:** Smoleńsk, Mazhaysk, Tarutina,on the Berezyna.

---

[3]IBID, p. 28
[4]Morawski, *Legia Nadwiślańscy*. p. 269

3rd REGIMENT OF THE VISTULA LEGION INFANTRY

This unit was formed 31 March 1808 as the 3rd Polish-Italian Legion.

Commanders: Col. Świderski, retired as battalion Chief; Col. Sykstus Estko from 14 July 1808; as Chief of the Vistula Legion, 9 May 1811; Maj. Michał Kosiński, 9 May 1811; Maj. Szott from October 1812.

Battles and Skirmishes: **1808:** the siege of Saragossa; **1812:** Smoleńsk, Taruntina, on the Berezyna.

4th REGIMENT OF THE VISTULA LEGION INFANTRY

The unit was formed 8 July 1809 under the designation of the 2nd Vistula Legion in Wolkersdorf under the command of Gen. Mikołaja Bronikowskiego. On 12 February 1810, the 2nd Legion was transferred to the 1st under the name of the 4th Infantry.

Commanders: Maj. Kazimiersz Tański until 2 August 1810; Battalion Chief Radomski; Col. Sykstus Estko, 9 May 1811 (Actually 1 January 1812).

Battles and Skirmishes: **1810:** Puebla-de-Senabria, Benevente; **1811:** Salinas, Penaranda; **1813:** Rogożno.

THE VISTULA INFANTRY REGIMENT

Formed on 18 June 1813 from the four regiments of the Vistula Legion.

Commanders: Col. Malczewski, killed 19 October 1813; Col. Kosiński.

Battles and Skirmishes: **1813:** Kratzen, Kulm, Schluckenau, Ebersdorf , Löbau, Neustadt, Borna, Leipzig; **1814:** the defense of Soissons, Arcis-sur-Aube.

THE VISTULA UŁAN REGIMENT (1st VISTULA UŁAN REGIMENT)

This unit was formed 20 March 1808 from the Ułans of the Polish-Italian Legion. It was transferred from Westphalian service to the French service on 18 June 1811 under the title of the 7th Lance Regiment (chevau-légers-lanciers).

Commanders: Col. Jan Konopka, Brig. Gen., August 1811; Maj. Dembiński; Col. Ignacy Stokowski, 13 October 1811, until the middle of July 1813; Kazimirsz Tański, 2 August 1813.

Battles and Skirmishes: **1808:** Tudela, Mallen, Alagon, the siege of Saragossa, Tudela, Almaraz; **1809:** Yevenes, Ciudad – Real, Santa Cruz, Alenbillas, Talavera de-la-Reina, Almonacid, Ocana; **1810:** Arquillos, Orgas, Tortosa, Rio Almanzor, Lorca; **1811:** Cor, Albuhera, Olivenza, Baza, Berlanga; **1813:** Budziszyn (Bautzen), Drezno, Pirna; **1815:** Ligny, Waterloo.

1ST HUSSAR REGIMENT

This unit was formed by a decree from Napoleon on 4 March 1807. It was organized in Warsaw on 27 October and transferred to the Polish-Italian Cavalry Regiment.

Commanders: Prince Jan Bielska Sułkowski; Michał Pruszak; Col. Józef Kalinowski.

2ND VISTULA UŁAN REGIMENT

Formed by decree 7 February 1811, later named the 8th Lancer Franco-Polish Regiment (chevau-légers-lancers) 18 May 1812.

Commanders: Col. Tomasz Łubieński, 7 February 1811

Battles and Skirmishes: **1812:** Krasne, on the Berezyn; **1813:** Bautzen, Kulm.

UNIFORMS

INFANTRY

The kurtka or habit-vest was dark blue with a yellow collar and facings. The waistcoat and trousers were white cloth. Ankle boots were worn with black or grey gaiters. The officers wore a dark blue czapka with a white or gold metal sunburst plate in front. The bottom of the czapka was black separated by a white band. It was edged white with a French cockade on the left and a carrot pompom. The enlisted wore a French shako with a triangle plate or sunburst, white cords, and French cockade. Grenadiers wore red cords and epaulettes and red banding on the top of the shako. The voltiguers had yellow epaulettes edged green and yellow banding on the top of their shako. The shako also had yellow cords. Musicians wore yellow czapkas with a white over red plume. They either wore a blue coat with yellow distinctions and pants or yellow jackets with blue facings.

Up to 1812, the 1st regiment had yellow lapels, cuffs, and turnbacks. The collar was dark blue, piped yellow. After 1812, they had a yellow collar piped white, yellow cuffs, and yellow lapels. The sappers had a black bearskin with a white metal plate. They wore white cords, a yellow bag edged white, and a black plume tipped yellow. They wore dark blue trousers with a yellow side stripe, a white apron, and belting.

The second regiment had yellow collar and turnbacks up to 1812. After 1812 they had yellow collars and dark blue cuffs piped yellow.

The 3rd regiment had yellow collars piped dark blue, yellow cuffs, and yellow turnbacks.
The 4th regiment had dark blue collars, yellow cuffs, and yellow turnbacks. After 1812 they had dark blue collars, piped yellow; dark blue cuffs, piped yellow.

In 1813, the regiment wore the same color uniform with a czapka topped either blue or yellow with a black bottom. The pants were either white with gaiters or dark blue with a yellow side stripe.

FLAGS AND STANDARDS

From 1808 to 1813, the regiment carried a French tricolor (from the fly) blue, white, and red. It was trimmed with gold fringe and the lettering in the center said, "L'EMPEREUR NAPOLEON AU RÉGIMENT POLONAIS".

CAVALRY

The lancers wore a blue kurtka with a yellow collar with yellow piping. The trousers wers dark blue with a double yellow stripe for parade or a single yellow with 19 buttons and leather inserts. The czapkas were nine inches tall, dark blue, edged in yellow metal with a sunburst front plate. The czapka had a white band between the bottom and top. The girdle had blue and yellow horizontal stripes. Between 1805-07, the uniform was dark blue with yellow collar and side pant stripe. The lapels and cuffs were dark blue with yellow edging. The epaulette on the right shoulder and antigulete on the left shoulder were both white. The czapka had a dark blue top with a white lambswool base and white cords. The French cockade was on the left surmounted by a gold pompom with a white over red plume. The lance pennant was blue over red with a white triangle on the fly. In 1808, the lance pennant was white over red. The second regiment had red over white. Around 1807, the czapka had a yellow top, white band, and black bottom. In 1808, the trumpeters wore yellow jackets with blue lapels. The collar and cuffs were edged blue prior to 1812. After 1812, the trumpeters wore a green uniform with a green topped czapka. The braid on the arms, collar, and lapels was gold and green. The pompom was red and the plume was yellow over green or green over yellow. The cords were white and red. In 1808, the greatcoat was dark blue with a yellow collar. By 1811, the greatcoat was light grey.

The first regiment (7th French Lancers) had a yellow collar, pointed yellow cuffs, lapels, and turnbacks. The elite company had a black lambskin busby with white cords, red plume, and yellow bag, trimmed white.
The second regiment (8th French Lancers) had a blue collar, trimmed yellow. The czapka had a French cockade on the left side and a red over white plume. The trumpeter's czapkas had the top part yellow. The kurtka was also yellow with dark blue lapels. The collar and cuffs were trimmed dark blue with dark blue seams. The trousers were dark blue with double yellow side stripes.

In 1813, the uniform was a dark blue kurtka with yellow collar, pointed cuffs, lapels, and turnbacks. The czapka was dark blue with a black lower half and white band. The cords were white with a French cockade on the left and black plume.

Though technically not part of the Vistula Lancers, the 9th regiment wore red topped czapkas trimmed white in 1812. The kurtkas were dark green with chamois lapels, cuffs, and collar with chamois piping. The trousers were red with a green side stripe. In 1813, the kurtka and trousers were dark blue.

FLAGS AND STANDARDS

The squadron standard was rectangular with rounded corners. It was vertical striped – from the fly – blue, white, and red. The corners had a wreath with the Roman numeral of the squadron at a 45 degree angle. The center was a laurel wreath with a brass voltiguer horn with a red plumed czapka on top. On the left side the top ribbon said "REPUBLIC FRANCAISE", the bottom said "LEGION POLONAISE", on the reverse it said "RZECZYPOSPOL-ITY FRANCUZKEIJ", and on the bottom "LEGII POLSKEIJ".

Fig. 108 Vistula Legion in 1810 (Bellange, Author's Collection)

Fig 109 Vistula Legion in Spain (JOB, Author's Collection)

Fig 110 Vistula Legion cap plate (Polish Army Museum)

Fig 111 8th Cheval Leger (Knötel, Author's Collection)

Fig 112 7th Vistula Lancers (Chełminski, Author's Collection)

Fig 113 8ᵗʰ Cheval Leger (Chełminski, Author's Collection)

Fig 114 9ᵗʰ Cheval Leger 1813-14 (Knötel, Author's Collection)

Fig 115 8ᵗʰ Cheval Leger (Knötel, Author's Collection)

THE IMPERIAL GUARD

THE POLISH GUARD REGIMENT OF LIGHT CAVALRY (1st LANCERS)

This unit was formed in Warsaw by the order of the Administrative Council on 19 February 1807. On 6 April 1807, by Imperial decree it was named as part of the Imperial Old Guard.

Commanders: Col. Wincenty Krasiński, 7 April 1807; Brig. Gen., 16 December 1811; Gen. Div., 18 November 1813.

Battles and Skirmishes: **1808:** Rio Seco, Burgos, Somo Sierra; **1809:** Esslingen, Wagram; **1812:** Wilno, Mochylów, Smoleńsk, Mało-Jarosławiec, Krasne, on the Berezyna; **1813:** Lützen, Bautzen, Reichenbach, Görlitz, Drezno, Peterswalde, Leipzig , Hanau, Nieder Isigheim; **1814:** St. Disier, Brienne, La Rothiére, Champaubert, Montmirail, Château-Thierry, Vauchamps, Villeneuve, Montereau, Troyes, Rocourt, Braisne, Béry-au-Bac , Craone, Laon, Reims, Fére-Champenoise, Arcis-sur-Aube, Vitry, St. Dizier, Bourget, Paris; **1815:** Waterloo.

3RD REGIMENT OF POLISH GUARD CAVALRY

The unit was raised by Napoleon in Wilno on 5 July 1812 and was and was included in the Young Guard. (The regiment under the command of Gen. Krasinski was No. 1; the Dutch Lancers were No. 2). The decree of 22 March 1813 transfered them to the 1st Regiment, which was completed at Friedberg on 11 April.

Commander: Brig. Gen. Jan Konopka, 5 July 1812; Maj. Kazimierz Tański.

Battles and Skirmishes: **1812:** Słonim.

LITHUANIAN-TARTAR SQUADRON

Formed by decree, 24 July 1812, assigned to the 3rd Guard Cavalry Lancers. On 22 March 1813 it was assigned to the 1st Guard Cavalry Lancers.

Commanders: Capt. Ułan.

3RD REGIMENT OF ÉCLAIREURS OF THE GUARD

Created by decree on 9 December 1813 in Givet, France. It was assigned to the 1st Guard Cavalry Lancers.

Commander: Maj. Jan Hipolit Kozietulski.

Battles and Skirmishes: see the 1st Guard Cavalry Lancers.

POLISH GUARD INFANTRY BATTALLION

Formed 2 October 1813.

Battles and Skirmishes: **1813:** Lützen, Bautzen, Reichenbach, Görlitz, Drezno, Peterswalde, Leipzig , Hanau, Nieder Isigheim; **1814:** St. Disier, Brienne, La Rothiére, Champaubert, Montmirail, Château-Thierry, Vauchamps, Villeneuve, Montereau, Troyes, Rocourt, Braisne, Béry-au-Bac , Craone, Laon, Reims, Fére-Champenoise, Arcis-sur-Aube, Vitry, St. Dizier, Bourget, Paris

UNIFORMS

GUARD LANCERS

The two Polish lancer regiments wore indentical style uniforms with variations in the coloring. For the first regiment, the czapka had a crimson felt top with white trim. The bottom part was black leather and the two were separated by a white cloth band two inches wide. The front plate was a yellow metal sunburst plate that featured either a crowned "N" or an imperial eagle. The top was edged in white as well, creating a Maltese cross. On the right side was a brass Maltese cross over a white/red/blue cockade. A white plume was atop this cockade. The fittings and chinscales were brass. The cords were white. The kurtka was blue with all facings crimson surmounted by silver lace. On the left shoulder was a white lanyard for troopers and silver and red lanyards for NCO's. On the right was white fringed epaulette; the buttons were silver.

The pantaloons were blue with a double crimson stripe down each side. On campaign, the pants had black leather inserts. The belting was white. The sword hilt and scabbard were yellow metal.

For buglers, the colors were reversed with the plume crimson, tipped white. There are also examples of buglers with light blue coats and pants with crimson/white piping. The top of the czapka was often white or light blue.

The 3rd Lancers had a similar uniform, but with gold braiding.

LITHUANIAN TARTARS

The shako was black felt with a green bag and red tassle. A yellow turban was wrapped around the base of the shako. In the front was a half moon under three stars. The collar shirt was dark green over which was a short-sleeved crimson waistjacket. The jacket was edged in gold with gold piping. The pantaloons were also dark green with two crimson side stripes and black boots. The lance penant was green over crimson. In 1814, the lance pennant was green over white and the uniform was draker blue. The sash was yellow and the vest was red with black trim.

3RD REGIMENT OF ÉCLAIREURS OF THE GUARD

The regiment wore a uniform of typical ułan pattern. The kurtka was dark blue with crimson collars and lapels piped white. The girdle had three white and two blue horizontal stripes. The trousers seem to have been grey in the field. The czapka had a crimson top with white piping, white band, and black base. The front sunburst plate was yellow metal with a white metal center and a gold imperial "N". The lance penant was white over red. The trumpeter wore a white kurtka with crimson distinctions and piping. The trousers were dark blue with double white side stripes. The czapka had a white top, trimed with crimson and red/white cords. The pompom was blue/red/white and the plume white over red.

INFANTRY BATTALION

According to Nafzinger and Knötel, a guard battalion was rasied on 2 October 1813. It served at Leipzig and Hanau. It was organized into four companies of 204 men each, plus an 11 man command staff. Their uniform consisted of a royal blue kurtkas with a blue collar and white lapels. The cuffs were scarlet with white cuff flaps. The turnbacks and piping were scarlet with white epaulettes. The trousers were royal blue with white gaiters. The headdress was a shako with a scarlet pompom and tuft over a Polish cockade. The boots were black and the belts white. [1]

---

[1]Nafziger, *Poles and Saxons of the Napoleonic Wars,* p 37

Fig 116 Lithuanian Tartars of the Guard 1813-1814 (Knötel, Author's Collection)

Fig 117 Trumpeter of the Guard Lancers 1807 -1810 (Jeziorkowski, Author's Collection)

Fig 118 Guard Light Cavalry 1807 (Frey, Brown University Collection)

Fig 119 Guard Lancer trumpeter 1812 (Knötel, Author's Collection)

Fig 120 Guard Lancer Officer 1812 (Frey, Brown University Collection)

Fig 121 Guard Lancer 1812 (Knötel, Author's Collection)

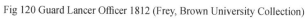

Fig 122 1st Guard Lancers (Vernet, Brown University Collection)

Fig 123 1st Guard Lancers in summer full dress (Frey, Brown University Collection)

THE COMING WAR - 1812

THE COMING WAR – 1812

An outcome of the success in 1809 and the role of Russia in that campaign was the stage was set for a future war between France and Russia over Poland. In anticipation of a war against Russia, Napoleon imposed an army on the Duchy of 60,000 men, which strained the finances of the land. The majority of the population and economically advantageous parts of the old Commonwealth still lay outside the borders of the Duchy, which would have made it more viable. The years 1810 to 1812 was a vast financial strain on the Duchy, but also allowed it to train for the upcoming war.

In February 1812, Napoleon concluded an agreement with the King of Saxony on preparations for war. The 5th, 10th, and 11th regiment of the Duchy each had four battalions and needed to be brought up to strength of 140 men per company. The rest of the regiments, not counting those in Spain, were to increase their company strength to 160 men. All the horse companies were to raise their strength from 100 to 120 men per company; the Emperor himself offering to garruntee the payment of these new troops.[1]

In June 1812, the Emperor established a General Confederation of the Kingdom of Poland. It was formally founded by Sejm of Duchy of Warsaw on 28 June 1812. It re-established a form of government very similar to the former Polish-Lithuanian Commonwealth, with Adam Kazimierz Cartoryski as its Marshal. The main goal of its activity was the re-introduction of Polish administration in the former Commonwealth territories of Lithuania, Belarus, and Ukraine that were to be liberated by La Grande Armée from Russian occupation. This ignored the rest of the lands still under control of Prussia and Austria as they were still Napoleon's allies. The confederation ceased to exist 30 April 1813.

In August 1812, it was decided that new six battalions of strzelcy (light infantry/rifles) would be raised in the liberated Lithuania. They were formed from outdoorsmen, foresters, and men who had an experience with hunting weapons, rifles, and muskets. All were volunteers, no recruits were accepted. They were issued Austrian muskets with rifled barrels (1807 Model), rifled carbines, and muskets. These sharpshooters were then organized into two regiments of three battalions each. But the amount of volunteers was disappointingly low (624 men) and only one regiment of two battalions was raised. This was known as the "Pulk Strzelców Litewskich" (Lithuanian Chasseur Regiment). This unit was mauled by the Russians at Kojdanow, Beresina River, and at Vilna. But the survivors, in contrast to other units, stayed in the ranks and retreated across Poland into Germany.

On the eve of war with Russia, Napoleon provided funds which allowed the Duchy to raise additional troops, which brought the Duchy's force up to approximately 75,000 men. A large group of new recruits and militia gave the Duchy 98,000 men at its disposal – which, while it was a goal, was never accomplished by the old Commonwealth. Upon invading Russia, a Lithuanian contingent of 16,000 men was added to the Duchy's forces.

The Polish contribution to the Grand Armeé was not wholly as a national force as in other corps. The largest concentration was centered on the Vth Corps made up of three divisions, plus artillery and cavalry elements. The cavalry was split up between the Vth Corps, the IVth corps of cavalry reserve, and attached to various divisions.

Polish cavalry were among the first to cross the Neman River on 28 June, and the forces fought with distinction throughout the campaign, culminating in the Battle at Borodino on 7 September. The Vth corps operated semi-independently as part of a flanking action that eventually forced the Russian army to retreat with heavy losses by both parties. General Dąbrowski helped to cover the retreat at the Berezina on the 28 November, where three Polish Generals of the Division and more than 200 officers received wounds. Of the 96,000 Polish troops who entered the campaign, more than 70,000 died on the march. Of all the troops, the Polish artillery returned to Warsaw without the loss of a single piece. [2]

[1] Nafziger, pg. 366
[2] Reddaway, pg. 233

Polish Armed Forces on the Eve of the 1812 Campaign

67,000 Polish from Duchy of Warsaw

12,000 Polish National Guard, depot companies, and garrisons in defence of Duchy of Warsaw

10,000 Polish in French service (Vistula Legion, 8th Chevauleger-Lancer, 1st and 3rd Guard Chevauleger-Lancer)

19,000 new formed regiments during campaign in Lithuania

108,000 Total

18th INFANTRY REGIMENT

This regiment wass organized by Confederation and the district of Grodno on 3 July 1812, under the name of the 1st Lithuanian Infantry.

Commander: Col. Aleksander Chodkiewicz, 13 July 1812

Battles and Skirmishes: **1813:** the defense of Modlin.

19TH INFANTRY REGIMENT

This was formed in Żmudź 1812.

Commander: Col. Konstantine Tyzenhaus, 13 July 1812.

Battles and Skirmishes: **1813:** the defense of Modlin.

20TH INFANTRY REGIMENT

Formed in Nowogródo in Lithuania 1812.

Commander: Col. Adam Bispink, 13 August 1812.

Battles and Skirmishes: **1813:** the defense of Modlin.

21st INFANTRY REGIMENT

Formed in Lithuania in 1812.

Commander: Col. Karol Przezdziecki, 13 July 1812; Col. Giełgud [3], 29 August 1812.

Battles and Skirmishes: **1813:** the defense of Modlin.

22nd INFANTRY REGIMENT

Formed in Mińszczyźnie in 1812.

Commander: Col. Stanisław Czapski, 13 August 1812.

Battles and Skirmishes: **1812:** around Bobruisk, around Kielce, Mińsk.

LITHUANIAN LIGHT INFANTRY REGIMENT

Formed in Mińszczyźnie in 1812.

Commanders: 1st Battalion, Lt. Col. Józef Kossakowski, 30 September 1812; 2nd Battalion, Col. Jan Grzymała, 6 December 1812; Jan Lubański.

Battles and Skirmishes: **1812:** Cimkowicze.

17th UŁAN REGIMENT

The regiment was formed in Lithuania from the counties: Wilno, Zawilejo, Brasława, Wiłkomira, Upitso, Rosieński, Szawelski, and Telszewski.

Commanders: Col. Michał Tyszkiewicz, 13 August 1812; Col. Franucszek Brzechffa, 1 March 1813.

Battles and Skirmishes: **1812:** Tylża, Labiau, Królewiec; 1813 Brandenburg, Sierakowo, Lubeka, Bornheft, Zeestadt.

---

[3]This is the ancestor of the British actor, Sir John Gielgud

18th UŁAN REGIMENT

The regiment was formed in 1812 in Lithuania.
Commander: Col. Karol Przezdziecki, 13 July 1812.
Battles and Skirmishes: **1812:** Kojdanów.

19TH UŁAN REGIMENT

The regiment was formed in 1812 in Nowogródko.
Commander: Col. Konstantine Rajecki, 13 July 1812.
Battles and Skirmishers: **1813:** Sierakowo.

20th UŁAN REGIMENT

The regiment was formed in 1812 in Lithuania.
Commander: Col. Obuchowicz, 13 July 1812.

21ST CHASSUER REGIMENT

The regiment was formed 22 September 1812 in Wilno from volunteers.
Commander: Col. Ignacy Moniuszko, 23 September 1812.

LITHUANIAN MOUNTED GENDARMES

This unit was formed to keep the lines of communication open in 1812. Napoleon accepted 200 of their ranks into the 1st Lancer Regiment of the Imperial Guard.
Battles and Skirmishes: **1812:** Berezina.

KRAKUS REGIMENT

This unit was formed by the decree of the Administrative Council, 20 December 1812, in fifty man sections from the Departments of: Kalisz, Krakow, Poznań, and Radom.
Commanders: Col. Aleksander Oborski, 20 March 1813; Józef Dwernicki, 1 January 1814.
Battles and Skirmishes: **1813:** Skarszew, Friedland, Georgenwalde, Strohweide, Neustadt, Frohburg, Luntzenau, Zehma, Rotha, Zetlitz, Wachau, Leipzig; **1814:** Claye, Paris.

9TH UŁAN REGIMENT OF FRANCO – POLISH CAVALRY

It was formed by decree on 23 February 1811 in Hamburg from mostly Poles.

SAPPER BATTALION

Formed by decree 30 March1810 with the 3rd Legion.
Commander: Maj. Maciej Kubicki.
Campaigns: **1812** and **1813**.

UNIFORMS

LITHUANIAN INFANTRY

The Lithuanian continguent seems to have worn a dark blue uniform with yellow distinctions. The pointed cuffs, lapels, collar, turnbacks, and shoulder strap piping were yellow on the kurtkas. The pants were also dark blue with a yellow side stripe. The czapka had a dark blue top and black base with a yellow band separating them. The czapka piping was yellow. There was a white Maltese cross cockade on the upper left of the czapka with a red ball pompom. The sunburst plate on the front sometimes featured the Lithuanian rider. All belting was white.

LITHUANIAN UŁANS

All the cavalry wore the typical ułan uniform pattern. The 17th had a dark blue uniform with crimson facings. The lance pennant was light blue over white. The czapka had a white cockade with a yellow Maltese cross on it. Over this was a blue, white, red plume. The 20th wore a green uniform with crimson distinctions and white epaulettes. The Czapka had a green top and a black fur base. The top piping was crimson. The lance pennant was red over white. In 1813, this was combined with the 16th regiment. The trumpeter for the 20th is depicted in a white coat with light blue distinctions. The trousers were red with yellow lace. The czapka had a white top with light blue piping, a black base, and yellow band separating them. The plume was yellow, white, and light blue.

LITHUANIAN MOUNTED GENDARMES

This unit wore a dark blue "surtout" with poppy red collars, cuffs, pipings, and turnbacks. The buttons, epauletes, and aguilettes were white, with the aguilettes worn on the left. The collar had white grenades. They had white breeches with knee length boots. Their headgear consisted of a black bicorne with white trim cockades and agraffes. This hat had a poppy red carrot shaped pompom. All belts were white. They carried a lance, carbine, saber, and a pair of pistols. The lance pennants were red over white.

KRAKUS

The Krakus were based on the customs of the Krakow region, and were similar to some troops raised during Kosciuszko's revolt. The initial uniform, according to Morawski, was worn from January to June 1813 based on Cossack cavalry – a long dark blue kaftan with a white lambskin collar, a red sash, and medium grey breeches. They wore a black lambswool colpak with a red bag, trimmed crimson. The saddle cloth was black lambswool trimmed red. The lance had no pennant. Alternatively, they wore a dark blue litwieka with crimson pointed cuffs and round collar. They had crimson confederatkas with white lambswool bands.

In later 1813 into 1814, the jacket was more a dark blue caftan with crimson pointed cuffs and collars, pipied white. On each breast there was a five cartridge pocket that was either plain blue or crimson cylindars with silver tops and bottoms on a white background. Officers' tunics had white or silver lace on the edges of the cuffs, collar, and trim. Officers wore double epaulettes in white metal. They wore a crimson sash around their waists. The hat was either a soft low crimson confederatka or a top stiff felt czapka, both without visors, but with a black lambswool band. If they had lance pennants they were swallow tailed blue over red or red over blue. The trousers were dark blue with a double crimson stripe on the outside leg. Eventually, units began using a "melon" style hat of crimson, over which, white felt strips radiated from the top crown to the white felt band at the base. A white cross cockade was worn on the left side with a heron feather attached to it. The saddle cloth was dark blue edged crimson and silver with a Polish eagle in the lower back corner. Instead of trumpeters, they used a buńczuk – this was a long strand of horse or yak hair attached to a pole surmounted by an ornament – usually a gold ball or crescent. The buńczuk could be white, black, or a combination thereof.

Fig 124 The Krakus Regiment (Chełminski, Author's Collection)

Fig 125 The Krakus Regiment (Gembarzewski, Author's Collection)

Fig 127 Cap plates from the period 1812-1814, Lithuanian and Polish motifs (Polish Army Museum)

Fig 126 Kurtka of the Polish Ułan regiment in 1814 (Polish Army Museum)

THE 1813 CAMPAIGN
AND THE END

THE 1813 CAMPAIGN

By the spring of 1813, the Duchy was able to make good on some of the losses from the previous campaign in Russia. There were still troops besieged in Gdansk and Zamość, who were not going to be able to help in the immediate future, but there were new troops raised in Modlin. General Dąbrowski was able to field a weak division to help in the Saxon campaign during May, but was forced to retreat from western Poland. By late August, Poniatowski had managed to move from Krakow with 21,000 soldiers toward Napoleon. By late September, the Emperor was moving towards Leipzig, following the defeat of several of his subordinates. The Poles met up with him there, forming the VIIIth corps and the IVth corps of the cavalry reserve.

Initially, Dąbrowski was active on the Prussian side of the Elbe and Poniatowski, guarding the operations from the Bohemian side. Because they were still able to field substancial numbers of cavalry, the Polish horsemen played an important part of screening the Emperor's forces.

The battle of Leipzig was fought over four days, from 16-19 October. Poniatowski was appointed a Marshal of France on the first day of battle. By the 19th of October, Napoleon was losing, his allies began to desert him, and his army was on the wrong side of the Elster and Parthe rivers. In the fighting that ensued during the French attempt to avoid being trapped, the VIIIth corps acted as the rear guard. The bridge over the Elster was blown prematurely and the wound Poniatowksi attempted to swim to safety on his horse, only to drown. In addition to the Marshal, almost 10,000 soldiers of the Duchy were killed, wounded, or taken prisoner. By the end of October, what was left of the Poles were under the command of Dąbrowski.

One of the innovations of the 1813 campaign was the introduction of the Krakus cavalry. In his experience against Cossack cavalry, Napoleon invisioned he could raise over 12,000 irregular light cavalry in the Duchy. Instead, the initial recruitment mustered only 2,000 riders. According to Wielecki, Poniatowski originally was going to place them among his existing units, but because of thier numbers and inexperience, he formed them into a special unit of vanguard soldiers at the suggestion of Gen. Uminski.[1]

By June 1813, there were three Krakus regiments, composed of four squadrons of 220 officers and men. They were banded together with the cuirassier regiment. They were trained differently from other cavalry units in that they relied on mobility, long-range reconnaissance, and flanking manuevers instead of massed charges. In September 1813, they showed thier mettle against Cossack cavalry near Eberbach.

Only 270 troopers survived Liepzig, but they served as the basis of a reconstituted regiment organized with the rest of the remaining Polish troops at Sedan in 1814. It was at Sedan that they acquired the distinctive melon beret. They remained with Napoleon through the defense of Paris. Some troopers joined the 1st Ułans in the Congress Kingdom.

4th UŁAN REGIMENT
Formed in May 1813 by Gen Dąbrowski at Wetzlarze.
Commanders: Col. Telesfor Kostanecki, killed 26 August 1813; Col. Tomasz Siemiątkowski, 29 August 1813.
Battles and Skirmishes: The campaign against Lützow's Partizans, Witenberg, Zanne, Jüterbog, Leipzig .

1ST COMPANY OF HORSE ARTILLERY
Formed in Cytawa (Saxony) in June 1813 by General de Division Dąbrowski.
Commander: Squadron Chief Jan Szwerin.
Battles and Skirmishes: The campaign in Saxony in **1813**, Dennewitz, Leipzig.

2ND COMPANY OF HORSE ARTILLERY
Formed in Cytawa (Saxony) in June 1813 with the VIII Corps of Prince Poniatowski.
Commander: Capt. Łukasz Dobrzański.
Battles and Skirmishes: The campaign in Saxony in **1813**, Dennewitz, Leipzig.

---

[1]Morawski, *Wojsko Księstwa Warszawskiego: Kawaleria.* Summary p. 4

UNIFORM VARIATIONS

In the 1813 campaign, there were eight ułan regiments – including two from Lithuania. According to Knoëtel, the ułans were dressed like the Vistula regiments with yellow facings on the lapels, collar, and cuffs along with the uniform piping. The lance penant was pictured as yellow over white.

The two hussar regiments were combined into one unit. The uniform was similar to the 13th Hussars, but substituted yellow for red on the collar, cuffs, and trouser stripe.

The 1st Chassuers folded in men of the 5th and substituted yellow for red on the collar, cuffs, piping, and trousers.

The horse artillery wore a chasseur style uniform, but in dark blue. The collar was black, with red piping around the collar, seams, and cuff. The epaulettes were red. They wore a black shako with red cords and plume. The shako had a white pcockade in the center.

THE 1814 CAMPAIGN AND AFTER

All that was left of the Polish forces after Leipzig were one infantry and five cavalry regiments. The Krakus had the honor of making the last attack in the battle for Paris. Once this was over, the remaing Duchy troops surrendered to Alexander I on the advice of Napoleon.[2] Article 19 of the Treaty of Paris, signed 11 April 1814, garrunteed the troops of the Duchy the right to return home with arms, baggage, maintenance of orders, and pensions in recognition of honorable service. In part because of the valor of the troops of the Duchy, Alexander invited many of the former soldiers to form the army of the new Kingdom of Poland army. This army, operating and developing an independent nature, was the basis for the troops that took part in the November Uprising of 1830.

A squadron of lancers followed Napoleon into exile on Elba, and finally through to Waterloo.

1ST UŁAN REGIMENT
Formed in Sedan in early January 1814.
Commanders: Col. Zygmund Kurnatowski; Col. Jan Tomicki, 1 January 1814; Col. Karol Madaliński, 5 April.
Battles and Skirmishes: **1814:** Brienne, Montmirail, Château-Thierry, Berry-au-Bac, Craonne, Laon, Arcis-sur-Aube, St. Dizier.

2ND UŁAN REGIMENT
Formed in Sedan in early January 1814.
Commander: Col. Tomasz Siemiątkowski; Michał Kossecki.
Battles and Skirmishes: **1814:** Montmirail, Châeau-Thierry, Berry-au-Bac, Craonne, Laon, Reims, Arcissur-Aube, St. Dizier, Paris.

HORSE ARTILLERY COMPANY
Made up from the two previous companies 1 January 1814 in Sedan.
Commander: Capt. Tomasz Konarski.
Battles and Skirmishes: **1814:** Brienne, Montmirail, Reims, Arcis-sur-Aube.

---

[2]Reddaway, pg. 234

EQUIPMENT AND ARMS

Any number of muskets was used from captured supplies as well as equipment provided by the state. The main weapon was based on the model 1777, modified in 1801. The calibre varied from 15.5mm to 17.5mm. It was about five feet long and weighed between 9-10 pounds. Some units used the 1786 model as well. It had a maximum range of 1,000 yards, but an effective range of 250 yards. Cavalrymen used the 1777 carbine that was only effective at about 30 yards. Lances were made of wood from ash trees, about 8.5 feet long and tipped with an iron point on the top and bottom. The lance pennant was about 2.25 feet long.

In Italy, between the years 1797 – 1799, the legions used Austrian muskets of the 1754, 1774, and 1784 issues. Some of the chasseur infantry were issued rifled carbines. By 1800, most of the troops were issued 1777 French Charlevilles made in Verona. When the Legion of the North was raised, they were given Prussian muskets of 1720 and 1782 models.

When the army of the Grand Duchy was formed, many were equipped with muskets of the 1801 variant, Russian arms, and some miscellaneous old Polish models. Between 1809 and 1811, most still carried Prussian muskets, but these were increasingly supplemented by Austrian 1807 models captured in the war with the Hapsburgs – many with rifled barrels. After 1811, the army was reequipped with French muskets of the 1793 and 1800/1801 patterns. Nafzinger says that at the end of the Russian campaign, in order to replace lost equipment and equip new recruits, 1808 Russian pattern muskets were used along with 1805 and 1809 Prussian model weapons.

The artillery was organized under the Gribeauval system with standardized calibres of 12-lbs 6-lbs and 6-inch howitzers. After the defeat of Austria in 1809 some infantry units were given small calibre 3 or 5-lb. regimental guns. The original ones used by the legions were French or Austrian. When the Duchy of Warsaw was organized, these were for the most part Prussian and Austrian guns. There was one 12-lb battery.

The Polish cavalry were equipped with several types of sabers:
Polish curved sabers (produced in liberated Galicia)
Prussian 1721 Model hussar curved saber
Prussian 1797 Model dragoon straight "pallash"
Austrian 1803 Model hussar curved saber
French IX, XI, and XIII Model curved and straight sabers
Russian sabers of various models

The cavalry were issued captured Prussian and Austrian carbines and French 1763 and Model 1786 carbines. Many pistols were the French Model 1777.

Fig 128 French 4-lb gun (Wikipedia)

Fig 129 French model of a 6-lb gun (Perry Miniatures)

Fig 130 6" howitzer (Wikipedia)

Fig 131 12-lb French gun (wikipedia)

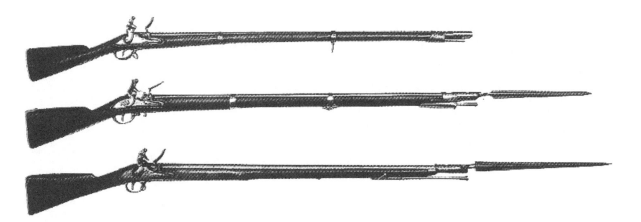

Fig 132 Muskets in use by the Polish infantry during this period from the top – Russian 1808, Austrian 1784 and English 1794 models (Polish Army Museum)

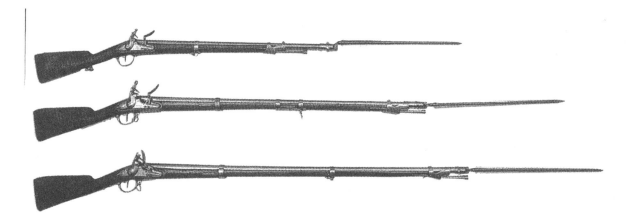

Fig 133 French muskets from the period – cavalry carbine, dragoon musket and infantry musket model 1777 (Polish Army Museum)

Fig 135 Virtuti Militari (Polish Army Museum)

Fig 134 Gen. Dąbrowski's general uniform showing the lace unique to Polish general officers (Polish Army Museum)

Ranks

The Polish Legions and the Army of the Duchy of Warsaw retained some rank distinctions unique to the Polish-Lithuanian forces, as well as incorporating French military insignias.

Lt. Gen. – two fringed epaulettes with thick braid and double lines of general lace in silver.

Maj. Gen. – two fringed epaulettes as above, but with only one line of general lace.

Chief of the Legion – one silver fringed epaulette on the right shoulder with four stripes placed on an angle.

Legion Major – same design as above, but with three stripes.

Chief de Battalion – same design as above, but with two stripes placed on an angle.

Battalion Major – same as above, but with one stripe.

Captain – one silver fringed epaulette on the right shoulder with four six pointed stars arranged in a square.

Lieutenant – same as above, but three stars arranged in a triangle.

2nd Lieutenant – same as above, but two stars in a line.

Ensign – same as above, but one star.

Staff Sergeant – two thick stripes at a 45 degree angle near the cuff.

Sergeant – one thick stripe at a 45 degree angle near the cuff.

Fourrier – one thick stripe at a 45 degree angle half way up the sleeve.

Corporal – two thin strips at 45 degree angle near the cuff.

APPENDICES:
BIOGRAPHIES AND BATTLES

APPENDIX I - SELECT BIOGRAPHIES

Wincenty Axamitowski (15 September 1760 - 13 January 1828) His mother was Tekla de Witte; the daughter of the engineer and General John de Witte who was prominent in the Polish army during the Saxon kings. He joined the army as a cadet in the Crown Artillery School in Warsaw in 1774. He was a second lieutenant in 1781. From 1783 he was in service as line officer.

He fought as a captain in the 1792 war with Russia as a company commander in the battles of Zielence and Ostróg. He was captured after later and was forced to temporarily take service in the Russian army where he was promoted to major. After the outbreak of the uprising of 1794 he returned to the Polish army, and fought as a captain in the defense of Warsaw. Kosciuszko accused him of clinging too closely to the Russians. After the uprising in Galicia he escaped to Italy. From 1797 he fought in the Legions, where he served as a chief of the battalion as well as organizing the Legion artillery. He defended Mantua and after its capitulation was captured by the Austrians. After his release on parole he returned to service. In 1801 he was the commander of the 2nd Demi-brigade sent to San Domingo. He was accused of questionable financial dealings and his reputation was viewed with suspect during the years 1803 – 1806. He fought at Jena in the French army and was placed in command of Poznan. He was promoted to the rank of general in 1806 in command of the artillery. From 1807, he was the commander of the artillery and engineering. As a result of disagreements with Prince J. Poniatowski

Fig 136 Gen Axamitowski in the uniform of the Legion artillery 1800 (Walski, Brown University Collection)

he was transferred to French service in 1808. In 1809 he was again service in the Polish Army as commander of the 2nd Infantry Brigade and commander of the 1st Division of the Department of Poznan.

During the 1812 campaign he was the deputy chief of staff for the King of Naples, Joachim Murat and in 1813 commanded a cavalry in Dąbrowski's division. He fought at Leipzig and Hanau before returning to the service of Murat. In 1814 campaign he commanded the French heavy cavalry brigade under General de Division Defranca. After the fall of Napoleon, he served as the deputy chairman of the Central Council of Administration of the Polish Corps. In 1815 he returned to the country and served in the army of the Congress Kingdom of Poland. He was the military commander of the department of Siedlce. In April 1816 moved to the reserve due to poor health.

Jérôme-Napoléon Bonaparte (15 November 1784 – 24 June 1860) was the youngest brother of Napoleon I and reigned as Jerome I, King of Westphalia, between 1807 and 1813. From 1816 onward, he bore the title of Prince of Montfort. After 1848, when his nephew, Louis Napoleon, became President of the French Second Republic, he served in several official roles, including Marshal of France from 1850 onward, and President of the Senate in 1852.

Napoléon Bonaparte (15 August 1769 – 5 May 1821) was a French military and political leader who rose to prominence during the French Revolution and its associated wars. As Napoleon I, he was Emperor of the French from 1804 until 1814, and again in 1815. Napoleon dominated European affairs for nearly two decades while leading France against a series of coalitions in the Revolutionary Wars and the Napoleonic Wars. He won the large majority of his 60 major battles and seized control of most of continental Europe before his ultimate defeat in 1815. One of the greatest commanders in history, his campaigns are studied at military schools worldwide and he remains one of the most celebrated and controversial political figures in Western history. In civil affairs, Napoleon implemented several liberal reforms across Europe, including the abolition of feudalism, the establishment of legal equality and religious toleration, and the legalization of divorce. His lasting legal achievement, the Napoleonic Code, has been adopted by dozens of nations around the world.

In 1809 the Austrians launched another attack against the French. Napoleon defeated them at the Battle of Wagram, dissolving the Fifth Coalition formed against France. After the Treaty of Schönbrunn in the fall of 1809, he divorced Josephine and married Austrian princess Marie Louise in 1810.

Escalating tensions over the existence of a Polish State and the Continental System led to renewed enmity with Russia. To enforce his blockade, Napoleon launched an invasion of Russia in 1812 that ended in catastrophic failure for the French. In early 1813, Prussia and Russia joined forces to fight against France, with the Austrians also joining this Sixth Coalition later in the year. In October 1813, a large Allied army defeated Napoleon at the Battle of Leipzig. The next year, the Allies launched an invasion of France and captured Paris, forcing Napoleon to abdicate in April 1814. He was exiled to the island of Elba. The Bourbons were restored to power and the French lost most territories they had conquered since the Revolution. However, Napoleon escaped from Elba in February 1815 and returned to lead the French government, only to find himself at war against another coalition. This new coalition decisively defeated him at the Battle of Waterloo in June. He attempted to flee to the United States, but the British blocked his escape route. He surrendered to British custody and spent the last six years of his life in confinement on the remote island of Saint Helena. His death in 1821, at the age of 51, was received by shock and grief throughout Europe and the New World. In 1840, roughly one million people lined the streets of Paris to witness his remains returning to France, where they still reside at Les Invalides.

Józef Grzegorz Chłopicki (14 March 1771 – 30 September 1854) He was born inVolhynia and ran away from school in 1785 to enlist as a volunteer in the Polish army. Chlopicki entered the army in 1785 and fought underKościuszko in the Uprising of 1794. Warsaw was surrendered to the Russians on November 8, 1794, after which Chlopicki went to France and joined the Army of the Cisalpine Republic under General Jan HenrykDąbrowski.He was present at all the engagements fought during 1792-1794, especially distinguishing himself at the Battle of Racławice, when he was General Franciszek Rymkiewicz's adjutant. Upon the formation of the Italian legion he joined the second battalion as major, and was publicly complimented by GeneralOudinot for his extraordinary valour at the storming ofPeschiera. He also distinguished himself at the battles of Modena,Busano, Casablanca and Ponto.

In 1807 he commanded the first Vistula regiment and distinguished himself at the battles ofEylau andFriedland. He was

Fig 137 Gen Józef Chłopicki (Author's collection)

awarded the Legion of Honor in Spain and was given the title of a French Imperial Baron for his heroism at the battle of Epila and the storming of Zaragoza. In 1809 he was promoted to be Brigadier General.In 1812, he fought at Smolensk and Moscow. At Smolensk he was seriously wounded, and on the reconstruction of the Polish army in 1813 was made a general of division.

Upon his return to Poland in 1814, Tsar Alexander I made him a General in the new Polish army with the rank of a general officer, but a personal insult from Grand Duke Konstantin resulted in his retiring into private life. At first he didn't join the November Uprising of 1830-31, but at the request of his countrymen accepted the dictatorship on 5 December 1830. Realizing the hopelessness of the insurrection, however, he quickly resigned on 17 January and joined the army as a private soldier. He fought at several battles including:Wawer (February 19) andOlszynkaGrochowska(February 20) he displayed all his old bravery, but was so seriously wounded at the Battle of OlszynkaGrochowska that he had to be conveyed to Krakow, where he lived in complete retirement until his death in 1854.

Prince Adam Kazimierz Czartoryski (1 December 1734 – 19 March 1823) The son of August Aleksander-Czartoryski, governor of Ruthenia, who gathered a great estate and founded prosperous workshops, Adam Kazimierz was educated in England and prepared to take over the Polish throne. But in the period when Poland was left without an elected king, Adam Kazimierz refused the crown (1763), which was accepted by his first cousinStanisław Augustus Poniatowski, who reigned as Stanisław II August as well as the future General Józef Poniatowski.

In 1765 he co-founded, The Monitor, the leading periodical of the Polish Enlightenment. In 1766 he reorganized the army of the Grand Duchy of Lithuania. In 1767 he joined the Radom Confederation. In 1768 he became the commander of the School of Chivalry (Corps of Cadets). In 1788-1792 he was Deputy fromLublin to the "Four-Year Sejm." Drawing closer the king once again, he became a leader of the Patriotic Party and co-founder of Poland's Commission of National Education.He supported the Polish Constitution of 3 May 1791, and headed a diplomatic mission to Dresden, attempting to convince Frederick Augustus III, Elector of Saxony to support the Commonwealth and accept its throne (after Poniatowski's future death). He refused to join theTargowica Confederation established to bring the Constitution down.

He was Marshal of the Convocation Sejm of 7 May - 23 June 1764, and of the Extraordinary Sejm of 26–28 June 1812, held in Warsaw. Thus he became Marshal of the General Confederation of the Kingdom of Poland.

Jan Henryk Dąbrowski (29 August 1755– 6 June 1818) Dąbrowski initially served in the Saxon army and joined the Polish-Lithuanian Commonwealth Army in 1792, shortly before the Second Partition of Poland. He was promoted to the rank of general in theKościuszko Uprising of 1794. After the final Third Partition of Poland, which ended the existence of Poland as independent country, he became actively involved in promoting the cause of Polish independence abroad. He was the founder of the Polish Legions in Italy serving under Napoleon since 1797, and as a general in Italian and French service he led the Wielkopolska Uprising of 1806 and contributed to the brief restoration of the Polish state following the Treaty of Tilst. He participated in the Polish-Austrian war and the French invasion of Russia until 1813. After Napoleon's defeat, he accepted a senatorial position in the Russian-backed Congress Poland, and was one of the organizers of the Army of Congress Poland. He did not always get along with Prince Poniatowski, but was a great Polish patriot.

Fig 138 Gen Jan Henryk Dąbrowski in the uniform of a Polish General 1812 (Polish Army Museum)

Louis-Nicolas d'Avout (10 May 1770 – 1 June 1823), better known as Davout, 1st Duke of Auerstaedt, 1st Prince of Eckmühl, was a Marshal of the Empire during the Napoleonic Era. His prodigious talent for war along with his reputation as a stern disciplinarian earned him the title "The Iron Marshal". He is ranked along withMasséna and Lannes as one of Napoleon's finest commanders. He was one of the few commanders in history to never be defeated on the field. His loyalty and obedience to Napoleon were absolute. Because of his reputation and skill he was allowed special triumphs and assignments including the governor-general of the newly created Duchy of Warsaw following the Treaty of Tilsit of 1807, and the next year created himDuke of Auerstädt.

Davout's military character has been interpreted as cruel, and he had to defend himself against many attacks upon his conduct at Hamburg. He was a stern disciplinarian, who exacted rigid and precise obedience from his troops, and consequently his corps was more trustworthy and exact in the performance of its duty than any other. For example, Davout forbade his troops from plundering enemy villages, a policy he would enforce by the use of the death penalty. Thus, in the early days of the Grande Armée, the III corps tended to be entrusted with the most difficult work. He was regarded by his contemporaries as one of the ablest of Napoleon's marshals. On the first restoration he retired into private life, openly displaying his hostility to the Bourbons, and when Napoleon returned from Elba, Davout rejoined him.

Joachim Mokosiej Denisko (b. approx. 1756 - d. approx. 1812) - In 1794 he led an unsuccessful expedition organized forVolhynia. From 1795 he was in Turkey, where he prepared the uprising while working with the Central Committee of Lvov. In1797 marched at the head of a small band (approx. 200 people) to Bukovina. He was defeated by the Austrian Army and peasant militia on 30 June at Dobronowa and fled to Turkey. He later rejected the offer for a commission in the Polish Legions. In 1798 he received amnesty from Russia and the return of his confiscated property, then served the Russians. He died in St. Petersburg.

Archduke Ferdinand Karl Joseph of Austria-Este (April 25, 1781 – November 5, 1850) was the third son ofArchduke Ferdinand of Austria-Este and of his wife Princess Maria Beatrice Ricciardad'Este. In 1805 in the war of the Third Coalition against France, Ferdinand was commander-in-chief of the Austrian forces with General Karl Freiherr Mack von Leiberich as his quartermaster general. In October his army was surrounded at Ulm. General Mack surrendered, but Ferdinand managed to escape with 2,000 cavalry to Bohemia. There he took command of the Austrian troops and raised the local militia. With a total of 9,000 men he set out for Iglau to distract attention from the Coalition's movements. He succeeded in holding the Bavarian division of Prince Karl Philipp von Wrede in Iglau thereby and preventing it from joining the Battle of Austerlitz.

In 1809 in the war of the Fifth Coalition against France, Ferdinand commanded an Austrian army of 36,000 men. In April he invaded the Duchy of Warsaw hoping to encourage a local uprising against Napoleon. But the Poles rallied to Prince Poniatowski. Ferdinand was defeated at the Battle of Raszyn, but managed to occupy Warsaw. In June, however, Ferdinand was compelled to withdraw from Warsaw, and to give up Kraków andGalicia as well.In 1815, Ferdinand commanded two divisions of the Austrian Reserve. The following year he was appointed military commander in Hungary.In 1830 Ferdinand was appointed military and civil governor of Galicia, taking up residence in Lviv. After the Revolution of 1848 he resided mostly in Italy.

Valerian (Valery) Wiktoryn Dzieduszycki (1754 – 10 March 1832) He was educated in Lwow and Vienna, earning honors from the Empress Maria Theresa and Joseph II. He was a reform supporter of the Four Year Sejm. After the establishment of the Constitution of May 3, he promised to release his top serf students from servitude. After the second partition, he moved to the district of Galicia because he would not submit to an oath of homage to the Tsarina.

In 1794 he was in the service of Kosciuszko in Lwow. During the Kosciuszko Insurrection he provided material and diplomatic support in trying to get aid from Austria. He attempted to mediate between the insurrection authorities and the court of Vienna to get the Austrian Archduke to accept the throne of the Republic. After the fall of the insurrection he became the leader of the Central Committee of Lwow and was arrested for attempting to incite an uprising in Galicia. As the head of the Central Committee of Lwow, he was the supreme authority of conspiracy in the area of the former territory of the Republic.Following his arrest, he was imprisoned from 1797 – 1800 by the Austrians in Olomouc. Dzieduszyckiwas released after promising to pledge loyalty to the state. Subsequently he settled in the country, retiring from political life and devoting himself to the study of farming and nature.

Stanislaw Fisher, also **Stanislaw Fischer** (1769 -18 October 1812) - A Polish General and Chief of Staff for the Army of the Duchy of Warsaw. After graduating from the Knights School, he joined the Wielkopolska Brigade under the command of Tadeusz Kosciuszko. He served under Kosciuszko during the Polish-Russian War of 1792, fighting at the battles of Polonny and Dubienka as a lieutenant. He was awarded the Knight's Cross of the Order of Virtuti Militari . He was captured at Maciejowice and imprisoned until paroled in 1796.

Fischer went to Paris and was instrumental in organizing the Danube Legion. He was captured in one of their first battles at Offenburg in June 1799 and was not released until 1800. He resigned in 1801 and lived as a civilian until 1807. When Dąbrowski came to Wielkopolska, Fischer was given command of a brigade and took part in the siege of Gdansk.   In 1807 he became an Inspector General of the Infantry; in 1808 became a brigadier general and chief of staff of the Duchy of Warsaw. Within two years, the army was effectively organized, especially the artillery. He was wounded in Raszyn and awarded the Commanders Cross of the VirtutiMilitari. In 1811 he organized the Duchy's forces for the war with Russia. In 1812 went to Moscow as the chief of staff for the V Corps under Prince Poniatowski. He fought in the Battle of Borodino and the capture of Moscow. During the retreat from Moscow, he fought in the rear guard and was killed at Winkowem on 18 October 1812 .

Fig 139 Gen. Stanisław Fisher (Polish Army Museum)

Fig 140 King Federic Augustus I (Dresden Galerie Neue)

Frederick Augustus I (23 December 1750 – 5 May 1827) was King of Saxony (1805–1827). He was also Elector Frederick Augustus III (Friedrich August III.) of Saxony (1763–1806) and Duke Frederick Augustus I (Polish: Fryderyk August I) of the Duchy of Warsaw (1807–1813). He succeeded his father in 1763 as elector Frederick Augustus III. His father and grandfather were both elected Kings of Poland, but Tsarina Catherine decided to offer the crown to Stanisław Augustus Poniatowski in 1763. He was named as successor to Stanisław Poniatowski under the May Constitution.

After the defeat at Jena in 1806 he made peace with Napoleon and was named both King of Saxony and titular ruler of the Duchy of Warsaw. Frederick Augustus remained a loyal ally to France even after the disastrous Russian campaign (1812–13). In the Battle of Leipzig(October 1813), his troops went over to Prussia and he was taken prisoner. At the Congress of Vienna in 1815, Frederick Augustus lost three-fifths of his territory to Prussia. He spent the rest of his life attempting to rehabilitate his truncated state.

Throughout his political career Frederick Augustus tried to rehabilitate and recreate the Polish state that was torn apart and stopped existing after the final partition of Poland in 1795, however he did not succeed - for this he would blame himself for the rest of his life.

Jozef Grabinski (1771- 1836) was a Colonel in the 1st Demi-brigade in 1801. He was a Brigadier General in 1807 and was commander of the Polish-Italian legion in 1808. He fought in Russia and later took part in the 1830 Uprising.

Michal Grabowski (1773 – 17 August 1812) He was the natural son of the King of Poland, Stanisław August Poniatowski and Elizabeth Grabowska. He remained under the care of his father the King and was groomed early for a career in the military. He was a major in the 5th Fusilier regiment at the time of the 1792 war with Russia and an Adjutant during the Kosciuszko Insurrection. He remained with the King after the third partition, but joined the Duchy's army as a colonel in the 1st Infantry Regiment in 1807. He was later promoted to brigadier general who saw action at Gdansk and Modlin. From 1809 to 1810 he was in command of the garrison at Gdansk. In 1812 he commanded the 1st Brigade of Kniaziewicz's 18thDivision of the Vth Corps. He was killed in action on 17 August 1812 during the storming of Smolensk.

Maurycy Hauke (1775 – 1830) His family was originally of German origin (Moritz von Hauke) and studied at the artillery school at Warsaw. He joined the Polish Army in 1790 as an engineer, served in the war against Russia in 1792 as well as the Kosciuszko Insurrection. He made his way to Italy and joined the legions and was commissioned a general when he returned to Poland in 1807. From 1809 to 1813 he was in command of the fortress at Zamość. His defense of Zamość in 1813 is considered one of the heroic actions of the campaign. In 1816 he was appointed Deputy Minister of War for Congress Poland and was given the title of Count.

Fig 141 Maurycy Hauke (Artist unknown)

Władysław Franciszek Jabłonowski (25 October 1769–29 September 1802) was a Polish and French general of mixed ancestry - the illegitimate child of Maria Dealire, an English aristocrat, and an unidentified African. He acquired the nickname "Murzynek" (loosely translated as "chocolate cake"). Maria Dealire's husband, the Polish nobleman KonstantyJabłonowski, accepted him as his son.In 1783 he was admitted to the French military academy at Brienne-le-Château. There he was a schoolmate ofNapoleon and Davout. In a climate of bullying, he was subjected to racist taunts, including from Napoleon. On graduation he joined the Régiment de Royal-Allemand where he attained the rank of lieutenant.

In 1794 he fought in the Kościuszko Uprising against Tsarist Russia. He took part in the battles ofSzczekociny, Warsaw,Maciejowice, and at Praga. In 1799 he was made a brigadier general in the Polish legions.From 1801 he was the commander of the Danube Legion. He was sent to Haiti by his own request prior to the rest of the legions in May 1802. He worked to put down the Haitian Revolution, but died from yellow fever on 29 September 1802 inJérémie, Haiti.

Fig 142 Władysław Franciszek Jabłonski (Artist unknown

Fig 143 Berek Joselewicz (Julius Kossak)

Berek Joselewicz (1764–1809) was a Jewish-Polish merchant and colonel in the Polish Army during the Kościuszko Uprising. He raised an all-Jewish cavalry unit that was the first Jewish military formation in the modern era. They took part in the 1794 defence of Praga where the unit was destroyed with few survivors. After the loss of Poland in the third partition, Joselewicz left for Galicia and then Italy where he joined the Polish Legions in command of a cavalry company. He fought at Trevia, Novi, Hohenlinden, Austerlitz and Friedland. He was awarded the Knight's Cross of the VirtutiMilitari and the Legion of Honor with a Golden Cross for his merits. He remained in the army as squadron leader in the 5th Mounted Chasseur Regiment for the Duchy of Warsaw in 1807. He was killed in the Battle of Kock in 1809 during an encounter with a unit of Austrian hussars where he was greatly outnumbered. His son, Josef Berkowicz (1789–1846), also fought in the Battle of Kock, and later served as a squadron chief during the November Uprising of 1830, during which he also attempted to convince Jewish soldiers to desert the Russian army and join the Poles.

Baron Karol Otto Kniaziewicz (4 May 1762 – 9 May 1842) attended the Knight School in Warsaw, participated in the Polish-Russian war of 1792 and the Kościuszko Uprising in the rank of a Major-General in 1794. He distinguished himself during the Napoleonic Wars in the Polish Legions as commander of the 1st Legion. In 1799 he was appointed to the position of a Brigadier General. From 1799 until 1801 he organized and commanded the Danube Legion, distinguishing himself during the Battle of Hohenlinden.

In 1812 he was a Brigadier General in the Grand Duchy of Warsaw, participating in the Russian Campaign of 1812. In 1814 he left Poland for France. During the November Uprising in 1830–1831 he served as representative of the "Polish National Government" in Paris. He was co-founder of the Polish library in Paris.

Fig 144 Karol Kniaziewicz (Polish Army Museum)

Jan Konopka (1777– 12 December 1814) was a lieutenant in the Kościuszko Uprising, captain of the Polish Legion in Italy, regiment commander in the Legion of the Vistula, as well as general of the French Army and the Duchy of Warsaw. Konopka has been described as "a brave man with cold mind in combat."

In 1792 he was a Second Lieutenant in the Ukrainian National Cavalry Brigade and took part in the Polish-Russian War of 1792. During theKościuiszko Uprising he fought as a lieutenant where he was wounded, and decorated. After the failure of the insurrection he emigrated to France and volunteered for the French army. In 1797 Konopka joined the Polish Legions in Italy with a rank of captain and took part in all of the Legion's campaigns.After the dissolution of the Legion, he returned to service in France as a Major. He was soon made a regiment commander in the Legion of the Vistula. He fought in the War of the Fourth Coalition and for his part in the Battle of Friedland was decorated with the Légiond'honneur. Subsequently he fought as part of Napoleon's forces in the Peninsular War In 1811 he was made a general of the French army after the Battle of Albuera and later of, Duchy of Warsaw, and a Baron of the French Empire.

During Napoleon's invasion of Russia in 1812 he was made the commander of the 3rd Lancers (Lithuanian) of the Guard. Most of his unit was captured, the rest scattered at Slonin(only the Lithuanian Tartar unit that was out on patrol escaped) and he was wounded and taken prisoner. After being released from prison in 1814 he was offered the command of the 1st Cavalry Brigade of Congress Poland, but he declined. Exhausted by wounds, prison, and fatigue he died the same year in Warsaw.

Kazimierz Józef Konopka (March 1769 - September 1805) He was the secretary to Hugo Kołłątajwhen he was Crown Vice Chancellor (1791). During the Kosciuszko Uprising joined a cavalry unit, gaining a reputation for his actions in Warsaw in May and June 1794 against alleged Russian sympathizers. He was exiled and went to Paris , where he joined a French hussar unit, fighting on the island of Corsica . In 1796 he joined the Polish Legions in Italy;commissioned as an officer (he held the rank of Major in 1798). He served in the cavalry, commanded a squadron and later the battalion. In 1801 he was adjutant Jan HenrykDabrowski . He died of a heart attack in 1805 in Bari, though his death is also listed as 1809.

Fig 145 Tadeusz Kościuszko (Karl Schweikart, National Museum of Warsaw)

Andrzej Tadeusz Bonawentura Kościuszko (4 or 12 February 1746 – 15 October 1817) Born to the minor nobility, he graduated from the Corps of Cadets in Warsaw and moved temporarily to Paris during the Bar Confederation. He returned to Poland in 1774, and then moved to North America in 1776 where he took part in the American Revolution as a Colonel, mustering out as a Brigadier General in 1783. After returning to Poland he was commissioned a Major General in the Polish-Lithuanian Army in 1789. He served with distinction during the 1792 war against Russia and organized an uprising against Russia in 1794 where he served as the head of the nation. Following his capture and imprisonment following the battle of Maciejowice he was pardoned by Tsar Paul in 1796. He was the leading force in Polish politics from 1793 until his death in 1817. Kościuszko did not believe that Napoleon would restore Poland in any durable form. When Napoleon's forces approached the borders of Poland, Kościuszko wrote him a letter, demanding guarantees of parliamentary democracy and substantial national borders, which Napoleon ignored. Kościuszko concluded that Napoleon had created the Duchy of Warsaw in 1807 only as an expedient, not because he supported Polish sovereignty. Consequently, Kościuszko did not move to the Duchy of Warsaw or join the new Army of the Duchy, allied with Napoleon.

Amilkar Anthony Kosinski (16 December 1769 - 10 March 1823) served in the army starting in 1792 and after the second partition, tried to raise insurrection in the Ukraine, but was forced to flee. During the Kościuszko Insurrection he was given the rank of captain during the defense of Warsaw. At the end of the insurrection, he emigrated to Italy. Unable to join the French Army he went to Nice to live in order to acquire citizenship, adopting the pseudonym "Amilkar". As a French citizen he enlisted in the army, fighting the Italian campaigns of 1795 and 1796. He supported Dąbrowski in the creation of the Polish Legions (from 1797 he was commander of the battalion). At that time, Kosinski earned the nickname "the first legionary". In 1798 he was promoted to colonel. After the surrender of Mantua in 1799 he was captured by the Austrian, was released in 1800. He served from 1802 as Chief of Staff of the General Inspectorate of Milan. After learning about the Polish Legions being sent to San Domingo, offered his servicesto Tsar Alexander I , but nothing came of this. Losing faith in further service in the Legions he resigned his commission in 1803.

He returned to service in 1806 alongside Dąbrowski, helping to organize the uprising in Wielkopolska. In 1807 he took part in the operations around Gdańsk and Tczew. He took over for Dąbrowski when he was wounded and led his divisions against Gdańsk. Later that same year he was awarded a campaign Knight's Cross of the Order of Military Virtue. After he was passed over for promotion by Prince Poniatowski in 1808, he resigned. During the 1809 campaign he commanded Polish troops, but resign when he was passed over for promotion again. In 1812 he was commissioned as a General de Division and organized the defensive line along the Bug River against the Russians. After the campaign was over he resigned from service.

Vincent Krasinski (30 January 1782 - 24 November 1858) Joined the national cavalry at eight years old, and as a ten year old was appointed lieutenant.

In early December 1806, after consulting withHenrykDąbrowski, he organized a Guard of Honour and received the rank of colonel.After the arrival of Napoleon in Warsaw was made a member of the imperial staff and was ordered to form a mounted regiment. On 4 April 1807 Krasinski receivedthe Legion of Honor, and was appointed him commander of the 1st Polish Guard Lancer. In 1808 the regiment was sent to Spain where it made its famous charge at Somosierra. In 1811Krasinski was appointed a Count of the Empire. He was promoted to Brigadier General in 1812. After returning from Moscow he was promoted to General de Division and stationed in Saxony. After Napoleon's abdication he brought the majority of Polish troops out of France.

Jean Baptiste Pelletier (1772 - 1862) Joined the artillery in 1794 and was the commander of the artillery as a colonel in 1808. He was appointed Inspector of the Artillery and Engineering for the Duchy of Warsaw in 1808. He helped create the topography department and took part in the 1809 campaign; helping in the capture of the fortress of Zamość. During the campaign in 1812 was captured by the Russians and returned to French service at the end of 1814. Later he went on to hold high command positions including the Military School in Metz as a Major General. He was a Brigadier General in the army of the Duchy of Warsaw, a Major General in the French army and commanded troops in the Polish army and was decorated with the Knight's Cross of the Order of the VirtutiMilitari.

Prince Józef Antoni Poniatowski (7 May 1763 – 19 October 1813) was born in Vienna, Austria and the son of Andrzej Poniatowski, the brother of the last king of Poland Stanisław II Augustus and a field marshal in the service of Austria. His father died when Józef was 10, Stanisław II Augustus then became his guardian and the two enjoyed a close personal relationship that lasted for the rest of their lives. Because of King Stanisław II August's influence that Poniatowski chose to consider himself a Polish citizen rather than Austrian, even though he transferred to the Polish army at the age of 26. Having chosen a military career, Poniatowski joined the Austrian imperial army where he was commissioned a Lieutenant in 1780, in 1786/1788 promoted to Colonel. Poniatowski fought in Austro-Turkish war and distinguished himself at the storming of Šabac on April 25, 1788, where he was seriously wounded.

When the Polish Army was reorganized in 1789 he was summoned back to Poland by his uncle to serve in the army. In October 1789, together with Tadeusz Kościuszko and three others, he received the rank of Major-General, and was appointed commander of a division in Ukraine On May 6, 1792 Poniatowski was appointed Lieutenant-General and commander of the Polish army in the Ukraine, with the task of defending the country against the imminent Russian attack. There Prince Józef was aided by Kościuszko and Michał Wielhorski. In the fighting, badly outnumbered and outgunned by the enemy, obliged constantly to retreat, but disputing every point of vantage, he turned on the pursuer whenever the Russian pressed too closely, and won several notable victories. He did not agree with the King's decision to join the Targowica Confederation and eventually resigned his commission. He returned to Poland to fight in Kościuszko's revolt, distinguishing himself around Warsaw. After the defeat in 1794 he returned to private life in Warsaw.

When Murat entered Warsaw, he negotiated with Poniatowski and declared him the Chief of Military Forces,

Fig 146 Prince Józef Poniatowski (Józef Grassi)

which alienated active leaders such as Dąbrowski and Zajączek. In July 1807, he was appointed the Minister of War for the Duchy and Head of the Army and sought to organize the army in conjunction with Marshal Davout. In March 1809 he was officially appointed Commander-in-Chief and despite multiple problems, led the army successfully against the Austrian invasion in 1809. He commanded the Vth Corps during the Russian Campaign and part of the right wing. Upon returning from Moscow, he reorganized the Polish forces and fought in the 1813 campaign at the head of the VIIIth Corps. He was made a Marshal of France on 16 October 1813 during the battle of Leipzig and was killed while covering the retreat.

Alexander Anthony John Rożniecki (12 February 1774 - 24 July 1849) A graduate of the Corps of Cadets, he joined the army in 1788 as a member of the Horse Guards. In 1789 he was promoted to lieutenant and joined a National Cavalry Brigade. He was promoted to captain in 1792 and fought in the Polish-Russian War in 1792. He took a leading place in the organization and conspiracy leading up to the Kósciuszko Uprising, being promoted to Vice-brigadier. In 1798 he joined the Polish Legions as a colonel, taking part in the campaigns of 1799 and 1801. He served as a Brig. Gen in the Danubian Legion as well as Commander of the Legion for a time. After the dissolution of the Polish Legions served in the corps of General. Massena . He participated in several campaigns in Italy and Germany, notably the Battle of Castelfranco in 1805. In 1806 he joined the Duchy of Warsaw's army and in 1807 was Inspector of the Cavalry. During the Polish-Austrian War of 1809, he showed flashes of brilliance as a commander, especially at Raszyn. His forces were the first to enter Krakow and overcame the last Austrian resistance in eastern Małopolska. In 1810 he was promoted to the rank of Maj. Gen. in charge of gathering intelligence for the war against Russia. During the 1812 campaign he was a cavalry commander of the IVth Corps of the Grand Armee; fighting at Mir and Borodino. In 1813 he was the Chief of Staff for the VIIIth (Polish) Corps. Wounded at Leipzig , he was captured by the Russians. After 1815 he became the commander of the Polish Cavalry and organized the Gendarmes. He was instrumental in supressing the patriotic societies within the Congress Kingdom and stayed with the Tsarist forces at the outbreak of the November Uprising.

Franciszek Rymkiewicz (1756 – 1799) - In 1778, after being refused admission to the Lithuanian army, he joined the Russian Army as a sergeant in theStarotulski infantry regiment. He rose quickly through the ranks, being promoted to officer in 1783 and Captain in 1787, taking part in campaigns against the Ottomans. Under the guise of health issues, he was allowed to resign from the Russian Army in 1790, but was unable to join the Polish Army before the end of the 1792 war with Russia. He was commissioned a major a Lithuanian Rifle battalion and was promoted to Lt. Colonel during the Kósciuszko Uprising, distinguishing himself during the siege of Warsaw. On 30 August he was promoted from Lt. Col. to Maj.Gen. He joined the Polish Legions in Italy and was killed in action at Adige in 1799.

Michael Sokolnicki (29 September 1760 – 24 September 1816) He was a graduate of the Knight School of the Corps of Cadets. He graduated as a lieutenant in engineering in 1780 and then spent several years traveling abroad to gain experience in military enginnering. In 1789, he was promoted to captain and organized the Lithuanian engineer corps. He was promoted to Lt. Col of the engineers in 1792. At the outbreak of the war with Russia he was made Quartermaster General of the Lithuanian Army, as well as in charge of engineering. During the Kósciuszko Uprising he was given the rank of Col. Ad organized a rifle corps in Wielkopolska, fighting at Warsaw, Wawrzyszcza,Kamiona, Bydgoszcz, Fordon and Toruń. He imprisoned in Russia after the defeat of the Uprising, but was allowed to return to Poland after Tsarina Catherine's death in 1796. In 1797 he assisted in the creation of the Danubian Legion and by 1800 he was in command of the Legion's infantry. He spent the next few years primarily in scientific pursuits, but took an active part in the 1806 campaign. With the creation of the army of the Duchy of Warsaw in 1807, he commanded forces at Raszyn, Falenty, Grochow, Mount Kawaleria and Sandomirz. In August 1809 he received promotion to Maj. Gen. as well as the Commander's Cross of the VirtutiMilitari. While recovering

Fig 147 Michaeł Sokolnicki (Józef Sonntag)

from illness he criticized Prince Poniatowski and was struck from the active army rolls of the Duchy. He served on Napoleon's Staff during the Russian Campaign and in 1813 was given command of the Polish VIIth's corps cavalry and later the IVth Corps.Sokolnicki returned to France with the remaining Polish forces and defended Paris. He was entrusted with bringing both Prince Poniatowski's and former King StanisławLeszynski's bodies back to Poland after the peace.

Piotr Strzyżewski (or Strzyżowski) (29 June 1777 – 6 January 1854) He was born to a noble family who held several offices in the Commonwealth. Strzyżewski graduated from the Knight's School in time to fight in the Kósciuszko Insurrection. He joined the 16th Infantry regiment as an Ensign and was quickly promoted to lieutenant. After the Uprising he stayed in Warsaw. Strzyżewski was among those who met the Emperor in Poznan in 1807, and impressed him with his fervour. Strzyżewski joined a local cavalry unit in Galicia when it was raised and eventually incorporated into the 3rd Cavalry Regiment. During the 1809 war against Austria he fought in several battles, suffering a head wound at Raszyn, but recovering enough to take part in the march on Zamość. He later formed a rifle battalion that took part in the battles in Eastern Galicia. Building up the force as he went east, he eventually built a sizable force that captured much of the area before he met Russian troops and the peace held the conquests in place. In honor of this initiative, he was promoted to Lt. Col. Of the 14th Cuirassiers Regiment in the Duchy's army. In 1810 he was transferred to the command of the 16th Lancers.

Józef Wielhorski (1759-1817).As an officer (rotmistrz) he fought in the Polish-Russian War of 1792 and later, as a colonel, in the Kościuszko Uprising. Tadeusz Kościuszkosent him to revolutionary France with the goal of obtaining help from the Committee of Public Safety, his requests for a French expeditionary corps were however futile. Under Napoleon, he would become (in 1797) a general in the Polish Legions, where he would be taken captive at the Siege of Mantua (1799). As a protest for the French-Austrian peace, he returned to partitioned Poland, but in 1809, with the France again at war with Austria, he would join the pro-French Polish forces and became a general in the Duchy of Warsaw, where he also became a deputy minister of war. He remained in the Duchy during Napoleon's invasion of Russia; in its aftermath, in the Congress Poland, he was a Minister of War and a member of its senate.

Fig 148 Józef Wielhorski (Polish Army Museum),

Józef Rufin Wybicki (1747 – 1822) An officer of the Polish Army who fought in the legions and best known for writing the words to MazurekDąbrowskiego (Dąbrowski's Mazurka), which was later adopted as the Polishnational anthem. He was to the Sejm of 1767 and later joined the Confederation of Bar, aimed at opposing the Russian influence and the King Stanisław August Poniatowski. Wybicki returned to Poland, in the 1770s was influential in the Commission of National Education. He then supported King Stanisław August Poniatowski and his proposed reforms. He participated in the Kościuszko Uprising and was a member of the Military Section of the Provisional Council of the Duchy of Masovia. After the failure of this insurrection he moved to France were he stayed in close contact with both Tadeusz Kościuszko and Jan HenrykDąbrowski. He worked with Dąbrowskito organize the Polish Legions in Italy; writing the Dąbrowski's Mazurka in 1797. He helped Dąbrowski organize the WielkopoloskaUprising in 1806.After the cre-

ation of the Duchy of Warsaw in 1807, he held a number of positions in its Department of Justice, and continued working for it after the Duchy's transformation into Congress Poland. In 1817 he became president of the Supreme Court of Congress Poland.

Prince Józef Zajączek (1752 - 1826)Started his career in the Polish-Lithuanian Army as an aide-de-camp to Hetman Franciszek KsaweryBranicki in the 1770's. He was Branicki'spolitical supporter, before joining the liberal opposition during the Great Sejm in 1790 becoming a radical supporter of the Constitution of 3 May 1791. He held the rank of general, during the Polish–Russian War of 1792 and KościuszkoUprising. After the partitions of Poland, he joined the Napoleonic Army, and was a general in Napoleon's forces until his wounding and capture during Napoleon's invasion of Russia in 1812. From 1815 he became involved in the governance of the Congress Kingdom of Poland, becoming the first Namestnik of Kingdom of Poland.

Fig 150 Józef Zajączek (Polish Army Museum)

APPENDIX II – BATTLES OF THE LEGIONS IN ITALY

Aulla (27 May 1799)
1st LEGION - Grenadier Battalion
LEGION CAVALRY- Cavalry Regiment

As part of an operation against Austrians around Fornovo. On 27 May Dąbrowski, personally led the reserve in an attack on Aulla. Hitting the enemy on the flanks, and drove them from their positions.The Austrians stopped and fortified themselves in Villafranca, but realizing that the Polish troops had surround the town with the chasseurs, and to were planning to assault it with the grenadiers. Subsequently the Austrians withdrew into Filattiéra, pursued by the Poles who pursued them to Pontremoli. In the meanwhile, the center column lost its way and was not able to arrive at Monte Sungo, before 8 a.m. On the same day, Dąbrowski entered Pontremoli he brought the center column from Monte Sungo, quickly attacked the enemy and routed them. The column pushed their outposts forward until they reached San Terenzo, where the Austrians were rallying. A detachment from this column continued to press on and attacked the Austrians at Sassalbo, forcing them to retreat beyondCollagna; into the Secchia valley and occupying the fortified position of Linari.

Bergheim (15 December 1800)
Danube Legion

Borghetto (25 May 1799)
1st LEGION - 1st Battalion, 2nd Battalion, 3rd Battalion
(seeCento-Croci below)

Bosco (24 October 1799)
1stLEGION - 1st Battalion, 2nd Battalion, 3rd Battalion, Grenadier Battalion
LEGION CAVALRY -Cavalry Regiment

The French pushed the Austrians back towards Alessandria from their starting position around Novi. On the 23rd, the Commander of the Army of Italy, Gen. Championnet, ordered Gen. Saint-Cyr to move from Genoa towards Acqui. He dislodged Gen Karackzay from the valleys around the Orba and Scrivia Rivers which they had been holding since Novi on 15 August.

Bosco (4 November 1799)
1st LEGION - 1st Battalion, Grenadier Battalion
LEGION CAVALRY - Cavalry Regiment

This battle at Bosco was a follow-up from the action on 24 October and a prelude to the combat at Novi on 6 November 1799.

Busano (4 July 1799)
1st LEGION - 1st Battalion

Calvi (9 December 1798)
1st LEGION - 1st Battalion, 2nd Battalion

Campo Forte (8 June 1799)
1st LEGION - 1st Battalion, 2nd Battalion, 3rd Battalion, Grenadier Battalion

On June 8, Macdonald changed his previously agreed to plans with Moreau and sent the Polish Divisionto Sassalbo. The 1st Battalion, led by Chef Brun, drove the enemy from their outposts at Cervarezza and Campo-Forte. On June 12, the Austrians tried to stop the advance of the Poles close to Grassano, at the mountains slopes. They deployed the infantry in line, and the cavalry along the plain. The Franco-Polish forces were deficient in cavalry, but the causeway which led toSassalbo, was almost impossible to pass with the horses.The enemy had deployed armed peasants bands to guard this in order to protect the passages. The battalion of Polish Chasseurs was split into two parts, on the flanks of the advance guard to the right of the Crostolo Creek. The peasants were soon dispersed by the Chasseurs, and the Austrians pushed forward some detachments to engage the Poles. The division continued to move forward, while the Austrians retreated in response to the pressure on their flanks until they reached the plain of Reggio. The Poles, camped at Vezzano, and placed their outposts in the hills in front of Rivalta. They took some prisoners and killed some hussars, while taking their horses, which could not cross the hedges nor jumped over the ditches. Many of the armed peasants were massacred without pity. On June 13, in the morning, the Polish division was ready to attack the enemy at Reggio, when it learned the Austrians had already left the place. The division passed through Reggio, along the road to Parma, to Quaresimo (today Codemondo). About midday, the army of Naples, led by Macdonald, arrived from Modena and reached the Polish rearguard.

Casa Bianca (16 January 1800)
1st LEGION - 2nd Battalion

Cassano (27 April 1799)
1st LEGION - 2nd Battalion

The Battle of Cassano d'Adda was fought on 27 April 1799 between the town of Cassanod'Adda and Milan. It resulted in a victory for the Austrians and Russians under Gen. Suvorov over Gen. Moreau's forces. With General Bonaparte in Egypt, the Second Coalition launched an invasion of French-occupied Italy. The French had suffered defeats atLegnago (26 March) and Magnano (4 April) which forced the French army to retreat. Gen Schérer, unable to contain the enemy at the Minico and Oglio rivers, turned the command over to Moreau.

Moreau deployed his divisions along the Adda River. The Austrians still made up the bulk of the allied army, since only three formations of Cossacks were present. Before the battle began, a Russian force under Gen. Bagrationoutflanked the French position by seizing a bridge over the Adda at Lecco on 26 April cutting off the French line of retreat. On 27 April, General of Cavalry Michael von Melas with additional Austrian divisions stormed the French positions at Cassano. Faced with this assault, plus Suvorov's attack, Moreau was forced to retreat.

Castiglione-Fiorentino (14 May 1799)
1st LEGION - 2nd Battalion
LEGION CAVALRY - Cavalry Regiment

Cento-Croci (26 May 1799)
1st LEGION - 1st Battalion, 2nd Battalion, 3rd Battalion, 3rd LEGION

On 18 May, Gen. Dąbrowski was ordered to occupy an area in the Apennines, under the command of General Merlin. The Austro-Russians already threatened to seize Spezia and to cut off there any communication with the army of Italy. Having no time to waste, Dąbrowski separated the legion, and gave orders to the 2nd Polish Battalion, under Col. Chłopicki, to reinforce the San-Pellegrino Pass, with the 3rd Demi-brigade, forming the right wing of the division, to cover the forces on the Modena Pass. The main force went through Lucca to Sarzana, but left a reserve of French troops and Polish cavalry. The enemy had advanced to Borghetto, then a series of towns along the Apennines. The 3rd Polish Battalion, reinforcing the Fivizzano Pass where it was joined by the 55th Demi-brigade under Col. Ledru. The 1st Battalion reinforced Borghetto, along with the 8th Demi-brigade. Dąbrowskihalted inSarzana with his grenadiers, chasseurs, and part of the cavalry under Forestier, to maintain a watch over the enemy at Aulla. He issued orders on the 19thto drive the enemy out ofPontremoli, and the Apennines. On 23 May he launched the attack, which seemed to progress well, except for the center column. Instead of encircling Pontremoli, the 3rd Polish Battalion left the town to its flank (according to the orders given) and joined, the reserve nearScorsetolo, instead of occupying Monte Sungo. If this column had continued as planned, none of the enemy would have escaped. The lst Polish Battalion, on the left wing, attacked the enemy, on the 25th, at Borghetto, and pushed it back. They continued the attack at Cento-Croci, and forced the Austrians to retreat with heavy losses.

Civita Castellana (4 October 1798)
1st LEGION - 1st Battalion

Civita Castellana (4 December 1798)
1st LEGION - 2nd Battalion, 3rd Battalion
      Battle of CivitaCastellana was fought between a Franco-Polish force of 10,000 troops (including 3,000 Poles under Kniaziewicz) under Gen. MacDonald and a Neapolitan force of approximately 40,000 troops under the Austrian Field Marshal Mack . The battle was won by an attack on the center and left of the Neapolitan troops, where the Polish troops rolled up the enemy's left flank. The victory allowed the French to gain control of Naples and establish the Parthenopaean Republic.

Cortona (13 October 1799)
1st LEGION - 3rd Battalion
LEGION CAVALRY - Cavalry Regiment

Erbach (16 May 1800)
Danube Legion
      The forces of the French Consulate, under Saint-Suzzane defeated an Austrian force under Baron Pál Kray. The French had 15,000 soldiers, while the Austrians had 36,000 soldiers, including 12,000 cavalry. The Austrians launched a strong attack against the French lines for 12 hours, but could not dislodge them but could not rout the French forces. While both sides suffered heavy casualties, the approach of Gen. St Cyr's corps forced the Austrians to retire.

Ferentino (29 July 1798)
1st LEGION - 1st Battalion
      The Legion was called in to put down a revolt in Ferentino, Frosinone and Terracina which they did with great ferocity.

Frankfurt (3 December 1800)
Danube Legion

Frosinone (28 July 1798)
1st LEGION - 1st Battalion
      The Legion was called in to put down a revolt in Ferentino, Frosinone and Terracina which they did with great ferocity.

Gaëta (30 December 1798)
1st LEGION - 1st Battalion, 2nd Battalion, 3rd Battalion
      The legion took part of the siege of the Fortress

Guastalia (13 December 1800)
POLISH LEGION – 7th Battalion

Höchstädt (19 June 1800)
Danube Legion
      Gen. Moreau feinted toward Ulm and marched toward Höchstädt. The campaign culminated in Kray's evacuation of Ulm which was one of Moreau's most resounding triumphs. Napoleon Bonaparte had given Moreau specific instructions about the conduct of the campaign, all of which Moreau had ignored. While Moreau wrecked

Austrian defenses in Germany, Massena and Desaix ran into stiff Austrian offensives in Northern Italy. The battle near Höchstädt, five days after the Austrian disaster at Marengo, allowed the French to take Munich and forced the Habsburgs to accept an armistice ended hostilities for the rest of the summer. In mid-November, the French ended the truce and Moreau inflicted another significant and decisive defeat atHohenlinden on 3 December 1800. The subsequent Peace of Lunéville stripped Austria of much of her Italian territories, and began to marginalize the Hapsburg influence in Central Europe.

Hohenlinden (3December 1800)
Danube Legion

The battle was fought under winter conditions, starting at dawn on the 3rd. The early part of the fighting was a mixture of tactical and strategic issues caused by the weather. A French column under Richepanse made headway in attacking the Austrian rear, but fell prey to caution before they could capitalize on their success.Around 11:00 AM, Gen. Decaen moved forward on the southern edge of the battlefield in support Gen. Drouet. The Danube Legion spearheaded this attack, pushing back Riesch's piecemeal attacks back to Albaching Heights, where the Austrians held firm. This attack allowed Moreau to order Genier and Grouchy forward in conjunction Ney which turned the battle into a rout

Lambach 1800
Danube Legion

A French column attacked retreating Austrians, capturing 1,000 wagons with provisions, weapons and ammunition

Legnano (26 March 1799)
2ⁿᵈ LEGION – 1ˢᵗ Battalion, 2ⁿᵈ Battalion, 3ʳᵈ Battalion

Magliano (1 December 1798)
1ˢᵗ LEGION - 1ˢᵗ Battalion, 2ⁿᵈ Battalion, 3ʳᵈ Battalion

Magnano (5 April 1799)
2ⁿᵈ LEGION – 1ˢᵗ Battalion, 2ⁿᵈ Battalion, 3ʳᵈ Battalion

Gen. Schérer deployed 41,000 soldiers including 6,800 cavalry against General Kray's 46,000-man army in northern Italy. Because Kray advanced at the same time as the French, Magnano is considerd a meeting engagement. On the east flank, Victor and Grenier defeated the outnumbered Mercandin, who was killed. They pressed north toward Verona. Kray committed Hohenzollern's reserve to assist Zoph's right flank division. Serurier engaged in a back-and-forth struggle all day but he finally seized his objective. Moreau pushed back the Austrians in his front, but did not score a notable success. Delmas was late, but he engaged Kaim and drove him back. At this point in the action, Schérer'suncoordinated attacks had spread his troops across a wide front. Kray launched his reserve at the victorious French right wing. This attack sent the right flank in retreat south and opened a large gap in the French battle line. Kray sent troops against the exposed right flank of Delmas and drove him and the rest of the French forces back in a disorderly retreat.

Malaussene (15 May 1800)
POLISH LEGION – 1ˢᵗ Battalion, 2ⁿᵈ Battalion, 3ʳᵈ Battalion

Mantua (12 April – 28 July 1799)
2ⁿᵈ LEGION – 1ˢᵗ Battalion, 2ⁿᵈ Battalion, 3ʳᵈ Battalion
LEGION ARTILLERY – Artillery Battalion

After a prolonged siege, General Kray attacked the fortress from its southern flank on 10 July which pushed back the French defenders with minimal Austrian casualties. Throughout the month, Austrian attackers inched parallels closer to the fortress walls. The Polish troops in the fortification supported the French troops along the parallels. Gen. Wielhorski gave great praised and supported the activity of the commander of the artillery Iakubowski, who was in Saint George's Fort. Eventually, it became necessary to evacuate that facility because of the hopelessness of their situation despite a strong defense. On 27 July, the Austrians opened a third parallel approaching-trench, which was close enough to open a breech. At 10 o'clock of that day, General Kray opened negotiation to surrender.

An additional article on the Capitulation Act, included by Kray, stated that all Austrian deserters "will be escorted to their respective regiments". In effect the majority of the soldiers of the Polish Legion were born in Poland and, for the partition of Poland, in the period between 1772 and 1795, they were Austrian citizens. Thus they were also enrolled in the Austrian units, which recruited in Poland. When the garrison left the citadel, The Austrians ordered the 2nd Polish Legion, which was in the middle of the French troops to stop in the town. The Austrian soldiers entered the ranks grabbing the Poles with brutal manners, insulting the officers, and then escorted them into the houses nearby. The complaints of Wielhorski and his Staff were useless and Axamitowski,who was charged with escorting theparolled Poles to France, had only 50 men, who could follow him to Lyon. All the Polish officers were led to Leoben in Styria, awaiting sentencing, while, the French commander Foissac-Latour, was accused by the Poles to be a traitor. He was imprisoned in a different location in order to avoid him face-to-face encounters with the Polish officers.

Novi (15 – 18 August 1799)
1st LEGION - 1st Battalion, 2nd Battalion, 3rd Battalion, Grenadier Battalion
LEGION CAVALRY - Cavalry Regiment

Joubert did not initially plan on fighting at Novi, but the position was well-suited for a defensive battle. Kray surprised the French pickets, but in turn instead of a flanking manoeuvre he was making a full frontal assault. On the extreme French right, Dąbrowski's division blockaded the Austrians in Serravalle Castle.The rest of the French troops held the high ground with a commanding view of the field. When the Austrians attacked in the center, Joubert personally led the counter-attack, but was mortally wounded.The French continued an active defense and Kray's left wing fell back to the bottom of the heights to reform. At this point Suvorov arrived and ordered a renewal of the attack.Over the course of the day each new attack was repulsed. Finally around 5:30pm the French line began to crumble and the Austrians broke into the town forcing the French to negotiate the narrow streets. Several French generals were captured, but many French soldiers were killed when they tried to surrender.

Novi (17 September 1799)
LEGION Cavalry Regiment

Novi (7 October 1799)
1st LEGION - 1st Battalion, 2nd Battalion, 3rd Battalion, Grenadier Battalion

Novi (22 October 1799)
1st LEGION - 1st Battalion, 2nd Battalion, 3rd Battalion, Grenadier Battalion

Novi (6 November 1799)
1st LEGION - 1st Battalion, 3rd Battalion, Grenadier Battalion
LEGION CAVALRY - Cavalry Regiment

Offenbach (12 July 1800)
Danube Legion

Ospedaletto (7 June 1799)
1st LEGION - 2nd Battalion

After the attack on Aulla, which pushed the enemy to Linari, the right column, consisting of the 2nd Polish

Battalion, under the Chief de Battalion DesPartes, went forward, on June 6, and attacked the enemy at Sillano on the Serchio on the 7th, routed them and continued the advance until Ospedaletto, where it was joined by a patrol of the center column. The main column was directed by Des Partes towards Frassinoro, where the Austrians threatened to fall onto his flank. The Austrians force was protected by mountains, and defended the ground step by step, however when they attackedimpetuously, they were forced to withdraw to Pavullo and Sassuolo. This Polish forces made their junction, on its right wing, with Montrichard's division, deployed in Pieve-Pelago, having made a withdrawal to the Apennines. At that point the Franco-Polish troops controlled the Apennines and all the passes, which led to the plain. Over the course of the action in the Apennines the Poles capturedsix artillery pieces at Aulla, as well as a large supply of badly needed cartridges. In addition a large quantity supplies from Pontremoli, and 600 prisoners, were captured from the enemy.

Peschiera (25-29 December 1800 and 1-11 January 1801)
POLISH LEGION – 1st Battalion, 2nd Battalion, 3rd Battalion, 4th Battalion, 7th Battalion
ARTILLERY - Artillery Battalion

This was a siege of the fortress as part of the campaigns in northern Italy that resulted in its capture from the Austrians

Pozzolo (23 October 1799)
1st LEGION - 1st Battalion, 2nd Battalion, 3rd Battalion, Grenadier Battalion
LEGION CAVALY - Cavalry Regiment

Rimini (March 1797)
LOMBARD LEGION - 2nd Battalion Light Infantry

Reggio (3 July 1797)
2nd LEGION – 2nd Battalion

Ronciglione (21 December 1799)
1st LEGION - 1st Battalion, 3rd Battalion

Salzburg (8 December 1800)
Danube Legion

San Leo (7 November 1797)
1st LEGION - 1st Battalion, 2nd Battalion, 3rd Battalion

San Terenzo (27 May 1799)
1st LEGION - Grenadier Battalion
LEGION CAVALRY - Cavalry Regiment

This was part of the campaign in the Apennines following the attack on Aulla. After the enemy was routed at Monte Sungo, the column pushed forward until they reached San Terenzo, where the Austrians tried to rally. The grenadiers and cavalry continued t push the enemy through there to Sassalbo.

Siege of Serravalli (1 – 10 November 1799)
1st LEGION - 2nd Battalion

Sezza (January 1799)
1st LEGION - 2nd Battalion

Sillano (25 May 1799)
1ˢᵗ LEGION - 2ⁿᵈ Battalion

Trebbia (17 June 1799)
1ˢᵗ LEGION - 1ˢᵗ Battalion, 2ⁿᵈ Battalion, 3ʳᵈ Battalion, Grenadier Battalion
LEGION CAVALRY - Cavalry Regiment

The Tidone River runs north into the Po west of Piacenza. With steep banks 2 to 3 metres high and a width of about 100 metres (109 yd), which gave the shore has some defensive value. On 17 June at 8:00 am the French opened their attack against Ott's Austrian's positions behind the Tidone. Victor had 18,700 soldiers with Victor's divisions on the right, Rusca in the center and Dombrowski on the left. As senior officer Victor should have assumed tactical control of the fight, but he stayed in Piacenza, resulting in poor coordination of the French effort. Nevertheless, the determined initial assault ousted the D'Aspre Jägers from their west-bank positions in the hamlets of Agazzino, Pontetidone and Veratto di Sopra. As Dombrowski's troops mounted a flank attack to the south, the troops of Victor's division fought their way to the village of Sarmato where they were held up by an Austrian artillery battery and two battalions of the Nádasdy Regiment. Chasteler was with Ott when the French attack started. He urged Ott to hold as long as possible and went back to find that his task force was hurrying on its way. At 1:00 pm Chasteler's men arrived and were thrown into the fight, but the French overran both Sarmato and its defending battery, forcing Ott's troops back to a position in front of Castel San Giovanni.Melas arrived shortly thereafter with three battalions of Austrian infantry and some squadrons of the Archduke Joseph Hussars. Suvorov arrived unexpectedly and tried to prod the soldiers back into formation. To make his pint Cossacks were employed to prod stragglers back into line. Chasteler's units were moved to the south to block a turning movement by Dombrowski's division. The Bagration Jäger Regiment veered off to the north while the four Russian combined grenadier battalions were committed to battle near Castel San Giovanni. Despite the odds turning against them, the French continued to mount spirited attacks. Gradually the Allies massed in two battle lines in front of Castel San Giovanni. By the end of the day, 30,656 Austrian and Russian troops were present to face the now-outnumbered French. The Allies recaptured Sarmato and recovered abandoned Austrian cannons, compelling the French to retreat. The French fell back stubbornly, taking advantage of cover to repulse Austrian cavalry charges. Salme's Advanced Guard covered the last stages of the withdrawal, forming square at Ca' del Bosco on the northern part of the battlefield. The shooting ended at nightfall with the Austrians holding the field.

Terracina (9 December 1798)
1ˢᵗ LEGION - 1ˢᵗ Battalion

Terracina (1799)
1ˢᵗ LEGION - 1ˢᵗ Battalion, 3ʳᵈ Battalion

Ulm (22 May 1800)
Danube Legion

Utelle (24 May 1800)
POLISH LEGION – 1ˢᵗ Battalion, 2ⁿᵈ Battalion, and 3ʳᵈ Battalion

Vaganza (26 March 1799)
2ⁿᵈ LEGION – 1ˢᵗ Battalion

Var (21 May 1800)
POLISH LEGION – 1ˢᵗ Battalion, 2ⁿᵈ Battalion, 3ʳᵈ Battalion

After a series of encounters in early April 1800, the Austrian army of Gen. Melas isolated Gen. Soult's corps from Masséna's army and laid siege to Genoa on 20 April 1800. After 18 April, Melas sent Elsnitz to drive Suchet toward France. Suchet's forces were involved in actions at Monte Settepani, San Giacomo,Loano, and Montecalvo between 10 April and 7 May. The 68th Line lost its colors in the last-mentioned battle After Bonaparte's offensive from the north, Suchet counterattacked along theVar River between 22 and 27 May. Moving across the unguarded Col de Tende, part of his corps captured 600 Austrians and seven guns at Monte Nave south of Cuneo.

Ventimiglia (11 June 1800)
POLISH LEGION – 1ˢᵗ Battalion, 2nd Battalion, and 3ʳᵈ Battalion

Verona (20 June 1797)
LOMBARD LEGION - 3ʳᵈ Battalion Fusiliers

On 26 March 1799 saw an Austrian army under Gen Kray battled a Republican army Gen. Schérer. The battle featured three separate actions on the same day. At Verona, the two sides battled to a bloody draw. AtPastrengo to the west of Verona, French forces prevailed over their Austrian opponents. AtLegnago to the southeast of Verona, the Austrians defeated their French adversaries. At Pastrengo, the French lost 1,000 killed, wounded, and missing out of 22,400 soldiers while inflicting 2,000 killed and wounded on the 11,000 Austrians. In addition, the French captured 1,500 men, 12 guns, two pontoon bridges, and two colors. At Verona, French losses numbered 1,500 killed and wounded plus 300 men and three guns captured out of a total of 14,500 men. The Austrians counted 1,600 killed and wounded and 1,100 captured out of 16,400 troops. The contest at Legnago cost the French 2,000 killed and wounded and 600 men and 14 guns captured out of 9,500 men. The Austrians lost 700 killed and wounded and 100 captured out of 14,000 soldiers.

Vigo (26 March 1799)
2ⁿᵈ LEGION– 1ˢᵗ Battalion

APPENDIX III - BATTLES OF THE DUCHY OF WARSAW

The 1806/07 Campaign
INFANTRY - 6th Regiment
CAVALRY - 4th Regiment of Chasseurs

This was fought during the Fourth Coalition, in 1806, when Prussia joined a renewed coalition, fearing the rise in French power after the defeat of Austria and establishment of the French-sponsored Confederation of the Rhine. Prussia and Russia mobilized for a fresh campaign, and Prussian troops massed in Saxony.

Napoleon decisively defeated the Prussians in a lightning campaign that culminated at the Battle of Jena-Auerstedt on 14 October 1806. French forces under Napoleon occupied Prussia, pursued the remnants of the shattered Prussian Army, and captured Berlin on 25 October 1806. They then advanced all the way to East Prussia, Poland and the Russian frontier, where they fought an inconclusive battle against the Russians at Eylau on 7–8 February 1807. Napoleon's advance on the Russian frontier was briefly checked during the spring as he revitalized his army. Russian forces were finally crushed by the French at Friedland on 14 June 1807, and three days later Russia asked for a truce. Under the Treaties of Tilsit in July 1807, France made peace with Russia, which agreed to join the Continental System. The treaty however, was particularly harsh on Prussia as Napoleon demanded much of Prussia's territory along the lower Rhine west of the Elbe, and in what was part of the former Polish–Lithuanian Commonwealth. These lands were incorporated into his brother Jérôme Bonaparte's new Kingdom of Westphalia, and established the Duchy of Warsaw (ruled by his new ally the King of Saxony). The end of the war gave Napoleon control of almost all of western and central Europe, except for Spain, Portugal, Austria and several smaller states.

The 1809 Campaign
CAVALRY - 4th Regiment Chasseurs, 9th Regiment Ulan
FOOT ARTILLERY - 1st Battalion, 2nd Battalion

The War of the Fifth Coalition was fought in the year 1809 centered on war against Austria, with Russia as a nomial French ally. Britain, already involved on the continent in the ongoing Peninsular War, sent another expedition, the Walcheren Campaign, to the Netherlands in order to relieve the Austrians, although this effort had little impact on the outcome of the conflict. After much campaigning in Bavaria and across the Danube valley, the war ended favourably for the French after the bloody struggle at Wagram in early July.

The resulting Treaty of Schönbrunn was harshest on Austria. Metternich and Archduke Charles did their best to preserve the Habsburg Empire and succeeded in making Napoleon seek more modest goals in return for promises of Franco-Austrian peace and friendship. Nevertheless, while most of the hereditary lands remained part of Habsburg territories, France received Carinthia, Carniola, and the Adriatic ports, while Galicia was given to the Poles and the Salzburg area of the Tyrol went to the Bavarians.

The 1812 Campaign
The Horse Artillery
FOOT ARTILLERY - 1st Battalion, 2nd Battalion

Began on 24 June 1812 when Napoleon's Grande Armée crossed the Neman River in an attempt to engage and defeat the Russian army. Napoleon hoped to compel Tsar Alexander I of Russia to cease trading with British merchants through proxies in an effort to pressure the United Kingdom to sue for peace. The official political aim of the campaign was to liberate the rest of Poland from the threat of Russia. Napoleon named the campaign the Second Polish War to gain further favor with the Poles and provide a political pretense for his actions.

Through a series of long marches, Napoleon pushed the army rapidly through Western Russia in an attempt to bring the Russian army to battle, winning a number of minor engagements and a major battle at Smolensk in August. Napoleon hoped the battle would mean an end of the march into Russia, but the Russian army slipped away from the engagement and continued to retreat into Russia, while leaving Smolensk to burn.

As the Russian army fell back, Cossacks employed a scortched earth policy to keep forage from the enemy. These actions forced the French to rely on a supply system that was incapable of feeding the large army in the field. Starvation and privation compelled French soldiers to leave their camps at night in search of food. These men were frequently confronted by parties of Cossacks, who captured or killed them. After a battle at Borodino in August, the French occupied Moscow without forcing Alexander to aceed to Napoleon's wishes. The retreat from Moscow, accompanied by an early winter in November, decimated the French forces. The Poles helped to protect the stragglers at the Berezina, allowing those that wee left to regroup in Lithuania.

The 1813 Campaign & The 1813 Campaign in Saxony
FOOT ARTILLERY - 1st Battalion, 2nd Battalion
HORSE ARTILLERY - 1st Company, 2nd Company

Napoleon vowed that he would create a new army as large as that he had sent into Russia, and quickly built up his forces in the east from 30,000 to 130,000 and eventually to 400,000. Napoleon inflicted 40,000 casualties on the Allies at Lützen (2 May) and Bautzen (20–21 May 1813) but he himself lost about the same number of men during those encounters. Both battles involved total forces of over 250,000 – making them some of the largest battles of the Napoleonic Wars to that point in time.

An armistice was initiated from 4 June 1813 and lasting until 13 August, during which time both sides attempted to recover from approximately quarter of a million losses since April. During this time Allied negotiations finally brought Austria over to the allies (like Prussia, Austria had slipped from nominal ally of France in 1812 to armed neutral in 1813). Two principal Austrian armies were deployed in Bohemia and Northern Italy, adding 300,000 troops to the Allied armies. In total the Allies now had around 800,000 frontline troops in the German theatre with a strategic reserve of 350,000.

Napoleon succeeded in bringing the total imperial forces in the region up to around 650,000 (although only 250,000 were under his direct command, with another 120,000 under Gen.Oudinot and 30,000 under Davout). The Confederation of the Rhine furnished Napoleon with the bulk of the remainder of the forces with Saxony and Bavaria as principal contributors. In Spain an additional 150–200,000 French troops were being steadily beaten back by Spanish and British forces numbering around 150,000. Thus in total around 900,000 French troops were opposed in all theatres by somewhere around a million Allied troops (not including the strategic reserve being formed in Germany).

Following the end of the armistice Napoleon seemed to have regained the initiative at Dresden, where he defeated a numerically-superior allied army and inflicted enormous casualties, while sustaining relatively few. However at about the same time Oudinot's thrust towards Berlin was beaten back and the French sustained several defeats in the north at Grossbeeren, Katzbach and Dennewitz. Napoleon himself, lacking reliable and numerous cavalry, was unable to fully take advantage of his victory, and could not avoid the destruction of a whole army corps at the Battle of Kulm, further weakening his army. He withdrew with around 175,000 troops toLeipzig in Saxony where he thought he could fight a defensive action against the Allied armies converging on him. There, at the so-called Battle of Nations (16–19 October 1813) a French army, ultimately reinforced to 191,000, found itself faced by three Allied armies converging on it, ultimately totalling more than 430,000 troops. Over the following days the battle resulted in a defeat for Napoleon, who however was still able to manage a relatively orderly retreat westwards. However as the French forces were pulling across the Elster, the bridge was prematurely blown and 30,000 troops (including many of the the Polish forces) were stranded to be taken prisoner by the Allied forces.

Napoleon defeated an army of his former ally Bavaria at the Battle of Hanau before pulling what was left of his forces back into France. Meanwhile Davout's corps continued to hold out in its siege of Hamburg, where it became the last Imperial force east of the Rhine.

The Allies offered peace terms in the Frankfurt proposals in November 1813. Napoleon would remain as Emperor of France, but it would be reduced to its "natural frontiers." That meant that France could retain control of Belgium, Savoy and the Rhineland (the west bank of the Rhine River), while giving up control of all the rest, including all of Poland, Spain and the Netherlands, and most of Italy and Germany. Metternich told Napoleon these were the best terms the Allies were likely to offer; after further victories, the terms would be harsher and harsher. Metternich's motivation was to maintain France as a balance against Russian threats, while ending the highly destabilizing series of wars.

Napoleon, expecting to win the war, delayed too long and lost this opportunity; by December the Allies had withdrawn the offer. When his back was to the wall in 1814 he tried to reopen peace negotiations on the basis of accepting the Frankfurt proposals. The Allies now had new, harsher terms that included the retreat of France to its 1791 boundaries, which meant the loss of Belgium. Napoleon adamantly refused.

Alagon (14 June 1808)
INFANTRY - 1st Regiment of the Vistula Legion
CAVALRY – The Vistula Ulan Regiment

Albuhera (16 May 1811)
Vistula Ulan Regiment

Beresford deployed his troops on the reverse slopes of such hills as could be found on the battlefield; unable to see the Allied army, Soult was still unaware that Blake's Spanish divisions had come up during the night. Thus, on the morning of 16 May 1811, the Marshal proceeded with his attempt to turn the Allied right flank. To approach Albuera village directly, the French would have to cross the Albuera River via a small bridge, and Soult's first move was to launch a strong feint attack in this direction. He sent Godinot's infantry brigade, flanked by Briche's light cavalry and supported by artillery, across the bridge towards the village. Four platoons of Vistula Ulans also crossed the river, but they were driven back by the 3rd Dragoon Guards. A Portuguese gun battery had been positioned to cover the approaches to the bridge, and as Godinot's skirmishers advanced they became engaged with Alten's KGL battalions, who were defending Albuera.

The battle raged back and forth with Beresford attempted to redeploy his forces in the face of French attacks. The musketry duel that developed between Colborne's brigade and Girard's left flank was so intense that both sides faltered. The French began to break, and were only kept in place by their officers beating them back with swords as they tried to retreat. The left of Colborne's brigade, assailed by both musket fire and grapeshot from Girard's supporting guns, tried to force the issue with a bayonet charge but were unsuccessful. On the right Colborne's men continued to trade volleys with the French and, seeing their resolve wavering, also fixed bayonets and charged.

As the brigade moved forward a blinding hail- and rain-shower hit the battlefield, rendering both sides' muskets useless. Under cover of the reduced visibility Latour-Maubourg launched two Polish cavalry regiments at Colborne's exposed right flank. Ploughing through the unprepared British infantry, the 1st Vistula Ulans and the 2nd Hussars virtually annihilated Colborne's first three regiments. Only the fourth, the 31st Regiment of Foot, was able to save itself by forming into squares. The cavalry pressed on against Colborne's supporting KGL artillery battery and captured its guns (although all but the howitzer were subsequently recovered).

Having captured five regimental flags and eight cannon the Ulans swept past the 31st's square, scattering Beresford and his staff, and attacked the rear of Zayas's line. Zayas met this assault while continuing to direct fire at Girard. By this time the rainstorm had cleared and Lumley, commanding Beresford's horse, could finally make out the devastation caused by the French and Polish cavalry. He sent two squadrons of the 4th Dragoons to disperse the Ulans, which they did, but the British troopers were in their turn driven off by a fresh hussar regiment that Latour-Maubourg had sent to cover the lancer's retreat. Closing on the action, the 29th Regiment of Foot (the lead regiment of Stewart's second brigade) opened fire on the scattered Vistula lancers. Most of this fusillade actually missed its intended targets and instead struck the rear ranks of Zayas's men. The Spaniards nevertheless stood firm; their actions very likely saved the allied army from destruction.

Some British sources claim that the Polish cavalrymen refused to accept any surrender by the British infantry, and deliberately speared the wounded as they lay. Tradition reports that the British 2nd Division swore to give no quarter to Poles following Albuera. According to Beresford, of the 1,258 men lost by Colborne's first three regiments, 319 were killed, 460 were wounded and 479 were taken prisoner. According to Soult's report the Vistula

Lancers had 130 casualties out of 591 troopers.

Alenbillas (22 May 1809)
Vistula Ułan Regiment

Almazaz (25 July 1808)
Vistula Ułan Regiment

Almazaz (24 August 1808)
4th Infantry Regiment

Almonacid (11 August 1809)
INFANTRY – 4th, 7th and 9th Regiments
CAVALRY – Vistula Ułan Regiment

The Battle of Almonacid was fought on 11 August 1809 between Sébastiani's IV Corps of the French Peninsular Army, which had withdrawn from the Battle of Talavera to defend Madrid, and theSpanish Army of La Mancha under General Venegas. After the decisive charges of Polish ułans, the battle resulted in a French victory.

After the battle of Aranjuez, General Venegas assumed the French only had a small and marched his army toward Toledo and meeting on 10 August at Almonacid. The army consisted of 22,000 infantry, more than 3,000 horses and 29 pieces of artillery, organized in five divisions commanded respectively by Luis Lacy, Gaspar de Vigodet,Pedro Agustín Girón, Francisco González de Castejón and Tomás de Zeraín. Miguel de los Ríos and the Marquess of Gelo served as Majors General of the cavalry and the infantry, while Brigadiers Antonio de la Cruzand Juan Bouligni were Commanders of Artillery and Engineers. They were so confident of victory that they disregarded all the established rules for camping out during times of military conflict, especially being so close to the enemy, who, the previous day, had crossed the Tagus River at Toledo and the Añover de Tajofords, settling in the nearby town of Nambroca, a league away from Almonacid.

After a council with his commanders, Gen Venegas decided to attack the French on 12 August in order to rest his troops. The French army anticipated this and appeared in front of the Spanish positions at half past five in the morning of 11 August, with 14,000 troops of the IV Corps commanded by Sebastiani, who attacked the Spanish without waiting for the reserve under the command of Dessolles and King Joseph Bonaparte in person to come up. The La Mancha army hastily positioned itself in front of Almonacid and on both sides in the following formation: Vigodet's division, a little behind, on the far right, with much of the cavalry; continuing to the left, Castejón's division was established on the Utrera hill, Zerain's division beside it covering the Santo hill, and Lacy's division closer at the Guazalate stream; the 3rd division, Girón's, acting as reserve, was spread between the heights of Cerrojones, on the extreme left and the key to the entire line of battle, and the Cerro de la Cruz or Castillo hill, named for the castle ruins on its summit.

After intense artillery barrage by both sides, Gen. Leval attacked with Polish and German-Dutch divisions on the Spanish left wing. The Bailén and Jaén battalions of the 3rd Division repelled the Poles, but received no reinforcement from the reserve. The Polish division was supported by the Germans coming up to their left, allowing the French army to storm the vital position of the Cerrojones at great cost (the three Polish regiments making up the division lost 47 officers). The French right was supported by a large body of troops advancing over the level ground at the foot of that hill, carrying out an envelopment on the extreme left, not stopped by a cavalry charge by the horsemen of Fernando VII and Granada, led by Colonel Antonio Zea and Commander Nicolás Chacón.
Vigodet's division intervened in time to prevent an immediate and disastrous defeat, speedily and skilfully carrying out a change of front, protected by lively fire from the Spanish guns. This manoeuvre delayed the pursuit of the disorganised forces of the centre and restored order on the left, where the Polish and German divisions threatened to surround the line completely and to cut off its retreat. The 2nd Division renewed the attack on the French who tried to break through this unexpected obstacle that was preventing them making the most of their victory. A large mass of Milhaud's dragoons charged towards the left, and in that last period of the battle the troops of Vigodet covered

themselves in glory.

Altenburg (2 October 1813)
CAVALRY – 1ˢᵗ Regiment of Chasseurs, 3ʳᵈ Regiment of Ulans

The raid at Altenburg on 28 September 1813 took place during the Allied autumn campaign in Saxony. The raid was carried out by the Streifkorp under the command of Saxon General Johann von Thielmann commanding seven regiments of Cossacks, a squadron each of Saxon Hussars and Dragoons, and a detachment of Saxon Freikorps numbering about 1,500 cavalry. The objective of the raid was to attempt harassment of the French lines of communication 25 miles (45 km) south of Leipzig shortly before the Battle of Leipzig. Thielmann surprised and routed a larger force of French cavalry, including Cavalry of the Imperial Guard and a small force of 2nd Baden Infantry Regiment (Infanterie-Regiment No.2 'Markgraf Wilhelm') nominally under the command of Lefebvre-Desnouettes numbering some 6,500. The French, completely surprised, broke and fled from Altenburg losing a third of their number (2,100), in the process running over the Baden infantry which was taken prisoner despite attempting to resist. Thielmann's force lost about 200 in casualties.

Aquila (21 July 1809)
INFANTRY – 2ⁿᵈ Regiment of the Vistula Legion

Operations in Aragon, Catalonia and Valencia (1811)
INFANTRY - 2ⁿᵈ Regiment of the Vistula Legion

Arcis-sur-Aube (21 March 1814)
INFANTRY – The Vistula Regiment
CAVALRY – Polish Guard Regiment of Light Cavalry (1ˢᵗ Lancers), 1ˢᵗ Ulan Regiment, 2ⁿᵈ Ulan Regiment
The Horse Artillery Company

Early on 20 March Napoleon set out for Arcis-sur-Aube, believing it was lightly held by the Austrians, in order to break out towards the Marne. On 20 March, Marshal Ney and General Sébastiani with 20,000 troops forced Field Marshal Wrede's 43,000 troops out of the Town of Arcis through bitter fighting. By 1:00 p.m. Napoleon arrived along the northern bank of the Aube River and crossed the bridge. A fierce cavalry battle developed in the late afternoon and into the night. At one point during the battle the Emperor barely avoided being taken prisoner through the protection of a single company of the Polish 1st Guard Lancer. During the night Schwarzenberg brought up 80,000 troops to face the French. Napoleon received reinforcements during the night, including units of the Imperial Guard, two cavalry formations, and one division from VIIth Corps commanded by Marshal Oudinot, giving 28,000 total troops. Schwarzenberg, suspecting a trap and yet unaware of his numerical advantage, did not attack until 3:00 p.m. on 21 March, by which time Napoleon realized he was not facing a small Allied force, broke contact with the enemy and ordered most French troops to recross the Aube River. A French rear guard commanded by Marshal Oudinot, bitterly held off the Austrians until 6:00 p.m., before falling back in good order and blowing the bridge over the Aube River behind them. The Austrians made no effort to pursue the retreating French, overnight the French were able to link up near Ormes with other French forces.

Arquillos (21 January 1811)
CAVALRY – The Vistula Ulan Regiment

Asturja (1809)
INFANTRY – 4ᵗʰ Regiment

Baranów (9 June 1809)
INFANTRY – 8ᵗʰ Regiment
CAVALRY – 2ⁿᵈ Regiment of Ulans, 5ᵗʰ Regiment of Chasseurs

Budziszyn (Bautzen) (19/20 May 1813)

CAVALRY - Vistula Ułan Regiment (19 May), 2nd Ułan Regiment (20 May), Polish Guard Regiment of Light Cavalry (1st Lancers)

After an intense bombardment by the Grand Battery and hours of continuis fighting, the French overpowered the first defensive lines of the allies and seized the town of Bautzen. Although the Prusso-Russian forces were about to be cut-off, Marshal Ney became confused while positioning his troops and allowed the allies to escape On the 21st the allies were set to be enveloped when Ney again foiled the Emperor's plans and the enemy escaped relatively intact.

Baza (4 November 1810)

INFANTRY – 7th Regiment, 9th Regiment
CAVALRY – Vistula Ułan Regiment

Sébastiani's IVth Corps attempted to capture the city of Murcia in August 1810, when he faced powerful defensive works under the command of Blake. Sébastiani was forced to retreat, but continued operations between Murcia and Adalusia for several weeks. Blake finally advanced from his lines in November, but allowed his line of march to become spread out with his advanced guard arriving at Baza. General Milhaud marched his cavalry to Baza, arriving on the morning of the 4th. Milhaud joined the 2,000 French infantry who were already holding Baza. General of Brigade Rey commanded a brigade from Sebastiani's 1st Division which included one battalion of the 32nd Line Infantry Regiment and three battalions of the 58th Line. Milhaud's 1,300-strong cavalry division was made up of the 5th, 12th, 16th, 20th, and 21st Dragoon Regiments and the Polish lancers of the Legion of the Vistula. The French also had two horse artillery batteries. Blake had 12 guns in addition to 8,000 infantry and 1,500 cavalry. Deploying on both sides of the main highway, Milhaud charged Blake's cavalry and routed it. As the Spanish horsemen galloped away, they disrupted their own infantry formations. When the French dragoons and Polish lancers bore down on the surprised and shaken Spanish foot soldiers, the men scattered in flight. Milhaud's horsemen cut Blake's vanguard to pieces, cutting down many soldiers and capturing many prisoners. But when the French encountered the second Spanish division drawn up in rough terrain, they refrained from attacking. Blake immediately ordered a retreat to Cúllar.

Belchite (18 June 1809)

INFANTRY - 1st Vistula Legion Regiment, 2nd Vistula Legion Regiment

After the British victory at Alcañiz on 23 May, Blake's forces attracted a surge of volunteers. Blake advanced down the Huerva River with two divisions on the left bank and one division under General Juan Carlos de Aréizaga on the right bank. A cautious Suchet initially fought on the defensive in the Battle of María on 15 June. The French general sent General of Division Laval with a 2,000-man brigade to watch Aréizaga while retaining the rest of his small corps to face Blake. After fending off Blake's attacks for several hours, Suchet went over to the attack when some French reinforcements arrived. He overwhelmed the Spanish right flank and compelled Blake to order a withdrawal. The next day, Suchet advanced against the combined forces of Blake and Aréizaga. Blake declined to fight and instead fell back; discouraged by defeat, 3,000 of Blake's new recruits deserted.

After joining with Aréizaga's division, Blake was only able to muster 11,000 infantry, 870 cavalry, and nine guns. He drew up this force on some hills in front of the town of Belchite. After Suchet ordered Laval to join him, he massed 12,000 infantry, 1,000 cavalry, and 12 artillery pieces for the battle. The French general paid no attention to the Spanish center and instead sent his two divisions to attack the enemy flanks. General of Division Musnier assaulted the Spanish left flank and began forcing it back into the town. General of Brigade Habert sent his soldiers against the opposite flank. Just as Habert's attack got rolling, a French shell blew up an artillery caisson in the Spanish right rear. The fire spread to some ammunition wagons and soon there was a titanic explosion as Blake's gunpowder supplies detonated. The Spanish soldiers panicked and fled with some throwing down thier arms.

Belzig (27 August 1813)
INFANTRY - 4th Regiment

Belzig was a side skirmish as part of the Battle of Hagelburg. This was one of the first battles fought by landwehr and newly formed reservists. Both a brainchild of Scharnhorst and others forming the Military Reorganization Committee.

Benevente (2 August 1810)
INFANTRY - 4thVistula Legion Regiment

Berezina (28 November 1812)
INFANTRY – 1st Regiment, 2nd Regiment, 12th Regiment, 14th Regiment, 15th Regiment, 16th Regiment, 17th Regiment, 1st Vistula Legion Regiment, 2nd Vistula Legion Regiment, 3rd Vistula Legion Regiment.
CAVALRY – 4th Regiment of Chasseurs, 9th Ulan Regiment, 13th Hussar Regiment, 15th Ulan Regiment, 2nd Vistula Ulan Regiment, Polish Guard Regiment of Light Cavalry (1st Lancers), Lithuanian Mounted Gendarmes

Napoleon's plan was to cross the Berezina River and head for Poland, while his enemies wanted to trap him there and destroy him. The original plan to cross the frozen river quickly proved impossible, as the usually frozen waterway had thawed and was now impassable. The nearby bridge at Borisov had been destroyed and most of the equipment to build a pontoon bridge had been destroyed a few days earlier. Fortunately for the French, the commander of the bridging equipment General Eblé had kept crucial forges, charcoal and sapper tools and only needed protection from Chichagov's force on the far west bank to span the river. Marshal Oudinot was given the task of drawing off the admiral and made a move towards the south. The plan worked, and Eblé's Dutch engineers braved ferociously cold water to construct the vital 100-metre bridge. Four Swiss infantry regiments acted as the rearguard. Cavalry quickly crossed it followed by infantry to hold the bridgehead. The Swiss suffered terrible losses (of the four Swiss Regiments of Oudinot's corps, only 300 soldiers survived), but managed to cover both positions and the retreat. A second structure opened within hours and cannons were taken across it to bolster the defensive perimeter. They arrived just in time, as Chichagov realised his error and attacked the 11,000 French troops. By midday of the 27th, Napoleon and his Imperial Guard were across, and the strategy now swung to saving the Swiss rearguard, which was fighting against Wittgenstein's arriving army. One of the spans broke in the late afternoon, but more feats of engineering skill had it repaired by early evening. The corps of Marshal Davout and Prince Eugene crossed, leaving Marshal Victor's IX Corps to hold off the enemy on the east bank. Boosting his firepower with artillery from across the river, Victor held out until after midnight, when his forces were able to join their colleagues, push Chichagov aside, and continue the retreat to France.

Berlanga (September 1811)
CAVALRY – Vistula Ulan Regiment

Béry-au-Bac (5 March 1814)
CAVALRY – The Polish Guard Regiment of Light Cavalry (1st Lancers), 1st Ulan Regiment

Bobruisk (20 November 1809)
CAVALRY – 7th Ulan Regiment

Bobruisk (July – November 1812)
INFANTRY – 22nd Regiment
CAVALRY - 15th Ulan Regiment

Borna (6 October 1813)
INFANTRY – The Vistula Regiment

Bornheft (8 December 1813)
CAVALRY - 17th Ułan Regiment

Borisov (21 November 1812)
INFANTRY - 1st Regiment, 6th Regiment, 14th Regiment
CAVALRY - 13th Hussar Regiment, 16th Ułan Regiment

The five different columns of the Grand Armee were converging on the Berezina crossings in mid-November. Victor and Oudinot were being pushed back by Wittgenstein and Kutuzov was following Napoleon. In the south Schwarzenberg had to move south-west to help Reynier, thus escaping from the trap. This also allowed Chichagov to slip past the French and Austrians and on 16 November he captured the important French supply depot at Minsk. Napoleon's options were quickly been reduced. He had already lost Vitebsk (7 November) and Polotsk, blocking the northern route. The loss of Minsk cut off a southern route, leaving him with one road out of Russian. This crossed the Berezina River at Borisov then made for Vilna and Kovno and eventually Konigsberg on the Baltic coast. Napoleon was now in a race with Admiral Chichagov to reach Borisov and capture its critically important bridge over the Berezina. Borizov wasn't entirely undefended. A small Polish force, under General Bronikowski, had been in the town since the fall of Minsk. More Poles, under Dombrowski, were on their way, and Napoleon also ordered Marshal Oudinot to move south and either reinforce Dombrowski or counter-attack if required. Napoleon also made the fateful decision to have his baggage train cut in half. Amongst the equipment lost was the pontoon train, although General Eblé, commander of the engineers, managed to save a few wagon loads of tools and key equipment.

Bourget (29 March 1814)
CAVALRY – The Polish Guard Regiment of Light Cavalry (1st Lancers)

Braisne (4 March 1814)
CAVALRY – The Polish Guard Regiment of Light Cavalry (1st Lancers)

Brandenburg (4 February 1813)
CAVALRY - 17th Ułan Regiment

Brienne (29 January 1814)
CAVALRY – The Polish Guard Regiment of Light Cavalry (1st Lancers)
ARTILLERY – Horse Artillery Company

The first battle of the 1814 Campaign took place near Brienne-le-Château, where Napoleon had attended military school in his early years. As the Allies advanced on France from three different directions, the French Emperor planned to attack and defeat each in turn. Napoleon's first target was the spread-out force of some 17,000 Russians (part of the combined Prusso-Russian Army of Silesia) under Field Marshal Blücher. To battle his old adversary, Napoleon had a force of some 30,000 troops, but most of these were just out of the recruiting camps with little training and no wartime experience. Napoleon had tried to envelopment Blucher's whole force near the Aube River, but allied cavalry captured a set of the Emperor's orders and Blucher avoided the trap. Additionally, rain had turned many area roads into mud, slowing Napoleon's advance. Napoleon finally caught up with Blucher near Brienne. Blucher, outnumbered, with only Russian Lt. General Baron Osten-Sachen's wing of his army on hand was forced to accept battle, as his army's baggage trains were too close – stuck on the muddy roads between Brienne and Dienville. The French emperor began the clash by pinning the enemy down while he organised a flanking attack. GeneralGrouchy's cavalry and horse artillery kept the Prussians occupied as Marshals Ney (with the Imperial Young Guard Corps) and Victor (commanding French II Corps) secured both the town of Brienne and its chateau. About dusk, the chateau was captured by the French, when Blucher thought the battle was nearly over, and was preparing for dinner. Blucher and his second-in-command General von Gneisenau only just managed to elude capture. During the heavy fighting Napoleon was almost taken prisoner by Russian Cossacks. The battle ended about midnight when the allies retreated. Blucher left behind some 4,000 casualties to France's 3,000.

Burgos (10 November 1808)
CAVALRY – The Polish Guard Regiment of Light Cavalry (1ˢᵗ Lancers)

The Battle of Burgos was also known as Battle of Gamonal, where a powerful French army under Marshal Bessières overwhelmed and destroyed the outnumbered Spanish troops under General Belveder, opening central Spain to invasion. Spanish history remembers this battle for the vain gallantry of the Guard and Walloon regiments under General de Quesada. Forming a rearguard for the shattered Spanish lines, these troops repelled repeated charges by General Lasalle's. The cost was high for the Spaniards, with only 74 of the 307 men in the rearguard surviving.

Calatayud (15 August 1809)
CAVALRY - 2ⁿᵈ Vistula Legion Regiment

La Carolina (20 January 1810)
INFANTRY – 9ᵗʰ Regiment

This action was part of the French attack in Andalusia. The main French attack towards La Carolina began on 18 January, as French troops began to advance up the passes. On 20 January the French forced their way through four separate passes, and the Spanish were forced to retreat south towards Jaen, away from the road to Seville. On 21 January Castejon's division, trapped between two French forces, was forced to surrender.

Champaubert (10, 14 February 1814)
CAVALRY – The Polish Guard Regiment of Light Cavalry (1ˢᵗ Lancers)

The Battle of Champaubert was the opening engagement of the Six Days Campaign. It was fought by a French force under Napoleon I against Russians and Prussians under Lieutenant General Count Olssufiev. Olssufiev pickets were overrun by 10:00 and although badly outnumbered, Olssufiev decided to fight rather than retreat. His decision was based on the mistaken hope that he would get reinforcements from Field Marshal Blücher in time to prevent a disaster. He was wrong, and Marmont crushed him. With no help coming and after five hours of fighting, the Russians had been forced to fall-back through Champaubert, and before they could reach Étoges, some of the corps was enveloped by Marshal Ney's cavalry corps.

Château-Thierry (12 February 1814)
CAVALRY – The Polish Guard Regiment of Light Cavalry (1ˢᵗ Lancers)

After winning a series of impressive tactical victories during the Six Days Campaign, Napoleon sought to deal what he hoped would be a final blow to the Prussians and end their participation in the Sixth Coalition against him. Having inflicted a defeat on Osten-Sacken and Yorck the previous day at the battle of Battle of Montmirail, Napoleon caught the Prussian rearguard under General Yorck on the Marne River near Château-Thierry. Sending Marshal Ney to lead the attack, the French broke into Blücher's ranks, inflicting heavy losses. Their attack was only stopped by some fortuitously placed Prussian batteries, allowing Yorck to withdraw in good order without suffering a rout. The Prussians had 1,250 casualties, the Russians 1,500, and the French 600. The French also captured nine cannons and much baggage and transport.

Chemnitz (9 October 1813)
INFANTRY – 1ˢᵗ Regiment, 16ᵗʰ Regiment

See Leipzig

Chorostków (1809)
CAVALRY – 3ʳᵈ Ulan Regiment, 8ᵗʰ Ulan Regiment, 16ᵗʰ Ulan Regiment
    See Razyn

Cimkowicze (November 1812)
INFANTRY – Lithuanian Light Regiment
Skirmish near Minsk

Ciudad Real (27 March 1809)
INFANTRY - 4th Regiment, 7th Regiment
CAVALRY – The Vistula Ulan Regiment
The Battle of Ciudad Real was fought on March 27, 1809, and resulted in a French victory under General Sebastiani against the Spanish under General Conde de Cartojal. The French 4th Corps (with an attached Polish division under general Valance) had to cross the bridge over the Guadiana River which was defended by the Spanish corps of Count Urbino Cartaojal. Polish lancers of the Vistula Legion under Colonel Jan Konopka charged through the bridge taking it by surprise, then outflanked Spanish infantry and attacked it from behind as the main French and Polish forces crossed the bridge, and attacked the Spanish front lines. The battle was over when undisciplined Spanish soldiers dispersed, and began to retreat in the direction of Santa Cruz.

Claye (1814)
CAVALRY – The Krakus Regiment

Coien (1810)
INFANTRY – 4th Regiment

Consuegra (1809)
INFANTRY – 4th Regiment

Cor (12 May 1811)
CAVALRY – The Vistula Ulan Regiment

Craone (7 March 1814)
CAVALRY – The Polish Guard Regiment of Light Cavalry (1st Lancers), 1st Ulan Regiment, 2nd Ulan Regiment
Marshal Blücher had recovered from his earlier setbacks more quickly than Napoleon Bonaparte had hoped, and so the French Emperor was forced to switch his attacks from the Austrian Field Marshal Schwarzenberg back to the Prussian commander. Moving with speed and aggression, the French pushed the Allies over the Aisne River and while Blücher planned his counter with some 85,000 men, his flanking army did not move fast enough. As a result, Napoleon's 37,000 troops struck Vorontsov's isolated from reinforcements. Napoleon's aim was to pin the Allies and then launch Marshal Ney, with a large cavalry force in a flanking move. Unfortunately for the French, the coordination was poorly timed. Consequently Ney not only suffered heavy casualties, including the cavalry commander Nansouty, but the Allies managed to extricate themselves from the situation. Craonne cost Blucher 5,000 casualties, while Napoleon lost some 5,400 he could npt afford.

Czaszniki (13 November 1812)
INFANTRY – 4th Regiment, 7th Regiment
On 13 November, Victor moved back toward Czaszniki to strike Wittgenstein to push him back across the Dvina River and buy Napoleon more time to withdraw across the Berezina River. On 15 November St. Cyr then received orders from Napoloen to withdraw. St. Cyr marched on Senno and Czereia with Wittgenstein's force behind him. From there, Victor was directed to Borisov to form the rear guard.

Czeryków (29 September 1812)
INFANTRY – 2ⁿᵈ Regiment, 3ʳᵈ Regiment, 12ᵗʰ Regiment, 15ᵗʰ Regiment, 16ᵗʰ Regiment, 1ˢᵗ Vistula Legion Regiment
CAVALRY – 4ᵗʰ Chasseur Regiment, 5ᵗʰ Chasseur Regiment, 9ᵗʰ Ulan Regiment, 12ᵗʰ Ulan Regiment, 13ᵗʰ Hussar Regiment

Czeczerynka (4 October 1812)
INFANTRY – 3ʳᵈ Regiment

Cźętochowa (1809)
INFANTRY – 5ᵗʰ Regiment
CAVALRY – 3ʳᵈ Ulan Regiment

Daroca (12 October 1809)
INFANTRY - 2ⁿᵈ Vistula Legion Regiment

Dennewitz (6 September 1813)
INFANTRY – 2ⁿᵈ Regiment
CAVALRY – 2ⁿᵈ Ulan Regiment
ARTILLERY – 1ˢᵗ Horse Artillery Company, 2ⁿᵈ Horse Artillery Company

Ney was advancing on Berlin with 58,000 men, encountering mixed elements of Prussian, Russian, and Swedish troops under the overall command of Crown Prince Charles of Sweden (formerly French Marshal Bernadotte) at Dennewitz. Ney had decided to move his entire army down a single road. While this allowed him to maintain communications with his entire army, the single road stacked his army for miles. As a result, the battle swayed back and forth with the arrival of fresh French and Allied reinforcements throughout its course. As a result of losses in Russia, lack of cavalry affected the French ability to screen their forces or carry on reconnaissance. This caused the French to attack strong allied positions. Ney initially pushed the French back, but Gen Bülow joined with reinforcements and assumed overall command. A see-saw battle developed, but just as the French appeared on the verge of a victory, Ney led the attack on the Allies personally and being unaware of the tactical situation due to a rainstorm on the battlefield, Ney ordered Oudinot to form a reserve. This withdrawal by Oudinot was perceived as a retreat and the Allies redoubled the attack. Under the pressure of this attack the French were forced back. Bernadotte arrived with the Swedish army on the French left flank. The French retreat then turned into a rout. The French suffered 10,000 casualties, the Allies some 7,000.

On the Dniestre (1812)
CAVALRY - 16ᵗʰ Ulan Regiment

Dobremiasto (5/6 June1807)
INFANTRY – 3ʳᵈ Regiment
CAVALRY - 5ᵗʰ Chasseur Regiment

At the beginning of June, Gen. Bennigsen launched an offensive against French forces in East Prussia. The Russian commander planned to trap Ney's corps between several converging columns. To occupy the French troops on Ney's left, Bennigsen sent Lt. Gen.von L'Estocq's Prussians to attack Marshal Bernadotte's troops at Spędy and ordered Lt. Gen. Dokhturov's Russians to assault Marshal Soult's men at Stolno. Although all three French Marshals were hard pressed by Benningsen, the Russian plan failed to coordinate their attacks. Afraid of being cut off, Bennigsen ordered a retreat on the night of the 7th as Napoleon instructed his forces to counterattack the Russians. The decisive Battle of Friedland was fought a week later on 14 June.

near Dresden (22 September 1813)
CAVALRY - 16ᵗʰ Ulan Regiment

near Dresden (9 and 10 November 1813)
CAVALRY - 16th Ulan Regiment

Dresden (13 October 1812)
CAVALRY - 13th Hussar Regiment

Dresden (27 August, and 7 October until 11 November 1813)
CAVALRY – The Polish Guard Regiment of Light Cavalry (1st Lancers)
      On the same day as Katzbach, Gen. Schwarzenberg, with over 200,000 men of the Austrian Army of Bohemia and accompanied by Francis II, Alexander I, and Frederick William III, attacked Saint-Cyr. In Dresden, French infantry manned the various redoubts and defensive positions. They hoped to last long enough for reinforcements to arrive.Napoleon arrived quickly and unexpectedly with reinforcements to repel this assault on the city. French counterattacks on the Great Garden in the southeast and on the allied center were successful, and by nightfall the French had regained almost all of Saint-Cyr's original positions. Although outnumbered three to two, Napoleon attacked the following morning (27 August), turned the allied left flank, and won an impressive tactical victory. The flooded Weisseritz cut the left wing of the Allied army, commanded by Generals von Klenau and Gyulai, from the main body. Marshal Murat took advantage of this situation to press the attack on the Austrians. Lt FM Baron Felsö-Kubiny's division of five infantry regiments was surrounded and captured by Murat's cavalry, which totaled 13,000 men, and 15 colours. Gyulai's divisions also suffered serious losses when they were attacked by Murat's cavalry during a rainstorm. With damp flints and powder, their muskets would not fire and many battalions became an easy prey to the French cuirassiers and dragoons. Napoleon was forced to leave the field do to illness and was unable to follow-up his which allowed Schwarzenberg to escape. The Coalition had lost some 38,000 men and 40 guns. French casualties totaled around 10,000.

Druja (November 1812) [Druya, Belrus]
CAVALRY - 10th Hussar Regiment

Dubrowno (1812)
CAVALRY - 16th Ulan Regiment

Düben (15 August 1813)
INFANTRY – 2nd Infantry

Düben (16 October 1813)
INFANTRY – 4th Regiment, 14th Regiment

Dynaburg (30 July 1812) [Daugavpils, Latvia]
INFANTRY – 5th Regiment, 10th Regiment
      In 1812, the fortress was attacked by the French Army of 24,000 men. The fortress was still under construction and was defended by 3300 men and 200 cannons.

Dyczkowo (4 July 1812)
INFANTRY - 15th Ulan Regiment

Dźwina (12 November 1812) [Daugava or Western Dvina River]
CAVALRY - 10th Hussar Regiment

Ebersdorf (6 September 1813)
INFANTRY – 1st Regiment, 15th Regiment, The Vistula Regiment

Eschfeld (9 October 1813)
INFANTRY – 15th Infantry Regiemnt

Marshal Murat made his headquarters at the castle. In the course of the preliminaries of the Leipzig campaign, troops were sent to Eschefeld to protect their lines of communication.

Esslingen (22 May 1809)
CAVALRY – The Polish Guard Regiment of Light Cavalry (1st Lancers)

Fére-Champenoise (28 March 1814)
CAVALRY – The Polish Guard Regiment of Light Cavalry (1st Lancers)

El Frasna (about 10 August 1809)
INFANTRY - 2nd Vistula Legion Regiment

Friedland (14 June 1807)
INFANTRY – 10th Regiment, 11th Regiment, 12th Regiment
CAVALRY - 5th Chasseur Regiment, 6th Ulan Regiment
ARTILLERY - 2nd Battalion of Foot

The army of Napoleon marched on Friedland, but remained dispersed on its various march routes, and the first stage of the engagement was an adhoc engagement. Gen. Lannes knew that support was nearby, but fixed Benningsen in place until the French were able to bring up 80,000 troops on the left bank of the river. The French eventually gained control of the river crossings and Benningsen was trapped on his side of the river. A cavalry fight developed between the French cavalry and Cossacks. French and Polish troops from Mortier's Corps drove Cossacks out of Schwonau, holding the enemy as Napoleon came up with an additional 40,000 troops. The Russian left was driven back despite attempts by their cavalry to counter-attack and much of the army was pushed into a bend of the Alle. Through a series of concerted attacks and deadly artillery, the Russians broke into a disorganized retreat over the river, with many men drowning. To the north the still unbroken troops of the right wing withdrew by using the Allenburg road; the French cavalry of the left wing, though ordered to pursue, remained inactive. French casualties numbered approximately 8,000 to 10,000 soldiers, while the Russians suffered over 30,000 in dead, wounded, and missing.

Friedland (17 August 1813)
CAVALRY - 14th Cuirassiers Regiment, Krakus Regiment

Frohburg (29 September 1813)
CAVALRY – Krakus Regiment

Fuengirola (13-15 October 1810)
INFANTRY - 4th Regiment

A small garrison of Polish 4th infantry regiment held a medieval Moorish fortress in Fuengirola against a much larger Anglo-Spanish expeditionary corps under Andrew Blayney. Blayney led an amphibious assault on Sohail Castle under heavy bombardment. The armada moved up the coast and landed a party 2 miles north who marched on the castle to convince the Poles to surrender. When that failed, the fortress was subject to bombardment. Despite lightweight calibre guns, the defenders managed to sink a gunboat that got too vlose to shore. After an assault by the 89th infantry was repulsed, Lord Blayney withdrew and built gun emplacements to reduce the fortifications. In the meantime, the Polish garrison of Mijas under Lieut. Chełmicki, alarmed by the artillery bombardment, snuck through the British lines and joined up with the defenders. Bronisz's garrison of Alhaurin was also alarmed and in the early morning of October 15 it marched to Mijas, where it clashed with a 450-strong Spanish-German unit sent there by Blayney and dispersed it in a bayonet charge. On the morning of October 15 the artillery bombardment destroyed one of the castle towers. Around 2:00 pm, HMS Rodneyand a similar Spanish warship arrived at Fuengirola bringing 932 men of the 1/82nd Regiment of Foot. To counter the threat, Captain Młokosiewicz decided to execute a surprise attack on the enemy artillery positions. Leaving the castle guarded mostly by the wounded, he led the remaining 130 soldiers in a sally. The besiegers were taken by surprise and, despite huge numerical superiority (approximately 10:1), the Spanish regiment protecting the artillery redoubt retreated in disorder. The guns were turned away from the castle and the Polish infantrymen started shelling the British positions. Although the artillery fire mostly missed its targets (there were no trained artillery officers in the Polish unit), it made the regrouping of British troops much more difficult.

After half an hour, Lord Blayney managed to reorganise his troops on the beach and ordered the assault of the artillery emplacement occupied by Polish forces. The outnumbered defenders blew up the gunpowder supplies and withdrew towards the fortress. However, before the British and Spanish forces could push any further, they were attacked on their left flank by the Polish garrison of Alhaurin that had just arrived on the battlefield. Approximately 200 rested and well-equipped Poles under Bronisz distracted the British long enough to allow Captain Młokosiewicz's force to regroup and strike the right flank of the British line. This near-simultaneous attack of Polish units, supported by approximately 30 French cavalrymen from the 21st Dragoon Regiment, surprised the enemy infantry, which soon began to waver. After Lord Blayney was taken prisoner by the Poles, his infantry sounded retreat and started a chaotic re-embarcation under the fire of their own, recaptured guns.

Fig 151 Polish Lancer in the countryside (Julisz Kossak, Author's Collection)

Fig 152 Vistula Lancers in Spain (Julisz Kossak, Author's Collection)

Gansenburg (1 October 1812)
INFANTRY – 5th Infantry

Siege of Gdańsk (19 March – 24 May 1807)
INFANTRY – 9th Regiment, 10th Regiment, 11th Regiment, 12th Regiment
CAVALRY – 1st Chasseur Regiment, 5th Chasseur Regiment, 6th Ulan Regiment (26 March)
ARTILLERY - 2nd Battalion of Foot

On 19 March 1807, around 27,000 French troops under Marshall Lefebvre besieged around 11,000 Prussian and Russian troops under Marshall Kalckreuth garrisoning the city of Danzig. As well as being an important heavily fortified port with 60,000 inhabitants at the mouth of the river Vistula, it was a direct threat to the French left - it lay within Prussian lands but to the rear of the French army as it advanced eastward. Danzig was also difficult to attack, being only accessible from the west – all other directions being covered either by the Vistula (N) or wetlands (S and E). Furthermore, it had precious resources (powder, grain, eau de vie, etc.) much needed by the Grande Armée in planning a substantial campaign in the east. The task of taking the city was in mid-February given to Marshal Lefebvre and his 10th corps. The 10th corps included two Polish divisions under General Jan Henryk Dąbrowski, one Saxon corps, one contingent from Baden, two Italian divisions and about 10,000 French troops, in total about 27,000 men and 3,000 horse. Inside Danzig were 11,000 men and 300 guns under the Prussian commander General Count Friedrich Adolf von Kalkreuth. Russian forces made an attempt between 10–15 May to bring 8,000 reinforcements to the city, led by General Kamensky, ferried on 57 transports under the escort of the British sloop of war Falcon and a Swedish ship of the line. Delays in Kamensky's departure allowed Lefebvre time to reinforce his positions, and the Russian troops were beaten back. A further attempt by the British 18-gun sloop Dauntless to bring a badly needed 150 barrels of gunpowder via the river failed. Dauntless ran aground near a battery, which bombarded her until grenadiers were able to capture her.

Danzig capitulated on 24 May 1807. Napoleon then ordered the siege of the nearby Weichselmünde fort, but Kamensky had fled with his troops, and the garrison capitulated shortly afterwards. The defenders had lost around 11,000 men during the siege, compared to the French losses of roughly 400 men. In recompense for Lefebvre's services, Napoléon granted him the title "Duc de Dantzig" in a letter to the Senate dated 28 May. On 9 September 1807, Napoleon established the Free City of Danzig, as a semi-independent state. This territory was carved out from lands that made up part of theKingdom of Prussia, consisting of the city of Danzig (now known as Gdańsk) along with its rural possessions on the mouth of Vistula, together with the Hel Peninsulaand the southern half of the Vistula Spit.

Gdańsk (1813)
INFANTRY – 5th Regiment, 10th Regiment, 11th Regiment
CAVALRY - 9th Ułan Regiment
From late January to 29 November 1813, Russian forces laid siege to the city and the French occupying forces withdrew on 2 January 1814.

Georgenwalde (4 September 1813)
CAVALRY – The Krakus Regiment

Gera (1813)
CAVALRY – 2nd Ułan Regiment

Skirmishes in Germany (29 January, 5, 24 March, 15 and 27 April, 1 November 1813)
INFANTRY – 5th Regiment

Gniew (2 March 1807)
See Tczew

Góra (3 May 1809)
INFANTRY – 6th Regiment, 12th Regiment
CAVALRY – 1st Chasseur Regiment, 5th Chasseur Regiment

Góra (30-31 May 1809)
INFANTRY – 6th Regiment, 14th Regiment (30/31 May)
Follow-up to the fight at Gorchow where the Austrians are defeated again

Góra-Piaseczno (2 June 1809)
CAVALRY – 7th Ułan Regiment

Görlitz (21 August 1813)
CAVALRY – The Polish Guard Regiment of Light Cavalry (1st Lancers)

Grabowo (14 June 1809)
CAVALRY – 7th Ułan Regiment

Grochów (24 - 25April 1809)
INFANTRY – 12th Regiment
CAVALRY - 2nd Ułan Regiment, 3rd Ułan Regiment
ARTILLERY – Horse Company
     Following the Austrian defeat in the Battle of Raszyn on April 19, the Polish forces commanded by Prince Józef Poniatowski left Warsaw undefended and withdrew to several fortresses located nearby (most notably to Modlin Fortress and Serock). The Austrians seized the Polish capital but the Austrian force was now seriously over-stretched and still hadan unbeaten enemy in the vicinity of Warsaw. In addition new Polish forces were being organized behind their lines in Wielkipolska. Archduke Ferdinand garrisoned Warsaw with 10,000 soldiers, and split his remaining forces, sending some 6,000 troops under Gen.von Mohr to the right bank of the Vistula, and the rest towards Toruń and other targets on the left bank. Across the river, Praga was initially garrisoned by a small force of 600 men. Mohr's force crossed the river near Karczew on April 24 and attempted to besiege the small Polish garrison. The following day the besiegers were assaulted in the rear from division-sized sortie from the Modlin Fortress under Gen. Michał Sokolnicki. In what became known as the Battle of Grochów, the spearhead of the Austrian force was defeated and the Poles withdrew successfully.

Grójec (18 April 1809)
CAVALRY – 3rd Ułan Regiment

Grodno (30 June 1812)
CAVALRY – 1st Chasseur Regiment, 12th Ułan Regiment
     Eugene crossed at Prenn on June 30 while Jerome moved VII Corps to Białystok, with everything else crossing at Grodno. The cavalry screened the army's approach while skirmishing with Russian cavalry from Bagration's forces.

Gross-Schweidnitz (3September 1813)
CAVALRY – 3rd Ułan Regiment

Grudziądz (1May – 9 July 1807)
INFANTRY – 2nd Regiment, 4th Regiment, 7th Regiment
     Siege of Prussian fortress (Graudenz)

Grzybów (18 May 1809)
INFANTRY – 2nd Regiment, 5th Regiment
CAVALRY - 5th Chasseur Regiment

Grzymała (1809)
CAVALRY - 8th Ułan Regiment, 16th Ułan Regiment

Haesslich (22 September 1813)
CAVALRY – 1st Chasseur Regiment

Hanau (30 October 1813)
CAVALRY – The Polish Guard Regiment of Light Cavalry (1st Lancers)
     Following Napoleon's defeat at the Battle of Leipzig earlier in October, Napoleon began to retreat from Germany into France. Wrede attempted to block Napoleon's line of retreat at Hanau on 30 October. Napoleon

arrived at Hanau with reinforcements and defeated Wrede's forces. On 31 October Hanau was in French control, opening Napoleon's line of retreat. The Battle of Hanau was a minor battle, but an important tactical victory allowing Napoleon's army to retreat onto French soil to recover and face the invasion of France.

Hellensdorf (14 November 1812)
CAVALRY - 13th Hussar Regiment, 16th Ulan Regiment

Herencia (June 1809)
INFANTRY – 9th Infantry

Horbaszewice (16 September 1812)
INFANTRY – 1st Regiment

Horodenka (1809)
INFANTRY – 3rd Ulan Regiment

Hrubieszów (4 February 1813)
INFANTRY – 6th Regiment

Jankowice (6 June 1809)
INFANTRY – 3rd Infantry

Jankowice (11 June 1809)
INFANTRY – 2nd Regiment, 8th Regiment, 14th Regiment
CAVALRY - 10th Hussar Regiment
    During the 1809 campaign, 6,300 Poles under Zajączek took on 11,000 Austro-Hungarians under Mondet resulting in a Polish loss with 1,200 casualties

Jedlińsk (9 April 1809)
CAVALRY - 8th Ulan Regiment

Jelnia (5 July 1812)
INFANTRY – 15th Regiment
CAVALRY – 6th Ulan Regiment, 9th Ulan Regiment

Jüterbog (6 September 1813)
INFANTRY – 2nd Regiment, 4th Regiment
CAVALRY – 4th Ulan Regiment
    See Dennewitz

Kalisz (13 February 1813)
CAVALRY - 15th Ulan Regiment, The Krakus Regiment
    This battle is the last of the ill-fated 1812 Russian Campaign or the start of the 1813 Spring Campaign. The pursuing Russian forces, leaded by Winzigerode, caught up the retiring Reynier's VII Corps. That Corps was relatively intact, after forming part of the French-Austrian right-flanking column under Schwarzenberg, and was a multinational force composed from Saxons, French and Wurzburgers formed in three divisions. At the time of the battle, it was reduced to around 9,000 infantrymen, 800 Saxon horse and 36 guns (not including some low-calibre regimental pieces). In addition, around Kalisz were 3,000 Polish infantry levies and 300 Krakus cavalry. The pursuing Russians, under Winzigerode, included the 2nd Infantry Corps of Eugene of Wurtemberg, the ad-

hoc Bachmetiev's Infantry Reserve corps and a large cavalry force under Trubezskoi and Lanskoi. The total force amounted to 6,000 infantry and 6,500 cavalry (mainly Cossacks) with 70 guns. All units were under-strength after heavy campaigning.

Kaługa (18 October 1812)
CAVALRY - 16th Ułan Regiment

After the battle of Borodino, Kutuzov realized that the Russian army would not survive one more large engagement and ordered the army to leave Moscow and retreat. At first it retreated in the south-east direction when the army reached the Moskva it crossed it and turned to the west. The army pitched camp in a village of Tarutino near Kaluga. At the same time small units of Cossacks continued moving along the Ryazanskaya road misleading French troops under the command of Murat. When he discovered his error he did not retreat but made camp not far from Tarutino in order to keep his eye on the Russian camp.

Kazimierzów (8 September 1812)
INFANTRY – 1st Regiment

Kępy (1809)
INFANTRY – 14th Regiment

Kirschenstein (19 August 1813)
CAVALRY – 1st Chasseur Regiment

Klecie (in the middle of October 1812)
INFANTRY - 22nd Regiment

Kobylin (5 June 1809)
CAVALRY – 7th Ułan Regiment

Kock (6 May 1809)
CAVALRY - 5th Chasseur Regiment
ARTILLERY – Horse Company

The Battle of Kock was fought in 1809 during the Napoleonic Wars, near the village of Kock in Poland. The battle saw the death of Polish Army Col. Berek Joselewicz, who had led an all-Jewish unit during the Kosciuszko uprisinig, fighting against Austria for the freedom of Poland.

Kojdanów (15 & 20 November 1812)
CAVALRY - 7th Ułan Regiment, 18th Ułan Regiment

Koła (1807)
INFANTRY – 7th Regiment

Siege of Kołobrzeg (April 1807)
INFANTRY – 1st Regiment, 9th Regiment, 10th Regiment

The Siege of Kolberg (now the Polish city of Kołobrzeg) took place from March to 2 July 1807 during the War of the Fourth Coalition. An army of the First French Empire and several foreign auxiliaries (including Polish insurgents) of France besieged the Prussian fortified town of Kolberg, the only remaining Prussian-held fortress in the Prussian province of Pomerania. The siege was not successful and was lifted upon the announcement of the peace of Tilsit. After Prussia lost the Battle of Jena-Auerstedt in late 1806, French troops marched north into Prussian Pomerania. Fortified Stettin (Szczecin) surrendered without battle, and the province became occupied by the

French forces. Kolberg resisted, and the implementation of a French siege was delayed until March 1807 by the Freikorps of Ferdinand von Schill operating around the fortress and capturing the assigned French commander of the siege, Gen. Perrin.

The French siege army was reinforced by troops from several German states as well as a Polish regiment. The Polish regiment, led by Col. Sułkowski, with a strength of 1,200 had been transferred from the siege of Danzig (Gdańsk) on 11 April and arrived on 20 April; it was the 1st infantry regiment of the Poznań legion raised by Gen. Dąbrowski on Napoleon's behalf, after a Polish uprising against Prussian occupation and French liberation of Prussian controlled. On 7 May, in a French reconnaissance attack, troops from the 1st Italian line infantry as well as the Polish, Württemberg and Saxon regiments assaulted the Wolfsberg sconce. During the fight, a Polish unit repelled a charge from the cavalry squadron of Schill's Freikorps (113 troopers). General Loison in a report to Marshal Berthier on 8 May stated that the Poles had stopped a charge of 600 Prussian cavalry in that action. Polish troops were extensively used, and according to Louis Loison, showed exceptional determination in the attacks on Wolfsberg sconce. The defenders were supported for a short time by the British corvette Phyleria and the Swedish frigate af Chapmann, the latter arrived on 29 April, and was armed with 46 guns (two 36-pounders, else 24-pounder cannons and carronades). On 3 June during the evening the supporting ships directed artillery fire on the Polish camp, which proved to be ineffective due to strong winds, three hours later an armed expedition of estimated 200 Prussians attempted to land on the beach, and was repulsed in intense fighting by the Polish regiment. On 2 July at noon, fighting ceased upon the announcement of the Prusso-French agreement to the Peace of Tilsit.

Konary (7 June 1809)
CAVALRY – 7th Ulan Regiment

Kosswig (15 August 1813)
INFANTRY – 2nd Regiment

Kozienice (4 June 1809)
CAVALRY – 7th Ulan Regiment

Królewiec (30 December 1812)
CAVALRY - 17th Ulan Regiment

Krakow (24 August 1813)
CAVALRY - 14th Cuirassiers

Krasne (14, 16, 17 November 1812)
INFANTRY – 4th Regiment, 1st Vistula Legion Regiment
CAVALRY – 2nd Vistula Ulan Regiment (14 Nov), The Polish Guard Regiment of Light Cavalry (1st Lancers) (17 Nov), 9th Ulan Regiment

During Napoleon's withdrawal, a 60,000 strong Grand Armée faced a Russian force of 70,000 under Gen. Kutuzov (70 thousand. soldiers). Kranse is 30 miles south-west of Smolensk, along the route from Russia to old Poland. On 15 November an advanced column of Napoleon's troops, consisting of Polish troops and VIIIth Corps, encountered Russian cavalry in the city attempting to block their path. The next day, Napoleon, came through with additional troops including cavalry regiments of Guards and broke through they lost much of their artillery. In order to allow the rest of the second column time to join the army, Napoleon decided to attack on 17 November. Kutuzov also decided to go on the offensive and obstruct Napoleon's troops. Early in the morning of 17 November, Napoleon moved the guard, cavalry and infantry division to attack and captured Uvarov, west of Krasne, forcing Kutuzov to abandon his original plan. The IIIrd Corps under Marshal Ney, remained in Smolensk and was not able to connect with Napoleon.

Kratzen (27 August 1813)
INFANTRY – The Vistula Regiment

Krymskoje (10 September 1812)
INFANTRY - 1ˢᵗ Vistula Legion Regiment

Kulm (30 August 1813)
INFANTRY – The Vistula Regiment
CAVALRY – 9ᵗʰ Ulan Regiment, 2ⁿᵈ Vistula Ulan Regiment

On 29 August, Vandamme attacked a Russian rearguard for the retreating Coalition army, with 34,000 soldiers and 84 guns at his disposal against 16,000 strong, under the command of Russian General Ostermann-Tolstoy. The situation was very dangerous for the allies; if Vandamme won the battle, the French would take the passes in the mountain, and the retreating Coalition army could be trapped by Napoleon. However, Ostermann-Tolstoy rallied all of his troops for a stiff defense, and soon Vandamme's troops were repulsed. Vandamme's situation changed the next day. A Prussian corps commanded by Gen. von Kleist attacked Vandamme's rear guard. Kleist then received help from a combined Russian and Austrian attack on his front, under the command of Generals Ostermann-Tolstoy and von Colloredo-Mansfield. In an attempt to repulse simultaneous attacks on his front and rear, Vandamme ordered his forces to form squadrons. The inexperienced French troops were unable to fend off the allies, and soon withdrew from the battlefield, with heavy losses, including Vandamme himself as a captured prisoner of war. There were two Polish regiments of Uhlans, part of cavalry divisions used by Vandamme to defend against enemy cavalry charges. One regiment, commanded by Colonel Maximilian Fredro (brother of playwright Alexander Fredro), was attacked after withdrawing to a defileand surrendered. The other regiment of Uhlans, under the command of Count Tomasz Łubieński (generally known in English as Thomas Lubienski) successfully withdrew.

La Rothiére (1, 2 February 1814)
CAVALRY - The Polish Guard Regiment of Light Cavalry (1ˢᵗ Lancers)

The Battle of La Rothière was fought on 1 February 1814 between the Napoleon's troops and the allied armies of Austria, Prussia, Russia, and German States previously allies with France under FM. Blücher. Attacked by a large force in severe weather conditions (wet snowstorm), the French managed to hold until they could retreat under cover of darkness. Multinational coalition forces used white shoulder bands to distinguish friends from foes during the battle. La Rothière was Napoleon's first defeat on French soil.

Labiau (29 December 1812 and 3 January 1813)
INFANTRY – 10ᵗʰ Regiment
CAVALRY - 17ᵗʰ Ulan Regiment

Troops that were part of MacDonald's corps retreating from Moscow fight a rearguard action

Laon (8 March 1814)
CAVALRY - The Polish Guard Regiment of Light Cavalry (1ˢᵗ Lancers), 1ˢᵗ Ulan Regiment, 2ⁿᵈ Ulan Regiment

Preliminary fighting on the evening of 8 March saw the French vanguard chase off a small Russian detachment from the village of Urcel on the Soissons road. They lost the element of surprise, but were force to repeatedly attack the Allied positions at Ardon and Semilly. Some troops from the Young Guard even reached the top of the hill before being driven back. Blücher was suffering from a fever and could not direct affairs as closely as he was accustomed during previous engagements. By 11:00 a.m., however, the fog had lifted and the Allied command staff had a clear view of the battlefield below. Blücher was operating under the impression that the French had 90,000 troops and was generally reluctant to have his troops launch any attacks. Blücher now decided to isolate Napoleon's western forces from Marmont's column to the east. A convincing Allied attack captured the village of Ardon, but the victorious Prussian infantry brigade was ordered to halt because Blücher feared that French forces to the east would outflank them. Renewed French assaults late in the evening of the 9th led to the capture of Clacy, a village on

Blücher's western flank. By the end of the first day of fighting, however, Laon still remained in Allied hands. Meanwhile, late on 9 March, Marmont's troops had attacked the village of Athies and driven off the Prussian advanced units. The Allies slammed into Marmont's troops and drove them back. At midnight on the 10th, Blücher decided on a bold outflanking maneuver intended to crush the French. A few more French attacks throughout the day produced no results, and Napoleon retired his forces late at night.

Lauterbach (21 September 1813)
INFANTRY – 6ᵗʰ Ulan Regiment

Leipzig (16 -19 October 1813)
INFANTRY- 1ˢᵗ Regiment, 2ⁿᵈ Regiment, 3ʳᵈ Regiment, 4ᵗʰ Regiment, 12ᵗʰ Regiment, 14ᵗʰ Regiment, 15ᵗʰ Regiment, The Vistula Regiment, Polish Guard Battalion
CAVALRY – 3ʳᵈ Ulan Regiment, 4ᵗʰ Ulan Regiment, 14ᵗʰ Cuirassier Regiment, Krakus Regiment, The Polish Guard Regiment of Light Cavalry (1ˢᵗ Lancers)
ARTILLERY – 1ˢᵗ Company of Horse Artillery, 2ⁿᵈ Company of Horse Artillery

During the retreat through Saxony, Napoleon attempted to take on the allied armies one at a time before they could combine their strength against him. Starting on the 16th there was a series of battles took place along the Pleiße River that was guarded by Polish troops at Dölitzand Markkleeberg. The fight at Markkleeberg was particularly hard fought, the the allied numbers eventually pushed the Poles back. There was continuous fighting at Wachau and Liebertwolkwitz where Napoleon was able to gain some tactical victories, but could not exploit them. The northern front opened with the attack by General Langeron's Russian Corps on the villages of Groß-Wiederitzsch and Klein-Wiederitzsch in the centre of the French northern lines. This position was defended by General Dabrowski's Polish division of four infantry battalions and two cavalry battalions. At first sign of the attack, the Polish division attacked. The battle wavered back and forth with attacks and counterattacks. General Langeron rallied his forces and finally took both villages with heavy casualties.

On 17 October, the Russian General Sacken attacked General Dabrowski's Polish Division at the village of Gohlis. In the end, the numbers and determination of the Russians prevailed and the Poles retired to Pfaffendorf. The French received only 14,000 troops as reinforcements at that point while, the coalition was strengthened by the arrival of 145,000 troops divided into two armies, one commanded by Russian General von Bennigsen from the Army of Bohemia's first line and the other, the Army of the North which consisted mainly of Swedish troops, commanded by Prince Charles John of Sweden. The Swedish prince was the ex-French Marshal Jean Baptiste Jules Bernadotte. He had been one of Napoleon's most trusted field marshals, but Napoleon had stripped him of command in 1810, which led to his defection to the Coalition cause.

By 18 October Napoleon realized that unless he could gain a victory and drive the allied armies apart, he would have to retreat or potentially be surrounded. He felt the garrison he was keeping in Leipzig was sufficient to keep his lines of communication open, but attempted to get an armistice from the major powers; which was declined. The allies threw all their weight against Napoloeon's lines, pushing the the French forces back through the environs of Leipzig back to the city. At this point the defections of Saxon and Württemberg to the allies put the whole line in jeopardy.

On the 19th the Emperor was withdrawing his army across the Elster River. Before this operation began, he promoted Prince Poniatowski to the rank of Marshal. The allies attacked the French lines early in the morning which resulted in vicious house-to-house fighting, but the French only stubbornly gave ground. At 1:00 pm the colonel in charge of blowing the bridge turned the task over to a corporal who ignited the fuses ahead of schedule, trapping a large portion of troops in the city. In the effort to escape across the river many soldiers drowned, including Marshal Poniatowski, who was commanding the rearguard.

Fig. 153 The Death of Poniatowski at Leipzig (January Suchodolski)

The Kingdom of Leon (1809)
INFANTRY – 4th Regiment

Lidzbark (Heilsberg) (10 June 1807)
CAVALRY - 5th Chasseur Regiment
     Bennigsen had fortified the area around Lidzbark facing the south-west approaches, where he was expecting the attack, though he thought he had time to complete all the defensive works. Moving quickly, troops under Murat, Soult and Lannes attacked from the north-west and overwhelmed the defenders and put the Russian force into retreat.

Skirmish Lithuania (16, 18, 21, 31 December 1812)
INFANTRY – 5th Regiment, 10th Regiment

Lancosa (1 May 1810)
INFANTRY - 2nd Vistula Legion Regiment

Ligny 16 June 1815
CAVALRY – Vistula Ułan Regiment (7th Cheval Leger)

Ljady (13 August 1812)
CAVALRY - 9th Ułan Regiment

Löbau (9 September 1813)
INFANTRY – The Vistula Regiment
    (See Ebersdorf)

Lorca (1810)
CAVALRY – Vistula Ułan Regiment

Lübeck 2 December (1813)
CAVALRY - 17th Ulan Regiment

Lubrin (1811)
INFANTRY – 9th Regiment

Luntzenau (30 September 1813)
CAVALRY – Krakus Regiment

Lunzenau 7 October 1813
INFANTRY – 1st Regiment
    See Penig

Lützen (2 May 1813)
CAVALRY - The Polish Guard Regiment of Light Cavalry (1st Lancers)

against Lützow's Partizans (1813)
CAVALRY - 4th Ulan Regiment

Malaga (5 February 1810)
INFANTRY – 7th Regiment, 9th Regiment
CAVALRY – Vistula Ulan Regiment
    The 5 February of 1810 a contingent of French and Polish troops captured the Spanish city of Malaga as part of the Napoleonic invasion of Spain. After being repelled at Bailen in 1808, French troops of the IVth Corps, commanded by Gen. Sebastiani, invaded Granad on 28 January and on 2 FebruaryAntequera. The city fathers of Malaga were willing to pay the French to avoid attackingthe city, but a military junta under Col. Abello led to hastily organized defensive works. The city resisted the French, including the Vistula Ulans, for over two hours before the defenders fled and left the city to be sacked. After the defeat, Gen. Sebastiani also fined the city $12 million for resisting.

Mallen 13 June 1808
INFANTRY - 1st Vistula Legion Regiment
CAVALRY – The Vistula Ulan Regiment
    The action at Mallen, was the second of three Spanish attempts to stop a French army under General Lefebvre-Desnouettes from reaching Saragossa. The first, on 8 June, had seen a force of Spanish levies under the command of the Marquis of Lazan suffer a heavy defeat at Toledo. Lazan, the older brother of Joseph Palafox, the Captain-general of Aragon, retreated to Mallen with the survivors from Toledo. There he was reinforced by more levies from Saragossa.
    Lazan placed his troops in a vulnerable position, which offered them no protection from the French artillery or from Lafebvre's Polish cavalry. A charge by the Polish lancers helped break the Spanish lines. The Spanish were forced to retreat for a second time, this time after suffering heavy casualties. In the aftermath Palafox himself led a third army out of Saragossa, for one final attempt to stop the Spanish, at Alagon on 14 June.

Maloyaroslavets (24 October 1812)
CAVALRY - 9th Ulan Regiment, 13th Hussar Regiment, The Polish Guard Regiment of Light Cavalry (1st Lancers)
    After leaving Moscow, Napoleon with an army of 108 000 soldiers and 570 guns went to Kaluga, to capture the Russian Army depot. At night on October 12 Beauharnais Corps along with Davout and the Imperial Guard (a total of 24 000 men) took Maloyaroslavets. In the morning, standing in the French troops were attacked by Docturov and Rajewski's corps supported by Platov's Cossacks (total 24 000 soldiers). Fierce fighting lasted 18 hours and

Maloyaroslavets changed hands eight times. In the end, the French managed to hold the town. Realizing that he was outnumbered and facing fierce resistence Napoleon abandoned the march on Kaluga and return to the route towards Smolensk . In the battle of the French lost 5,000 killed and wounded, while the Russians – 6,000.

Maria (15 June 1809)
INFANTRY - 1st Vistula Legion Regiment

The Battle of María (15 June 1809) saw a small Spanish army led by Joaquín Blake y Joyes face an Imperial French corps under Louis Gabriel Suchet. After an inconclusive contest earlier in the day, Suchet's cavalry made a decisive charge that resulted in a French victory. Though the Spanish right wing was crushed, the rest of Blake's army got away in fairly good order after abandoning most of its artillery.

Marjampol (1812)
CAVALRY - 16th Ułan Regiment

Mazhaysk [Możajsk] (5 and 7 September 1812)
INFANTRY – 2nd Regiment, 3rd Regiment, 8th Regiment, 12th Regiment, 15th Regiment, 16th Regiment, 1st Vistula Legion Regiment, 2nd Vistula Legion Regiment
CAVALRY – 3rd Ułan Regiment, 4th Chasseur Regiment, 6th Ułan Regiment, 8th Ułan Regiment, 9th Ułan Regiment, 10th Hussar Regiment, 11th Ułan Regiment, 12th Ułan Regiment, 13th Hussar Regiment, 14th Cuirassier Regiment, 16th Ułan Regiment

The-almost-12-hour battle took place outside the town of Mozhaysk at the Battle of Borodino field located west of Moscow. The Battle of Borodino was preceded by a fighting near the village of Shevardino which had a spate of strategic commanding points. Col. Toll, the Quartermaster for the Russian Army, picked the site for the battle. The Polish forces were under the command of Prince Poniatowski, who commanded the right flank of the French line. The Prince initially had trouble coordinating his attacks and although he was eventually successful, the delays did not allow Napoleon to fully exploit his control of the battlefield.

Medyna (26 and 28 October 1812)
INFANTRY – 2nd Regiment, 15th Regiment
CAVALRY – 4th Chasseur Regiment, 12th Ułan Regiment

Mińsk (15 November 1812)
INFANTRY - 22nd Regiment

Mir (9 - 10 July 1812)
CAVALRY - 2nd Ułan Regiment, 3rd Ułan Regiemnt, 7th Ułan Regiment, 11th Ułan Regiment, 13th Hussar Regiment, 15th Ułan Regiment, 16th Ułan Regiment

The Battle of Mir was a largescale cavalry battle that featured three Polish Lancers brigades against Russian cavalry, ending in the first major Russian victory in the French invasion of Russia. Russian Gen. Platov had eight Cossack regiments and two Don Cossack Batteries deployed south of the village of Mir, when one brigade of the Polish Fourth Light Cavalry attacked his advance posts, numbering about 100 men. These advance posts had the dual job of both observation and sentry duty; trying to entice the enemy to attack; ambushes of a hundred men were set up farther down the road to Mir, on either side of it. Gen. Rosniecki's Polish troopers clashed with Russian Gen. Vasilchikov's cavalry, in vicious hand-to-hand combat with fairly even losses. Ułans followed up the combat by sweeping through the village to attack Platov's main force. A third Polish brigade attempting to join the fight was encircled and broken by Cossacks, after which the entire Polish force gave ground, driven back with the aid of Russian Hussars. After the arrival of the Akhtyrka Hussars, Dragoons, and other reinforcements, the battle raged for six more hours, shifting to the nearby village of Simiakovo. Platov defeated the enemy there, and moved on to Mir, where he inflicted further losses on the enemy before tactically withdrawing. A complete rout was only averted by

Tyszkiewicz's brigade, which covered the Polish retreat.

Modlin (5 February – 1 December 1813)
INFANTRY – 3rd Regiment, 17th Regiment, 18th Regiment, 19th Regiment, 20th Regiment, 21st Regiment

After the defeat of the Grande Armée at Moscow, the fortress was taken over by the forces of the Duchy of Warsaw. On 5 February 1813 the Russian army of 36,000 soldiers arrived to the fortress and laid siege to it. The Polish forces under Dutch general Herman Willem Daendels defended the fortress until 1 December 1813. It was the last of the French fortresses along the Vistula to capitulate.

Mohylow (22 July 1812)
INFANTRY - 17th Regiment
CAVALRY - The Polish Guard Regiment of Light Cavalry (1st Lancers)

The Russian Gen. Bagration was trying to join up with Gen. de Tolly after French forces took Mogilev and blocked the Dneiper crossing. Bagration sent Gen Rayevski against five French divisions led by Marshal Davout, who had over 28,000 troops present, including 3 infantry divisions and a large number of cavalry, but only a fraction of the French Corps was engaged in this battle. Meanwhile, the Russians had deployed around 20,000 troops but only engaged only a single corps against the enemy. Davout was able to repulse the Russian attackers throughout his line, then launched a counterattack and pursued the Russians for about a league. The battle prevented Bagration from joining the main Russian army under de Tolly at Vitebsk, forcing Bagration to retreat to Smolensk.

Monbella (9 December 1810)
INFANTRY – 4th Regiment

Montmirail (11 February 1814)
CAVALRY - The Polish Guard Regiment of Light Cavalry (1st Lancers), 1st Ulan Regiment, 2nd Ulan Regiment
ARTILLERY – Horse Company

The battle was fought near Montmirail, France, during the Six Days Campaign resulting in the victory for Napoleon, with 20,000 men and 36 cannons, against a Russian force under Gen. Osten-Sacken and Prussians under Gen. Yorck, each numbering about 18,000.

Montereau (18 February 1814)
CAVALRY - The Polish Guard Regiment of Light Cavalry (1st Lancers)

Montril (21 August 1811)
INFANTRY – 9th Regiment

Moro (1811)
INFANTRY – 9th Regiment

Murviedra (Saguntu) (taken 28 October 1811)
INFANTRY - 1st Vistula Legion Regiment
Seige taken 28 October 1811

Nadarzyn (14, 17, 19 April 1809)
CAVALRY – 2nd Ulan Regiment (19 April), 3rd Ulan Regiment
Part of the Raszyn campaign

Narwa (13 May 1807)
INFANTRY – 2nd Regiment

Nieder Isigheim (30 October 1813)
CAVALRY - The Polish Guard Regiment of Light Cavalry (1st Lancers)

Neustadt (15 September 1813)
INFANTRY – 15th Regiment, The Vistula Regiment
CAVALRY – 6th Ulan Regiment, 8th Ulan Regiment, Krakus Regiment
      Lead up to Leipzig

New and Old Castile (1809)
INFANTRY – 4th Regiment

Nibork (1807)
INFANTRY – 3rd Regiment, 7th Regiment

Neugat (7 November 1812)
INFANTRY – 5th Regiment, 10th Regiment

Nowe Miasto (10 June 1809)
CAVALRY - 5th Chasseur Regiment

Ocana (10 September 1809)
INFANTRY – 7th Regiment

Ocana (19 November 1809)
INFANTRY – 7th Regiment, 9th Regiment
      French forces under Marshal Soult and King Joseph Bonaparte decisivelydefeated a Spanish army under Gen. de Aréizaga, which suffered its greatest single defeat in the Peninsular War. The Spanish forces lost 19,000 killed, wounded, prisoners and deserters out of a total force of 51,000, mostly due to the French use of their cavalry.

Ocana (19 January 1810)
INFANTRY – 4th Regiment
CAVALRY – The Vistula Ulan Regiment

Ojos Negros (23 November 1809)
INFANTRY - 2nd Vistula Legion Regiment

Olivenza (19-23 January 1811)
CAVALRY – The Vistula Ulan Regiment
      Marshal Soult captured the Portugese fortress after his armies' breached the walls, forcing the surrender of 4,000 Spanish troops from the Army of Extremadurea.

Orgas (1810)
CAVALRY – The Vistula Ulan Regiment

Ortelsburg (9 May 1807)
CAVALRY – 3rd Ulan Regiment

Ośnicka (1809)

INFANTRY – 14th Regiment

Ostrovno (25 - 26 July 1812)

CAVALRY – 6th Ułan Regiment, 8th Ułan Regiment

A rearguard action fought in the opening phases of Napoleon's advance into Russia between Oster-mann-Tolstoy's rearguard of Barclay de Tolly's 1st Western Army and Murat's advance guard of the Grande Armée. The Russians were eventually forced to retreat into Vitebsk, but they held up the French for two days.

The French advance was led by General Nansouty's 1st Cavalry Corps, with Marshal Murat close behind. The first clashes, between Nansouty's advance guard and Russian cavalry, were won by the Russians. Murat's advance guard then arrived, and the French got the better of their adversaries. Osterman-Tolstoy deployed his troops in two lines just to the west of Ostrovno, defending the main road to Vitebsk. The 11th Division (Nikolay Bakhmetyev) was posted in the front line with the 23rd Division (Aleksey Bakhmetyev) in the second line. The Ingermanland Dragoons were posted on the left of the Russian front line, the Sumsk Hussars in the second line. On the French side General Saint Germain's cavalry division was on the left, part of Bruyères's cavalry division formed the right and the rest of his cavalry along with the 8th Légere were in the centre. General Delzons' division was further west on the road.

The battle started with a Russian cavalry attack, led by the Ingermanland Dragoons. This ended in failure when the French cavalry counterattacked. In the centre the French skirmishes were taking a heavy toll of the Russians. The Russian infantry attempted to drive them back, but once again the French cavalry defeated them. The French were less successful when they attempted to attack. The Russians had a strong defensive position with their flanks secured by woodland, and Russian infantry held firm despite heavy losses to artillery fire. Osterman-Tolstoy's own attacks were also repulsed, and eventually the arrival of French reinforcements forced him to retreat east. Overnight both sides received reinforcements. The Russians held their positions for most of the day before finally retreating to Vitebsk.

Oszmiana (30 June 1812)

CAVALRY - 9th Ułan Regiment

Penaranda (1 June 1811)

INFANTRY - 4th Vistula Legion Regiment

Pankratowice (21 November 1812)

INFANTRY - 1st Regiment

Paris (30 March 1814)

CAVALRY – The Polish Guard Regiment of Light Cavalry (1st Lancers), Krakus Regiment, 2nd Ułan Regiment

Early in the morning of March 30 the Coalition attack began when the Russians attacked and drove back the Young Guard near Romainville in the center of the French lines. A few hours later the Prussians, under Blücher, attacked north of the city and carried the French position around Aubervilliers, but did not press their attack. The Württemberg troops seized the positions at Saint-Maur to the southwest, with Austrian troops in support. The Russians attempted to press their attack but became caught up by trenches and artillery before falling back before a counterattack of the Imperial Guard. The Imperial Guard continued to hold back the Russians in the center until the Prussian forces appeared to their rear. The Russian forces then assailed the Montmartre Heights, where Joseph's headquarters had been at the beginning of the battle. Control of the heights was severely contested, and Joseph fled the city. Marmont contacted the Coalition and reached a secret agreement with them. Shortly afterwards, he marched his soldiers to a position, where they were quickly surrounded by Coalition troops; Marmont then surrendered, as had been agreed.

Passenheim (3 and 30 May 1807)
CAVALRY – 3rd Ułan Regiment

Penig (7 – 9 October 1813)
INFANTRY - 1st Regiment
CAVALRY – 1st Chassuer Regiment, 3rd Ułan Regiment
         From the first until the thirty-frist of October Penig was the scene of a running battle upto and after the battle at Leipzig. The fight over the bridge in town controlled access across. On the 8th 500 to 600 Polish infantry occupied and defended this hill overlooking the bridge. On the 9th the Poles were pushed back from the bridge and the city was taken again.

Perdiguera (7 June 1809)
INFANTRY - 2nd Vistula Legion Regiment

Peterswalde (16 November 1812)
CAVALRY - 13th Hussar Regiment, 16th Ułan Regiment, The Polish Guard Regiment of Light Cavalry (1st Lancers)

Pińczów (9 July 1809)
CAVALRY – 6th Ułan Regiment

Pitterbach (20 August 1813)
CAVALRY - 14th Cuirassiers

Pirna (17 September 1812)
CAVALRY - 13th Hussar Regiment

Pirna (9 October 1812)
CAVALRY - 13th Hussar Regiment

Pirna (17 October 1813)
INFANTRY – The Vistula Regiment

Pirna (17 November 1813)
CAVALRY - 16th Ułan Regiment

Podhajce (18 July 1812)
CAVALRY - 15th Ułan Regiment

Pomorze 1807
INFANTRY – 11th Regiment
         Gdansk and Pommerania

Praga (25, 27 April 1809)
INFANTRY- 1st Regiment
CAVALRY – 2nd Ułan Regiment
         Raszyn campaign

Przedborz (8 July 1812)

CAVALRY – 2ⁿᵈ Ułan Regiment

Puebla-de-Senabria (29 July 1810)
INFANTRY - 4ᵗʰ Vistula Legion Regiment

Pułtusk (25 December 1806)
CAVALRY – 1ˢᵗ Chasseur Regiment

Raguhn (15 August 1813)
INFANTRY – 2nd Regiment

Radzymin (25, 26, 27 April 1809)
INFANTRY – 6ᵗʰ Regiment (25th)
CAVALRY – 1ˢᵗ Chasseur Regiment (25th), 3ʳᵈ Ułan Regiment (26, 27)
ARTILLERY – Horse battery

    The Radzymin battlefield is approximately 12 miles north-east of Warsaw. On the heels of Grochow, the Polish army mounted another attack on the overstretched Austrian lines at Radzymin. The town was held by relatively small Austrian forces consisting of the 2nd and 3rd Battalions from the 63rd Graf Baillet Infantry Regiment and a detachment of hussars. The Polish force was similar in size and consisted of a squadron of ułans under Capt. Piotr Strzyżewski and a single infantry battalion from the 6th Infantry Regiment under Julian Sierawski. The force was supported by a single 2-gun battery of mounted artillery. During the night of 24 April the Polish force left Serock and crossed the Narew, reaching Radzymin before daylight. In the early hours of 25 April the force attacked the town from two sides in a synchronised attack. The Austrians withdrew to the town's centre, but soon their cavalry was forced to retreat altogether and the infantry battalions were isolated. After a brief fight at close quarters, the two Austrian battalions with their remaining 37 officers surrendered.

    Polish losses were 19 killed and 27 wounded. The losses for the Austrians included approximately 2,000 prisoners of war and many killed and wounded. Although the battle was not a decisive defeat for the Austrians, it was one of a series of skirmishes they lost on the eastern bank of Vistula. On May 2 and May 3 the entire corps under Gen. Mohr was defeated at Ostrówek and its pontoon bridge across the river was destroyed, thwarting any further attempts to advance further east. This gave Poles enough time to leave the Austrians locked in Warsaw and liberate much of Galicia without much opposition from the enemy.

Raszyn (19 April 1809)
INFANTRY – 1ˢᵗ Regiment, 3ʳᵈ Regiment, 6ᵗʰ Regiment, 8ᵗʰ Regiment
CAVALRY – 1ˢᵗ Chasseur Cavalry, 3ʳᵈ Ułan Regiment
ARTILLERY – The Horse Artillery

    The battle at Raszyn was important because it ws the first action by the reconstituted Polish Army since the Partitions. The Austrian army under Archduke Ferdinand invaded the Duchy of Warsaw in April 1809 in the hopes of a quick victory. Polish troops under Prince Poniatowski along with some Saxon units made their initial stand at Raszyn, south of Warsaw. The battlefield's terrain is dominated by several villages and by the Utrata River, which is often unfordable in April. The only way to cross the river is at the towns of Raszyn, Dawidy or Michalowice, which were all under Polish control. After an initial bombardment starting at 2 pm, the Austrian infantry attacked the Polish skirmishers around 3 pm. The Poles gradually yielded terrain to the attacker. Austrian attempts to outflank the Polish position near Jaworowo were without success. After the village of Falenty was captured at 4 pm Poniatowski launched a counterattack which pushed the Austrians from the town and re-establishing the Polish line. Around 5 pm a combined attack was launched against Raszyn. Repulsed by the Saxon units, the Austrians called up reinforcements and took the town around 7 pm but where unable to progress beyond the outskirts of the village. The Poles counterattacked again at 9 pm and drove the Austrians from Raszyn but were unable to recapture the causeway. Fighting progressed until 10 pm when the Poles withdrew from the battlefield. After the Austrian army pulled back from the battle line, Prince Poniatowski ordered his forces to withdraw towards Warsaw. Since the city fortifications were in a very bad shape and their Saxon allies withdrew towards the west, Poniatowski decided to leave Warsaw undefended and withdraw to several fortresses located nearby (most notably to Modlin Fortress and Serock). The capital was seized with little opposition, but it was a Pyrrhic victory since the Austrian commander diverted most of his forces there at the expense of other fronts.

Reichenbach (22 May 1813)
CAVALRY - The Polish Guard Regiment of Light Cavalry (1st Lancers)

After their defeat at Bautzen the Allied Coalition retreated towards the south-east in two columns of weary soldiers in order to cross the Neisse River. Their rearguard, commanded by Eugen of Wurttemberg and comprising his 2nd Russian Corps, remained in Reichenbach and was caught by Reynier's VII Corps, which had not fought at Bautzen, along with the 1st Cavalry Corps. Napoleon himself arrived to the battlefield and sent in the Guard Light cavalry to push the allies back further.

Reims (13 March 1814)
CAVALRY – The Polish Guard Regiment of Light Cavalry (1st Lancers), 1st Ułan Regiment, 2nd Ułan Regiment
ARTILLERY – Horse Company

Retascon (4 September 1809)
INFANTRY - 2nd Vistula Legion Regiment

Rio Almanzor (November 1810)
CAVALRY – The Vistula Ułan Regiment

Rio Seco 14 July (1808)
CAVALRY – The Polish Guard Regiment of Light Cavalry (1st Lancers)

Rocourt (3 March 1814)
CAVALRY – The Polish Guard Regiment of Light Cavalry (1st Lancers)

Rogożno (10 February 1813)
INFANTRY - 4th Vistula Legion Regiment

Rohaczew (8 September 1812)
CAVALRY - 15th Ułan Regiment, 16th Ułan Regiment

Romanówo (14 July 1812)
CAVALRY – 1st Chassuer Regiment, 12th Ułan Regiment, 13th Hussar Regiment

Ronda (1810)
INFANTRY – 7th Regiment

Ronda (1811)
INFANTRY – 9th Regiment

Rosslau (15 August 1813)
INFANTRY – 2nd Regiment

Rotha (8 October 1813)

CAVALRY – Krakus Regiment

Roźki (5 April 1809)
CAVALRY – 1st Chasseur Regiment, 2nd Ulan Regiment, 5th Chasseur Regiment

Rożniszewo (6 January 1809)
CAVALRY - 8th Ulan Regiment

Ruda (12 May 1807)
INFANTRY – 1st Regiment

Ruda (16 May 1809)
INFANTRY - 1st Regiment

Ruda (5 June 1809)
INFANTRY – 1st Regiment

Rumberg (17 August 1813)
CAVALRY – 1st Chasseur Regiment

Skirmish in Russia (28 September 1812)
INFANTRY - 5th Regiment, 10th Regiment

Skirmish in Russia (2, 7, 15 and 23 October 1812)
INFANTRY - 5th Regiment, 10th Regiment

Skirmish Russia (17, 18 November 1812)
INFANTRY - 5th Regiment, 10th Regiment

St. Disier (27 January 1814)
CAVALRY – The Polish Guard Regiment of Light Cavalry (1st Lancers)

St. Disier (26 March 1814)
CAVALRY – The Polish Guard Regiment of Light Cavalry (1st Lancers), 1st Ulan Regiment, 2nd Ulan Regiment
The first Battle of St-Dizier was fought on January 26, 1814, and resulted the victory of French under Napoleon against Russians under General Lanskoy. Napoleon and his troops had left Ligny the day before; Lanskoy held St-Dizier with 800 dragoons, and he left the town to join Blücher.

The second battle occurred on March 26, 1814 and resulted the victory of French under Napoleon against Russians under Gen.Wintzingerode. This was Napoleon's penultimate victory. Coming up on the right bank of the Aube River, Napoleon was informed by MacDonald that a large part of the Allied army was advancing on his rear guard. Napoleon chose to present his whole army for battle at St Dizier, but MacDonald's information was incorrect; Napoleon found only a body of cavalry under the command of General Wintzingerode, whom Napoleon's troops quickly put to flight.

Salinas (March 1812)
INFANTRY – 7th Regiment, 4th Vistula Legion Regiment

Sandomierz (13, 17, 18 May 1809)
INFANTRY – 6th Regiment, 8th Regiment

CAVALRY – 2nd Ulan Regiment, 5th ChasseurRegiment, 6th Ulan Regiment
ARTILLERY – T he Horse Companies

Sandomierz (27, 29 May1809)
INFANTRY – 3rd Regiment

Sandomierz (6 June 1809)
INFANTRY – 3rd Regiment

Sandomierz (7, 9 and 12, 13, 15, 16 June 1809)
INFANTRY - 1st Regiment, 2nd Regiment (15, 16), 3rd Regiment, 6th Regiment, 12th Regiment
CAVALRY - 1st Chasseur Regiment, 6th Ulan Regiment (15, 16)

    Sandomierz was a major fortress in south-western Poland, in what wwas considered Galicia. It was originally taken on 18 May, then a siege between 26 May and 18 June 1809. The Austrian commander was Archduke Ferdinand with 11,000 men and the Poles under Gen. Sokolwicki with 5,000 men. It lost, then recovered again later in the month.

Santa Cruz (28 March 1809)
INFANTRY – Vistula Ulan Regiment

Santa Fe (14 June 1809)
INFANTRY - 2nd Vistula Legion Regiment

Siege of Saragossa (15 June – 14 August 1808 and 20 December 1808 – 21 February 1809)
INFANTRY - 1st Vistula Legion Regiemnt, 2nd Vistula Legion Regiment, 3rd Vistula Legion Regiment
CAVALRY – Vistula Ulan Regiment

    Gen. Lefebvre initially reached Zaragoza on 15 June 1808and was outnumbered by the Spanish, who had around 11,000 troops. Lefebvre immediately launched an attack on the city expecting the Spanish wouldquickly givein. In the first assault the French broke into the western part of the city and their Polish cavalry broke through the Santa Engracia gate but could make no progress inside the city and were forced to retreat. The French, however, received more substantial reinforcements with a force of 3,000 led by General Verdier arriving on 26 June 1808. As General Verdier was senior to Lefebvre he took over command of all the troops. Further reinforcements continued to arrive including some siege artillery. On 28 June 1808 Verdier attacked Monte Terrero on the southern bank of the Huerva River. Monte Terrero was a hill that dominated the south of Zaragoza and should have been strongly fortified but was not. As a result the hill was captured with ease and the Spanish commander, Colonel Vincento Falco, was subsequently court-martialled and shot.Verdier was now able to use the heights as a base for his siege artillery. Starting from midnight on 30 June 1808 thirty siege guns, four mortars, and twelve howitzers opened fire on Zaragoza and kept firing continuously.

    A second assault was made by the French on 2 July 1808 with twice the strength of the first assault. Although the fixed defences in Zaragoza had suffered heavily from the bombardment, the barricades were still intact and Gen. Palafox had returned to take command. The French penetrated the city in several places but were unable to make any further progress and once again were forced to retreat. This assault became famous for the story of the Maid of Zaragoza: Agustina Zaragoza. Her lover was an artillery sergeant at the Portillo Gate. The entire crew of his gun were killed before they could fire off their last round. Agostina ran forward taking the lighted match from her dead lover's hands and fired the cannon. The French were hit by a round of grapeshot at close range and their attack was broken. Palafox said he personally witnessed this event and Agostina was commissioned as a sub-lieutenant. Verdier therefore decided not to make any further assaults and settled down for a siege but could never fully blockade the city.

    By 4 August, having captured other surrounding heights the French began a heavy artillery bombardment, silencing the Spanish guns and made several breaches in the walls. At 2pm Verdier launched a massive assault with thirteen battalions in three columns and penetrated deep into Zaragoza. By evening the French had taken half of the city but the Spanish counter-attacked and pushed the French out except for a small wedge. The fighting continued for several days but the assault had effectively failed ensuring the failure of the siege. On 19 July 1808 the surrender of Gen. Dupont's army at Bailén made continuation of the siege untenable. Finally on 14 August 1808 Verdier blew up all the strongpoints he held and withdrew.

Schluckenau (4 September 1813)
INFANTRY – The Vistula Regiment

Sere (18 November 1812)
CAVALRY - 13th Hussar Regiment, 16th Ułan Regiment

Seidenberg (31 August 1813)
CAVALRY – 1st Chasseur Regiment

Sierakowo (12 February 1813)
INFANTRY – 22nd Regiment, 23rd Regiment
CAVALRY - 17th Ułan Regiment, 19th Ułan Regiment
Sierakow was one of the last battles of the Napoleonic era on Polish soil. The 17th and 19th Ułans, supported by Polish infantry and local guard units fought a battle for the bridge over the Warta against Cossacks under Count Alexander Chernyshev. Under heavy rifle and artillery fire soldiers of the Duchy of Warsaw held off the Russians before withdrawing.

Sierra Morena (1810)
INFANTRY – 7th Regiment

Skarszew (12 February 1813)
CAVALRY – Krakus Regiment

Skenditz (18 and 19 October 1813)
INFANTRY – 2nd Regiment

Słonim (19 and 20 October 1812)
CAVALRY – Lithuanian Regiment of Guard Light Cavalry (3rd Lancers)

Słupca (4 May 1809)
CAVALRY – 3rd Ułan Regiment

Smolany (1812)
INFANTRY - 9th Regiment

Smoleńsk (17 August 1812)
INFANTRY – 2nd Regiment, 3rd Regiment, 7th Regiment, 8th Regiment, 12th Regiment, 15th Regiment, 16th Regiment, 1st Vistula Legion Regiment, 2nd Vistula Legion Regiment, 3rd Vistula Legion Regiment
CAVALRY – 4th Chasseur Regiment, 5th Chassuer Regiment, 8th Ułan Regiment, 9th Ułan Regiment, 13th Hussar Regiment, 16th Ułan Regiment, The Polish Guard Regiment of Light Cavalry (1st Lancers)
For the first month and a half of his of his invasion of Russia, Napoleon attempted to entice the Russian armies to battle, but also keep them apart so he could throw the full weight of his arms on them. He failed in this

attempt through August as the Russians linked force at Smolensk on 4 August. In early August Napoleon developed the plan for his famous manoeuvre of Smolensk. The Dnieper flows west from Smolensk to Orsha then turns south and flows towards Kiev. Napoleon decided to move his army across the Dnieper east of Orsha, then advance east along the south bank of the river. This would bring him to Smolensk while the Russians were still on the north bank of the river, and allow him to cut the roads to Moscow. The Russians would either have to offer battle on ground of Napoleon's own choice or retreat north, abandoning Moscow without a battle.

On 7 August the Russians briefly threatened to disrupt Napoleon's plans when they began a short-lived offensive between the Dnieper and the Dvina. On the following day the Cossacks won a minor victory over French cavalry at Inkovo. This alerted Napoleon to the Russian plans, and also alarmed Barclay de Tolly, who feared that it would trigger an overwhelming French attack. He stopped his advance west and instead moved north-west from Smolensk, then halted. Napoleon had cancelled his move on Smolensk, but by 10 August it was clear that the Russians were no longer a threat north of the Dnieper. The move to the Dnieper resumed, and on the night of 13-14 August General Eblé's engineers built four bridges across the river. By the morning of 14 August most of Napoleon's army had crossed to the south bank and the advance east began. The French largely wasted 15 August. Napoleon held a review of part of his army to celebrate his birthday, but the French missed their best chance to capture Smolensk.

In 1812 the main part of Smolensk was on the south bank of the Dnieper. The smaller New Town, or St. Petersburg suburb, was on the north bank, connected to the Old Town on the south bank by a bridge. The Old Town was protected by a four mile long medieval town wall, protected by 32 towers, an earthwork fort called the 'Royal Citadel' in the south-east and a more modern covered way and glacis. The fortifications weren't in great condition, the walls couldn't carry cannons, and there were suburbs outside the defences. Rayevsky realised that his main task was to delay the French and give Bagration and Barclay de Tolly time to reach the city and so he deployed most of his men outside the suburbs. The bulk of his infantry (23 battalions) were posted to the west and south of the Old City, with two infantry battalions and the cavalry in the east and four battalions within the city to act as a reserve. The Russians had 72 guns. 18 were massed in the Royal Citadel and the rest were spread out around the towers.

The night of 16-17 August reinforcements arrived in the form of Davout's and Poniatowski's corps. Within Smolensk Rayevsky was withdrawn to the north bank to rejoin Bagration's army and was replaced by Dokhturov's troops from Barclay de Tolly's army. Bagration was camped to the east of the town and Barclay de Tolly was approaching from the west. The main French attack came on 17 August. This time three corps were involved, but the attacks weren't very effective. The suburbs were eventually taken but the massive medieval walls turned out to be much more effective than anyone had expected. The French artillery did massive damage to the Old Town, helping trigger a fire that destroyed most of the city, but the Russians held on to the walls.

During the night of 17-18 August Dokhturov retreated to the New Town and destroyed the bridge over the Dnieper. At about 2am on 18 August the French realised that the Old Town had been deserted and men from I and III Corps rushed into the burning city. A force of Württembergers and Portuguese even managed to wade the Dnieper near the bridge ruins, but Bagration's rearguard was able to pin them down.

Fig 154 Gen. Fisher Charging (Author's Collection)

Early on 18 August most of Bagration's army began to move east to guard the Moscow road against a possible French outflanking manoeuvre. Barclay de Tolly followed late on 18 August, but Bagration had moved very quickly and a dangerous gap developed between the two armies. Luckily for the Russians Napoleon wasted another day on 18 August, and the pursuit didn't really begin until 19 August. Even then there was brief chance that the French could have won a major victory. Bagration had failed to properly guard an important crossroads at Lubino, eighteen miles to the east of Smolensk. When Napoleon realised that the Russians were heading east he sent General Junot east along the south bank of the river with orders to cross at Prudichevo and seize the crossroads. This would prevent Barclay de Tolly from escaping to the east and allow the main army to catch him. Junot did eventually get across the river, but refused to attack. This left Ney and Murat to attack the Russian rearguard at Valuntino, but the Russians held their ground and Barclay de Tolly was able to slip away to the east.

Sobota (27 May 1809)
INFANTRY – 6ᵗʰ Ulan Regiment

Somo Sierra (30 November 1808)
CAVALRY – The Polish Guard Regiment of Light Cavalry (1ˢᵗ Lancers)
Because the Spanish forces were not easily outflanked by infantry movement alone, and Napoleon was impatient to proceed, he ordered his Polish Chevaux-Légers escort squadron of 125 men, plus some other members of the regiment totalling 450 troopers to charge the Spaniards and their fortified artillery batteries. The commander of the third squadron, Jan Kozietulski, supposedly announced, "Lekka jazda kłusem!" ("Light cavalry at the trot!") and, passing the little bridge, added, "En avant, Vive l'Empereur!" (Forward, long live the Emperor!"). The chevaux-légers found themselves under fire from the second battery, so they had no choice but to press the attack as the horses were already moving full tilt forward and were unable to stop. They took the second and third batteries, but only a few chevaux-légers reached the last battery, and the Spanish attempted to recapture it. It was then that Napoleon saw his chance and immediately committed the other squadrons.

The charge was led by Kozietulski, but he lost his horse after taking the first battery. The squadron was then joined by Lt. Andrzej Niegolewski, who had previously been on reconnaissance with his soldiers. The charge was continued under Dziewanowski, and when he fell from the horse after taking the third battery, by Piotr Krasiński. The charge which continued to the last battery was led by Niegolewski, who survived almost by miracle when Spanish attacked him (he received nine wounds from bayonets and two carbine shots to the head). When the fourth battery was taken Napoleon ordered his Chasseurs of the Guard, and 1st squadron of Poles led by Tomasz Łubieński to resume the attack and repulse Spaniards from the Pass.

defense of Soissons (1814)
INFANTRY – Vistula Infantry Regiment, Polish Guard Battalion

Spandau (1812)
INFANTRY – 9ᵗʰ Regiment

Spandau (April 1813)
INFANTRY – 4ᵗʰ Regiment

Strohweide (6 September 1813)
CAVALRY - 14ᵗʰ Cuirassiers, Krakus Regiment

Stublau (14 January 1813)
INFANTRY – 10ᵗʰ Regiment

Studzianka (29 November 1812)
INFANTRY – 3rd Regiment

Sulejów (16 June 1809)
CAVALRY – 7th Ulan Regiment

Szczytno 13 April 1807
CAVALRY – 3rd Ulan Regiment

Talavera (28 July 1809)
INFANTRY – 4th Regiment, 7th Regiment
CAVALRY – Vistula Ulan Regiment

After forcing the French to withdraw from Portugal, an Anglo-Spanish Army attempted push the enemy further into Spain. On the 27th, the French attempted the crossing of the Alberche River, but were attacked and contained by the allied forces. At dawn on the 28th the French attempted to attack the British left wing, but were repulsed. On the other flank an artillery duel combined with cavalry clashes made no further headway although the Vistula Ulans acquitted themselves against the enemy cava;ry. Under the cover of darkness the French forces left the field.

Tarragony (28 June 1811)
INFANTRY - 1st Vistula Legion Regiment

Tarnopol (14 July 1809)
CAVALRY – 3rd Ulan Regiment, 8th Ulan Regiment, 15th Ulan Regiment, 16th Ulan Regiment

Tarutina (4 & 18 October 1812)
INFANTRY - 1st Vistula Legion Regiment, 2nd Vistula Legion Regiment (4 Oct), 3rd Vistula Legion Regiment (4 Oct)
CAVALRY – 8th Ulan Regiment (4 Oct), 9th Ulan Regiment (4 Oct)

Regarding the battle on the 4th, the Polish attack fell on the 48th Jaeger regiment. The infantry tried to form a square with two battalions, but could not form in time and were ridden over. The infantry fought hard, but many fell. In some cases they rose later and fired into the rear of the Polish cavalry before being disbursed.

Tczew (23February 1807)
INFANTRY – 9th Regiment, 11th Regiment, 12th Regiment
CAVALRY – 1st Chasseur Regiment, 5th Chasseur Regiment, 6th Ulan Regiment

The entry of Napoleon into the former Polish territories in Prussia during the 1806-07 campaign raised the hopes of the patriots that Napoleon's armies and the Polish Legions would restore the nation. In response to this there was an uprising in Wielkopolska and Gdańsk Pomerania was encouraged by Dąbrowski. Insurrectionists led by Dąbrowski attempted to capture key locations and supplies to wrest control of these areas from Prussia. On 23 February 1807 there was a general assault on Tczew, which was after several assaults by newly rasied units containing many veterans of the Kościuszko Uprising..

Teruel (10 February 1810)
INFANTRY - 2nd Vistula Legion Regiment

Tłuste (26 June 1812)
CAVALRY - 15th Ulan Regiment

Tokarska (1809)

INFANTRY – 8th Regiment, 14th Regiment

The Austrians were advancing north towards the village Tokary near Płock during the 1809 campaign, when they decided to cross the Vistula to attack Płock. In Płock there was a company of the 8th infantry, some National Guard units and the 14th infantry who hastily drew up defensive works to defend against the Austrian crossing. The Poles repulsed 3,000 enemy infantry accompanies by artillery and force the enemy to withdraw.

Toledo (9 August 1809)

INFANTRY – 4th Regiment, 7th Regiment, 9th Regiment
CAVALRY - Vistula Ułan Regiment

After the Battle of Talavera, General Sebastiani, with 20 000 soldiers, attacked the Spanish army of Gen. Venegas composed of 28 000 soldiers. The decisive battle took place on the right wing of Sebastiani's army where the 7th and 9th regiments of the Duchy of Warsaw attacked a castle on a hill, supported by the 4th, but outnumbered by the defenders. The 7th was surrounded by Spanish cavalry, but managed to escape by fixing bayonets and capturing the objective. The 9th also captured their objective when they were suddenly recalled by an aide of Gen. Sebastiani. At the same time, the Polish lancers, led by Col. Konopka, defeated the Spanish horse and went to the rear of Venegas' army. The Spaniards were then forced to retreat towards the Sierra Morena Mts. The Spaniards lost 2,000 killed and 3,000 prisoners, while the French and the Poles lost 1,500 dead and wounded.

Toledo (9 August 1809)

INFANTRY - 7th INFANTRY

Torre la Carcel (8 February 1810)

INFANTRY - 2nd Vistula Legion Regiment

Tortosa (4 July 1810)

INFANTRY - 2nd Vistula Legion Regiment
CAVALRY – Vistula Ułan Regiment

Torun (15-19 May 1809)

INFANTRY – 10th Regiment, 11th Regiment, 12th Regiment

During the initial stages of the 1809 campaign where the Austrians were stopped at Radzymin and Ostrówki, Archduke Ferdinand decidedto switch to attacking the Polish forces on the left bank of the Wistula, cutting off potential retreat into Saxony and potentially making Poniatowski stop operations in Galicia. Torun was not prepared for a proper defense, but the Governor and Commander was a veteran of the Kościuszko Uprising – Gen. Stanisław Woyczyński. He had approximately, 3,600 men from the reiments, but many of them were new recruits, many without proper uniforms.

Gen. Mohr, commanding the Austrian troops launched a dawn attack with the 48th Infantry. Despite orders, from Gen. Woyczyński, Col. Mielżyński did not withdraw his men into the fortications and was surprised by the enemy. In turn, Col. Brusch did not follow orders to go around the earthworks and tried to attack head-on and was beaten back. Eventually the Polish troops were forced to retreat, but Gen. Woyczyński refused to surrender. Because no heavy guns were brought up the siege could not progress and eventually Archduke Ferdinand ordered the Austrian troops to return to Warsaw.

Tremedal (25 November 1809)

INFANTRY - 2nd Vistula Legion Regiment

Troyes (24 February 1814)

CAVALRY – The Polish Guard Regiment of Light Cavalry (1st Lancers)

Tudela (9 June 1808)
CAVALRY – Vistula Ulan Regiment

Tudela (23 November 1808)
INFANTRY - 2ⁿᵈ Vistula Legion Regiment
CAVALRY – Vistula Ulan Regiment

On the morning of 23 November 1808 Lagrange's infantry and two cavalry brigades were sent towards Cascante. The rest of the force was sent along the Ebro towards Tudela. The initial French attack was carried out in a piecemeal fashion by the vanguard when it was realised that the Spanish were not in position. Although this attack was repelled it showed the weakness of the Spanish positions, especially the three mile gap between Castaños and La Peña's force at Cascante.

By noon on 23 November 1808 they had received orders to move: La Peña to close the gap at Tudela and Grimarest to Cascante. Both men failed to carry out these orders other than La Peña moving two battalions and a detachment of provincial Grenadiers to Urzante. La Peña's lack of initiative allowed the two French cavalry brigades of Colbert and General of Brigade Alexandre, vicomte Digeon to pin him in place. The second French attack was made with much greater force. On the French left General of Division Morlot's division attacked Roca's division on the heights above Tudela. On the French right General of Division Mathieu's division made a frontal assault on the smaller O'Neylle division while also making outflanking moves. The attacks on both left and right were successful with both Spanish divisions being pushed off the ridges they occupied. The French cavalry under General of Division Lefebvre-Desnouettes charged the gap between Roca and Saint-Marcq causing the collapse of the Spanish right.

Tyniec (13 February 1813)
INFANTRY – 2ⁿᵈ Regiment

Tilsit (24 June 1812)
INFANTRY – 5ᵗʰ Regiment, 10th Regiment

Tilsit (28 December 1812)
INFANTRY – 5ᵗʰ Regiment, 10ᵗʰ Regiment
CAVALRY - 17ᵗʰ Ulan Regiment

Venta Nueva (20 January 1810)
INFANTRY – 7ᵗʰ Regiment

Vera (1810)
INFANTRY – 7ᵗʰ Regiment

Usza (21 November 1812)
INFANTRY – 14ᵗʰ Regiment

Utera (15 March 1811)
INFANTRY – 9ᵗʰ Regiment

Utera (3 June 1811)
INFANTRY – 9ᵗʰ Regiment

Vauchamps (14 February 1814)
CAVALRY – The Polish Guard Regiment of Light Cavalry (1ˢᵗ Lancers)

Villastar (12 and 14 February 1810)
INFANTRY - 2nd Vistula Legion Regiment

Villel (16 February 1810)
INFANTRY - 2nd Vistula Legion Regiment

Villeneuve 14 February 1814
CAVALRY – The Polish Guard Regiment of Light Cavalry (1st Lancers)

Vitry (23 March 1814)
CAVALRY – The Polish Guard Regiment of Light Cavalry (1st Lancers)

Wachau (18 and 19 October 1813)
INFANTRY – 3rd Regiment, 12th Regiment
CAVALRY – 1st Chasseur Regiment, 3rd Ułan Regiment, 6th Ułan Regiment, 8th Ułan Regiment, Krakus Regiment

The Russian II Infantry Corps attacked Wachau near Leipzig with support from the Prussian 9th Brigade. The Russians advanced, unaware that French forces were waiting. The French took them by surprise on the flank, mauling them. The Prussians entered Wachau, engaging in street to street fighting. French artillery blasted the Prussians out of Wachau and the French recovered the village.

Wagram (6 July 1809)
CAVALRY – The Polish Guard Regiment of Light Cavalry (1st Lancers)

Walkow (16 November 1812)
INFANTRY – 5th Regiment, 10th Regiment

Walutina Gora (19 August 1812)
CAVALRY - 8th Ułan Regiment

Wały (5 May 1807)
INFANTRY – 1st Regiment, 3rd Regiment

Waterloo (18 June 1815)
CAVALRY – Vistula Ułan Regiment (7th French Cheval Legere), The Polish Guard Regiment of Light Cavalry (1st Lancers)

Weida (4 October 1813)
CAVALRY - 14th Cuirassiers

Wisła (The Vistula)(11 May 1809)
INFANTRY – 1st Regiment

Wiaźma (3 November 1812)
INFANTRY – 2nd Regiment, 15th Regiment
CAVALRY - 9th Ułan Regiment

The battle of Wiaźma or Vyazma involved the rearguard of the Grand Armee and a Russian force under Gen. Miloradovich. The Russians attempted to encircle and destroy Davout's corps, and was thwarted, but still resulted in a defeat for the retreating French and a disruption of their plans. After the southern route to Smolensk was blocked following the Battle of Maloyaroslavets (24 October), the army began to breakdown into large groups of stragglers, at some points more than 60 miles long. Marshal Ney replaced Davout on the 2nd as the commander of the rear guard. They were continually harassed by 5,000 Cossacks under Ataman Platov. Gen. Miloradovich moving from the south, found a gap in the line between Davout, Eugene and Poniatowski's Corps just outside Wiaźma that was an opportunity to destroy the French Corps.

The Russian general sent his cavalry to attack Davout from the west, while Platov attacked from the east, supported by an artillery barrage from the nearby heights. This succeeded in capturing the baggage train, but had not waited for infantry support, so he could not capitalize on the initial surprise. Hearing the cannon fire, two of Eugene's Italian divisions and one of the Polish divisions came Davout's aid. Many of Davout's units took shelter behind Eugene's, but then they came under increasing fire and had to fall back. Because of their precarioust position Davout, Eugene and Poniatowski agreed to fall back to Wiaźma, where they were eventually assisted by Ney's troops. Kutusov was nearby, but attack cautiously, which allowed the bulk of the disorganized forces to slip away as Ney stabilized the line of retreat.

Wiązownia (1 May 1809)
CAVALRY - 5th Chasseur Regiment

After the fighting at Radzymin, Praga and Grochow, the Polish forces crossed the Vistula and started to occupy areas that were formerly part of the Austrian occupation. The Polish forces move into Wiązownia and quickly pushed out Austrian skirmishers

Wielatów (11 May 1809)
CAVALRY – 3rd Ułan Regiment

Wieniawka (17, 20 July 1809)
CAVALRY – 3rd Ułan Regiment, 8th Ułan Regiment, 15th Ułan Regiment

Wilejka (July 1812)
CAVALRY - 9th UŁAN REGIMENT

Wilno (10 December 1812)
INFANTRY – 15th Regiment
CAVALRY – The Polish Guard Regiment of Light Cavalry (1st Lancers)

Winkowo (4 October 1812)
CAVALRY – 6th Ułan Regiment
See Tarutina

Witebsk (26 and 27 July 1812)
CAVALRY - 8th Ułan Regiment

During Napoleon's initial invasion of Russia, he engaged the Russia rearguard at Witebsk (or Vitebsk) undr generals Konovnitsyn and Pahlen. Napoleon attempted to envelope General de Tolly's forces near Witebsk, but the Russian forces fought a delaying action that allowed the bulk of the forces to escape to Smolensk.

Wittenberg (11 August 1813)
INFANTRY – 2nd Regiment

Wittenberg (21 & 27 August 1813)
CAVALRY – 4th Ułan Regiment

Wittenberg (10 October 1813)
INFANTRY – 4ᵗʰ Regiment

Włodawa (6 May 1809)
CAVALRY – 6ᵗʰ Ulan Regiment

Woronowo (2 October 1812)
INFANTRY - 1ˢᵗ Vistula Legion Regiment
CAVALRY - 8ᵗʰ Ulan Regiment

Woronow (18 and 20 October 1812)
INFANTRY – 2ⁿᵈ Regiment, 8ᵗʰ Regiment, 12ᵗʰ Regiment
CAVALRY - 5ᵗʰ Chasseur Regiment (Oct 18), 10ᵗʰ Hussar Regiment (Oct 20), 13ᵗʰ Hussar Regiment (Oct 20)

Wrzawy (12 June 1809)
INFANTRY – 1ˢᵗ Regiment, 2ⁿᵈ Regiment, 6ᵗʰ Regiment, 8ᵗʰ Regiment
CAVALRY – 1ˢᵗ Chasseur Regiment, 2ⁿᵈ Ulan Regiment, 5ᵗʰ Chasseur Regiment
ARTILLERY – Horse Artillery

On 10 June Prince Poniatowski moved a large portion of the troops across the San River into Galicia when he discovered an Austrian division in the area of Wrzawy. Thearea is marshy and cross-crossed with dikes used to prevent the flooding from the Vistula and San. The Prince took up a defensive position in the old course of the San. The right wing was commanded Lt. Col. Obetyński with three infantry companies and two field guns, situated between Wrzawy and Dabrowa. The left wing was underthe command of Lt. Col. Dainena with two companies and a rearguard of five companies near the bridge. The center was commanded by Col. Malachowski with nine companies and one gun. The Austrians made several attacks along the causeway defended by the Polish grenadiers who fought with bayonets to force them back. The Austrians attempted to make a flanking attack through the villages on the left flank with a few squadrons of cavalry and artillery. Prince Poniatowski personally led the 2nd Ułans to counter-attack and stopped the enemy drive. At the same time Lt. Col. Obertyński repulsed an attack of Austrian infantry and Cuirassiers with the help of Gen Rożniecki's cavalry. The Austrian's had to pause at this stage late in the afternoon due to lack of ammunition. The Poles lost about 100 men, the Austrian's 200, but both sides claimed victory. The Austrians were able to keep Polish forces from operations south of the San and they were forced to withdraw.

Ximenes de a Frontera (25 September 1811)
INFANTRY – 4ᵗʰ Regiment

Yevenes (24 March 1809)
CAVALRY – The Vistula Ulan Regiment

At Yébenes, the Vistula ułan regiment clashed with multiple regiments of Spanish cavalry. Gen. Valance's Polish Division left Toledo on 20 March and were supposed to bivouac in Orgaz, but the lancers chose to stay in Los Yébenes, even though it was more difficult to potentially defend. The 591 men were quartered throughout the village, while fifth company was deployed in the center of the village. During the night and with the fog of the morning, the New Army of LaMancha had moved into position to attack the regiment. The Spanish had several ranks of cavalry, plus two batteries of horse artillery. Surprised, the Poles quickly ordered a retreat. As the squadrons left, the 5th company formed the rearguard. Col Konopka then encountered the Royal Carabineer Regiment, who he promptly charged. The lancers took the Spanish cavalry by surprise and pushed them back. The command made it past the road into the open fields and prepared a defensive line. Finally, they made their way to Mora, but had suffered significant losses. More than men, the regiment had also lost all their baggage train and the banners which Joséphine de Beauharnais had given them as a gift when they were in Italy in 1802.

Zaleszczyki (18 April 1809)
CAVALRY – 3rd Ułan Regiment

Zaleszczyki (12, 15 and 18 June 1812)
CAVALRY - 15th Ułan Regiment, 16th Ułan Regiment

Zamość (15 - 20 May 1809)
INFANTRY – 2nd Regiment, 3rd Regiment, 6th Regiment, 12th Regiment
CAVALRY – 3rd Ułan Regiment, 6th Ułan Regiemnt
ARTILLERY – Horse Artillery
    The Poles under General Pelletier with 2,500 men captured Zamość on 20 May 1809 defended by 2,500 Austro-Hungarians under the command of Gen. Pulski.

Zamość (1813)
INFANTRY – 3rd Regiment, 6th Regiment, 13th Regiment, 17th Regiment
CAVALRY – 3rd Ułan Regiment
    The siege of Zamość occurred 2 October to 22 December 1813 pitting 4,500 Poles under Hauke against 7,000 Russians under von Radt

Zanne (26 August 1813)
CAVALRY - 4th Ułan Regiment

Zatory (9 May 1807)
CAVALRY – 2nd Ułan Regiment

Zawady (16 May 1809)
CAVALRY – 3rd Ułan Regiment

Zawadzka (1809)
INFANTRY – 14th Regiment

Żarnowiec (11 July 1809)
INFANTRY – 5th Regiment, 10th Regiment

Fig 155 The Battle of Smolensk (W. Kossak)

Fig 156 The Battle at Tczew (W. Kossak)

Zeestadt (10 December 1813)
CAVALRY - 17th Ulan Regiment

Zehma (4 October 1813)
CAVALRY – 6th Ulan Regiment, Krakus Regiment

Zetlitz (9 October 1813)
CAVALRY – Krakus Regiment

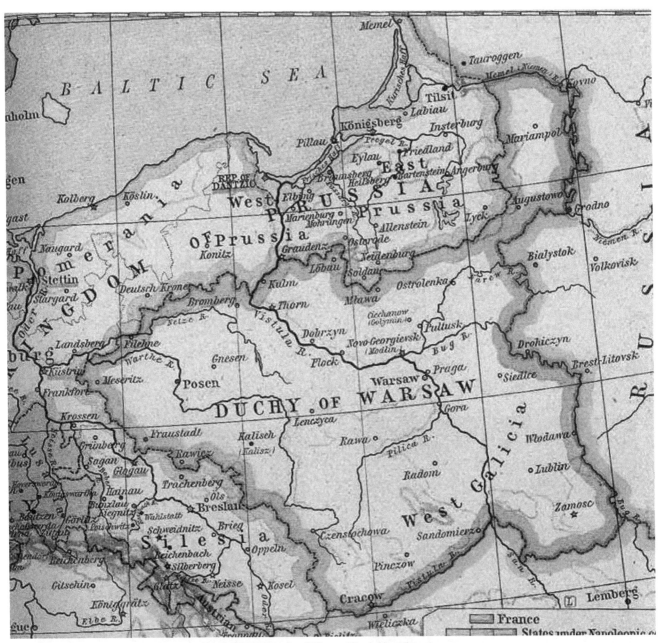

Fig 157 The Duchy of Warsaw (Cambridge History)

Chronology of the Polish Legions

1795
The Third Partition of Poland

1796

December	Gen. Dąbrowski arrives in Milan with the objective of forming a corps from Polish emigres

1797

9 January	Convention of San Marco signed with Gen. Bonaparte officially creates a Polish auxilary corps for the Cisalpine Republic
March	Legion garrisons Mantua and fights at Brescia
April	Legion used to suppress Verona uprising
July	Denisko crosses the Dneister into Galicia
18 October	Treaty of Campo Formio ends fighting with Austria

1798

April	Legions were designated, "1st and 2nd demi-brigades"
May	Legion occupies Rome
December	Legion fights in the Kingdom of Naples

1799

5 April	Battle of Magnano – Gen. Rymkiewicz killed
April – July	Seige of Mantua, Gen. Wielhorski and Polish soldiers turned over to the Austrians
17-19 June	Battle of Trebbia, Dąbrowski wounded

1800

January	Formation of the Danube Legion
25 December	Start of the siege of Peschiera

1801

9 February	Treaty of Luneville creates the short peace with Austria
21 December	The Legions were reorganized by the French into three French demi-brigades

1802

25 March	Peace of Amiens creates the only peace of the Napoleonic Wars
July	The first demi-brigade is sent to Haiti
December	The second demi-brigade is sent to Haiti

1805

Polish troops in Italy renamed "The Polish Legion" and attached to the Kingdom of Italy

1806

Legions attached to the Kingdom of Naples

1807

February	Legions renamed "Polish-Italian legion" in Silesia

1808

31 March	Legions renamed the Vistula Legion
	Vistula Legion sent to Spain

1812

	Vistula Legion sent to Poland for invasion of Russia
June	Invasion of Russia begins

1813

January	The Vistula Regiments are reformed from the 4th Vistula Legion
15-19 October	The Battle of Leipzig

1814

January	The Vistula Legion is reorganized again at Sedan
April	The Legions are disbanded

Fig 158 The Poles at Sammosierra (Vernet, Brown University Collection)

Chronology of Military Operations for the Polish-Austrian War of 1809

APRIL

14	The Austrians cross the Duchy's borders along the Pilica River
15	The first skirmish at Mogielnica
17	A skirmish at Coniew
19	The battle of Raszyn (the Poles and Saxons beat back an Austrian attack, then initiate a tactical withdrawal)
21	Both sides agree to a 48-hour truce for the Polish Army to evacuate Warsaw
23	The Austrians occupy Warsaw and Poniatowski moves his HQ to Zegrze
25	The battle of Grochow (Polish victory)
27	The battle of Radzymin (Polish victory)

MAY

5	Skirmish at Kock (death of Joselewicz)
10	Siege of Płock by the Austrians
14	Polish forces move toward Lublin
15	The siege of Toruń (eventually broken off by the Austrians)
18	Sandomierz captured by Polish forces
20	Zamość captured by Polish forces
21	Austrians are repulsed in a skirmish near Wilanow
26	Austrians attempt to cross the Vistula near Żerań, but are pushed back by Polish forces
27	Lwow is captured by Polish forces

JUNE

2	Prince Poniatowski is appointed to head the Provisional Government by the Military Council for Lithuania and Galicia
2-3	Austrians abandon Warsaw, Gen. Krasicki defends Sanok against Austrian forces
11	The battle of Jedliński
12	The battle of Gorzycami (Wrzawami) both sides fight to a stand-off
18	The battle of Zaleszczyce
18	Archduke Ferdinand attacks Sandomierz

JULY

1	The battle of Jeiorna (Franco-Galician units defeat Austria)
3	The battleof Zagrobla (Franco-Galician units defeat Austria)
5	Prince Poniatowski begins offensive operations south of Radom
11	Franco-Austrian truce goes in effect
14	Gen Rożnecki almost clashes with Austrian/Russian troops in Krakow
15	Prince Poniatowski continues operations around Krakow
16	The battle of Chmielówka under the leadership of Franco-Galician units commanded by Peter Strzyżewski.

OCTOBER

14	The Treaty of Schonbrunn provides increased territory for the Duchy of Warsaw, with the exclusion of the liberated territories west of Lwow.

Chronology of 1812

JUNE
28   The Grand Armée, led by Polish Cavalry, crosses the Neman River into Russia

AUGUST
17   The Battle of Smolensk resulting in an allied victory
19   The Battle of Valutino resulting in an allied victory

SEPTEMBER
7   The Battle of Borodino results in an allied victory
14   Napoleon enters Moscow

OCTOBER
19   Napoleon retreats to Smolensk
24   Allied forces are defeated at Maloyaroslavets

NOVEMBER
16-17   Allied forces are defeated in a two day battle at Krasnoi
26-28   The Grand Armée crossed the Berezina

DECEMBER
14   The remnants of the Grand Armée reach Wilno

LIST OF ILLUSTRATIONS

Origins of the Polish Legions – Jan Henryk Dąbrowski – Commander of the Polish Legion in Italy (Julian Kossak, author's collection) p.6

Fig. 1 Northern Italy during the initial operations of the Polish Legions 1797 – 1800, p8

Fig. 2 Gen. Dąbrowski's Polish Legion uniform (Polish Army Museum), p9

Fig 3 Grenadier in the Polish Legion in Italy 1796 (New York Public Library), p.11

Fig 4 Fusilier in the Polish Legion in Italy 1796 (New York Public Library), p.11

Fig 5 Danube Legion in 1800 by Knötel. Fusilier, Grenadier, Hussar, Horse Artillery in jacket, Ułan, Horse Artillery in dolman (Author's Collection), p.12

Fig 6 Operations in Haiti 1802-1804 (Wikipedia), p.14

Fig 7. Poles in San Domingo (January Suchodolski), p.15

Fig 8 Dąbrowski in Italy 1800 (Walski, Brown University Collection), p.17

Fig 9 The Siege of Danzig 1807 (Lorenz, Brown University Collection), p.19

Fig 10 Polish infantry of the Lombard Legion 1796 (Walski, Brown University Collection), p.20

Fig 11 The 1st Legion – I, II, III Battalions 1797 (Walski, Brown University Collection), p.20

Fig 12 Legion Cavalry Officer 1799 (JOB, Author's Collection), p.22

Fig 13 Polish Infantry 1799 (Maciej Szcezpamczyk, Wikipedia), p.22

Fig 14 Danube Legion Chasseur (author collection), p.23

Fig 15 Danube Legion Grenadier (author Collection), p.23

Fig 16 Polish Legionnaire in summer dress in Haiti, p.24

Fig 17 Officer of the 114 demi-brigade in San Domingo by an English officer, p.24

Fig 18 Legion Cavalry, Grenadier and Artillery 1800 (Walski, Brown University Collection), p.27

Fig 19 Legion Cavalry of the Lombard Cavalry (Gembarzewski, Author Collection), p.27

Fig 20 Artilleryman of the Legion 1800 (Walski, Brown University Collection), p.29

Fig 21 Flag of the Legion Artillery 1800 (Polish Army Museum, Author's Collection), p.29

Fig 22 114th Demi-brigade 1802 (Walski, Brown University Collection), p.31

Fig 23 Banner of the Legion Infantry 1801 (Polish Army Museum), p.31

Fig 24 Flag of the Kingdom supposedly sewn by the wife of Gen Dąbrowski in 1807 (Polish Army Museum), p.34

Fig 25 The Coat of Arms of the Duchy of Warsaw (Steifer, Wikipedia), p.35

Fig 26 Infantry of the Duchy 1807 Voltigeur and Fusilier (Author's Collection), p.36

Fig 27 General de Brigade 1809 (Bronisław Gembarzewski, Brown University Collection), p.36

Fig 28 Operations around Warsaw 1809, p.37

Fig 29 Duchy of Warsaw 1807 – 1813 (Author's Collection), p.42

Fig 30 Poniatowski's Guides 1809 (Chełminski, Author's Collection), p.43

Fig 31 13th Regiment Grenadier (Gembarzewski, Author's Collection), p.43

Fig 32 Aide to General du Division (Gembarzewski, Brown University Collection), p.44

Fig 33 Grenadiers of the Gdańsk Free State (Knötel, Author's Collection), p.44

Fig 34 Poniatowski at Raszyn (Juliusz Kossack, Author's Collection), p.45

Fig 35 Stanisław Mielżyński battles the Austrians at Torun (Wojcieck Kossack, Author's Collection), p.45

Fig 36 Polish Ułan attacks an Austrian Cheval Leger in 1809 (Marinet, Brown University Collection), p.46

Fig 37 An example of an eagle used with Polish regimental standards (Polish Army Museum), p.47

Fig 38 Official version of the czapka plate – 1st regiment infantry, p.47

Fig 39 The Polish courier (Finart, Brown University Collection), p.48

Fig 40 2nd Infantry NCO's czapka of a fusilier company (Polish Army Museum), p.50

Fig 41 3rd Infantry czapka for a drummer (Polish Army Museum), p.50

Fig 42 An officer's Uniform from 1810 (Polish Army Museum), p.51

Fig 43 Fusiliers and NCO's of the 2nd Infantry (Chełminski, Author's Collection), p.51

Fig 44 Drum Major and Drummer of the 2nd Infantry /Grenadier and Officer of the 5th Infantry in 1808 (Knötel, Author's Collection), p.51

Fig 45 Czapka of the 4th Infantry voltigeurs 1807-1808 (Polish Army Museum), p.51

Fig 46 Drummer of the 4th Infantry (Author's Collection), p.52

Fig 47 Voltigeur 4th Infantry / Grenadier 17th Infantry 1809 (Knötel, Author's Collection), p.52

Fig 48 5th Infantry Fusilier 1812 (Author's Collection), p.52

Fig 49 5th Infantry Grenadiers (Chełminski, Author's Collection), p.52

Fig 50 Drummer 13th, Drum Major 1st, National Guard Drummer, 4th Drummer Infantry (Chełminski, Author's Collection), p.53

Fig 51 Infantry officers – Voltigeurs, Grenadiers and Fusiliers 1812 (Gembarzewski, Author's Collection), p.53

Fig 52 8th Infantry in attack (Chełminski, Author's Collection), p.53

Fig 53 10th Infantry, voltigeurs (Brown University Collection), p.53

Fig 54 11th Infantry NCO czapka 1808-1814 (Polish Army Museum), p.54

Fig 55 Infantry colorguard (Gembarzewski, Author's Collection), p.54

Fig 56 Voltigeur trumpeter (Gembarzewski, Author's Collection), p.54
Fig 57 Voltigeurs and grenadiers (Gembarzewski, Author's collection), p.54
Fig 58 Foot artillery in action (Chełminski, Author's Collection), p.55
Fig 59 Officer and cannonier in 1807 (Gembarzewski), p.55
Fig 60 Field artillery in action 1812 (Gembarzewski), p.55
Fig 61 Field artillery in summer dress 1812 (Gembarzewski), p.55
Fig 62 Sappers (Gembarzewski), p.56
Fig 63 Engineer and officer (Chełminski, Author's Collection), p.56
Fig 64 Jewish National Guard of Warsaw (Brown University Collection), p.57
Fig 65 Officer's uniform Lublin National Guard (Polish Army Museum), p.57
Fig 66 National Guard of Warsaw (Chełminski), p.57
Fig 67 Wilno National Guard cap plate, p.57
Fig 68 Line voltigeurs, Veteran and Krakow National Guard in 1812 (Knötel, Author's Collection), p.58
Fig 69 Veteran (Gembarzewski, Author's Collection), p.58
Fig 70 1st Legion cavalry in 1807 – NCO, Horse Artillery, Trooper and Trumpeter (Knötel, Author's Collection), p.59
Fig 71 Cuirassier uniform 1809 – 1812 (Polish Army Museum), p.60
Fig 72 14th Cuirassier in 1812 (Author's Collection), p.60
Fig 73 14th Cuirassier in 1812 (Gembarzewski, Author's Collection), p.60
Fig 74 Cuirassier trumpeter (Chełminski, Author's Collection), p.60
Fig 75 1st Chasseurs (Gembarzewski, Author's Collection), p.61
Fig 76 1st Chasseurs Elite Company 1812 (Author's Collection), p.61
Fig 77 1st Chasseurs 1810-1812 – Trumpeter, Officer, Trooper and Elite (Gabrys, Author's Collection), p.62
Fig 78 4th Chasseurs 1810-1812 – Officer, Trumpeter, Elite and Trooprt (Gabrys, Author's Collection), p.62
Fig 79 4th Chasseurs 1809-1814 Officer's jacket (Polish Army Museum), p.63
Fig 80 5th Chasseurs 1810-1814 Officer's jacket (Polish Army Museum), p.63
Fig 81 4th Chasseurs (Chełminski, Author's Collection), p.63
Fig 82 5th Chasseurs (Chełminski, Author's Collection), p.63
Fig 83 5th Chasseurs 1810-1812 – Elite, Trooper, Trumpeter, Officer (Gabrys, Author's Collection), p.64
Fig 84 5th Chasseurs – Trumpeter, Officer, Trooper (Knötel, Author's Collection), p.64
Fig 85 10th Hussars – Elite, Trooper, Trumpeter, Officer (Gabrys, Author's Collection), p.66
Fig 86 10th Hussars (Gembarzewski, Author's Collection), p.66
Fig 87 Trumpeter 13th Hussars (Chełminski, Author's Collection), p.66
Fig 88 2nd Ułans - Trumpeter, Officer, Trooper and Elite (Gabrys, Author's Collection), p.68
Fig 90 2nd Ułans – Trumpeters (Chełminski, Author's Collection), p.68
Fig 91 3rd Ułans – Trooper (Chełminski, Author's Collection), p.68
Fig 92 3rd Ułans - Elite, Trooper, Trumpeter and Officer (Gabrys, Author's Collection), p.69
Fig 93 6th Officer, 7th Trumpeter, 6th Trooper and 7th Trooper Ułans (Gabrys, Author's Collection), p.69
Fig 94 7th Ułan officer with a regimental adjutant (Chełminski, Author's Collection), p.70
Fig 95 8th Ułan (Gembarzewski, Author's Collection), p.70
Fig 96 8th Ułans – Trooper, Elite, Trumpeter and Officer 1810-1812 (Gabrys, Author's Collection), p.70
Fig 97 8th Ułan uniform jacket and czapka (Polish Army Museum), p.71
Fig 98 8th Ułan trooper (Author's Collection), p.71
Fig 99 9th Ułan Elite, Trooper, Trumpeter, Officer 1810-1812 (Gabrys, Author's Collection), p.71
Fig 100 11th Ułan in winter dress (Chełminski, Author's Collection), p.72
Fig 101 17th Ułan jacket and czapka (Polish Army Museum), p.72
Fig 102 Elite Ułan company (Gembarzewski, Author's Collection), p.72
Fig 103 The Horse Artillery in action at Raszyn (Wojciech Kossack, 1913), p.73
Fig 104 Horse Artillery officer's uniform 1809-1812 (Polish Army Museum), p.74
Fig 105 Horse Artillery trumpeter 1809 (Chełminski, Author's Collection), p.74
Fig 106 Horse Artillery in action 1812 (Gembarzewski, Author's Collection), p.74
Fig 107 Gendarmes and Train Drivers (Chełminski, Author's Collection), p.75
Fig. 108 Vistula Legion in 1810 (Bellange, Author's Collection), p.80
Fig 109 Vistula Legion in Spain (JOB, Author's Collection), p.80
Fig 110 Vistula Legion cap plate (Polish Army Museum), p.80
Fig 111 8th Cheval Leger (Knötel, Author's Collection), p.80
Fig 112 7th Vistula Lancers (Chełminski, Author's Collection), p.81
Fig 113 8th Cheval Leger (Chełminski, Author's Collection), p.81
Fig 114 9th Cheval Leger 1813-14 (Knötel, Author's Collection), p.81
Fig 115 8th Cheval Leger (Knötel, Author's Collection), p.81
Fig 116 Lithuanian Tartars of the Guard 1813-1814 (Knötel, Author's Collection), p.84

Fig 117 Trumpeter of the Guard Lancers 1807 -1810 (Jeziorkowski, Author's Collection), p.84

Fig 118 Guard Light Cavalry 1807 (Frey, Brown University Collection), p.84

Fig 119 Guard Lancer trumpeter 1812 (Knötel, Author's Collection), p.84

Fig 120 Guard Lancer Officer 1812 (Frey, Brown University Collection), p.85

Fig 121 Guard Lancer 1812 (Knötel, Author's Collection), p.85

Fig 122 1st Guard Lancers (Vernet, Brown University Collection), p.85

Fig 123 1st Guard Lancers in summer full dress (Frey, Brown University Collection), p.86

Fig 124 The Krakus Regiment (Chełminski, Author's Collection), p.92

Fig 125 The Krakus Regiment (Gembarzewski, Author's Collection), p.92

Fig 126 Kurtka of the Polish Ułan regiment in 1814 (Polish Army Museum), p.92

Fig 127 Cap plates from the period 1812-1814, Lithuanian and Polish motifs (Polish Army Museum), p.92

Fig 128 French 4-lb gun (Wikipedia), p.96

Fig 129 French model of a 6-lb gun (Perry Miniatures), p.96

Fig 130 6" howitzer (Wikipedia), p.97

Fig 131 12-lb French gun (wikipedia), p.97

Fig 132 Muskets in use by the Polish infantry during this period from the top – Russian 1808, Austrian 1784 and English 1794 models (Polish Army Museum), p.97

Fig 133 French muskets from the period – cavalry carbine, dragoon musket and infantry musket model 1777 (Polish Army Museum), p.97

Fig 134 Ranks, p.98

Fig 135 Virtuti Militari (Polish Army Museum), p.98

Fig 136 Gen Axamitowski in the uniform of the Legion artillery 1800 (Walski, Brown University Collection), p.100

Fig 137 Gen Józef Chłopicki (Author's collection), p.101

Fig 138 Gen Jan Henryk Dąbrowski in the uniform of a Polish General 1812 (Polish Army Museum), p.102

Fig 139 Gen. Stanisław Fisher (Polish Army Museum), p.104

Fig 140 King Federic Augustus I (Dresden Galerie Neue), p.104

Fig 141 Maurycy Hauke (Artist unknown), p.105

Fig 142 Władysław Franciszek Jabłonski (Artist unknown), p.105

Fig 143 Berek Joselewicz (Julius Kossak), p.105

Fig 144 Karol Kniaziewicz (Polish Army Museum), p.106

Fig 145 Tadeusz Kościuszko (Karl Schweikart, National Museum of Warsaw), p.109

Fig 146 Prince Józef Poniatowski (Józef Grassi), p.108

Fig 147 Michaeł Sokolnicki (Józef Sonntag), p.109

Fig 148 Józef Wielhorski (Polish Army Museum), p.110

Fig 149 Józef Wybicki (Author's Collection), p.110

Fig 150 Józef Zajączek (Polish Army Museum), p.110

Fig 151 Polish Lancer in the countryside (Julisz Kossak, Author's Collection), p.133

Fig 152 Vistula Lancers in Spain (Julisz Kossak, Author's Collection), p.133

Fig. 153 The Death of Poniatowski at Leipzig (January Suchodolski), p.142

Fig 154 Gen. Fisher Charging (Author's Collection), p.153

Fig 155 The Battle of Smolensk (W. Kossak), p.161

Fig 156 The Battle at Tczew (W. Kossak), p.161

Fig 157 The Duchy of Warsaw (Cambridge History), p.162

Fig 158 The Poles at Sammosierra (Vernet, Brown University Collection), p.164

BIBLIOGRAPHY

Bowden, Scotty & Charlie Tarbox. *Armies of the Danube 1809*. Empire Games Press: Arlington 1980

Von Brandt, Heinrich. *In the Legions of Napoleon: The Memoirs of a Polish Officer in Spain and Russia 1808 – 1813*. Translated and edited by Jonathan North. Stackpole Books: Mechanicsburg. 1999

Chandler, David G. (Editor). *Dictionary of the Napoleonic Wars*. Macmillan Publishing Co: New York. 1979

Chełmiński, J. *l'Armeé du Duché de Varsovie*. Paris 1913

Chlapowski, Dezydery, translated by Tim Simmons. *Memoirs of a Polish Lancer*. Emperor's Press: Chicago. 1992

Chodzko, Leonard. *Histoire Des Légions Polonaises enItalie, sous Le Commandement du GénéralDombrowski*, Volumes 1-2.Publié Par J. Barbezat: Geneve. 1829

Rickard, J (24 March 2012, Battle of Ostrovno, 25-26 July 1812), http://www.historyofwar.org/articles/battles_ostrovno.html

Elting, Col. John R. *Napoleonic Uniforms Vol I*. Macmillan Publishing Co: New York. 1993

Elting, Col. John R. *Napoleonic Uniforms Vol II*. Macmillan Publishing Co: New York. 1993

Elting, Col. John R. *Napoleonic Uniforms Vol IV*. Emperor's Press: Rosemont. 2000

Gembarzewski, Bronisław. *Wojsko Polskie: Księstwo Warszawskie 1807 – 1814*. Gebethner & Wolff: Warszawa. 1905

Gill, John H. *Thunder on the Danube: Napoleon's Defeat of the Hapsburgs. Vol. III Wagram and Znaim*. Frontline Books: London 2010

Haythornthwaite, Philip J. *The Napoleonic Source Book*. Facts On File: New York 1990

Humbert, René & Lienhart Le Docteur. *Les Uniformes de l'Armée Française Recueil D'Ordonnances de 1690 á 1894*. Leipzig: Libraire M. Ruhl 1898

Hughes, Major-General B.P. *Firepower: Weapons Effectiveness on the Battlefield, 1630-1850*. Sarpedon: New York. 1997

Kannik, Preben. *Military Uniforms of the World in Color*. Macmillan Publishing Co: New York. 1974

Morawski, Ryszard and Dusiewicz, Andrzej. *Wojsko Polskie w Służbie Napoleona: Legiony Polskie we Włoszech*. Karabela: Warszawa. 2010

Morawski, Ryszard and Wielecki, Henryk, *Wojsko Księstwa Warszawskiego: Kawaleria*. Wydawnictwo Bellona: Warsaw. 2000

http://www.napolun.com/mirror/napoleonistyka.atspace.com/polish_army_2.htm

Ryszard Morawski and Sławomir Leśniewski. *Wojsko Polski w Służbie Napoleona: Legia Nadwiślańska , Lansjerzy Nadwiślańscy*. Karabella: Warszawa. 2008

Nafziger, George. *Napoleon's Invasion of Russia.* Presidio Press: Novato 1988

Nafziger, George; Wesolowski, Mariuz T.And Devoe, Tom.*Poles and Saxons of the Napoleonic Wars*. Emperor's Press: Chicago. 1991

Over, Keith. *Flags and Standards of the Napoleonic Wars.* Bivouac Books Ltd: London 1976

Pachoński, Jan. *Generał Jan Henryk Dąbrowski 1755-1818*. Warszawa: Wydawnictwo Ministeria Obrony Narodowej. 1981

Pachoński, Jan. *Legiony Polskie: PrawdaiLegenda 1794 – 1807 – Tom I, Działalność Niepodległościowai Zaczątki Legionów 1794 – 1797*. WydawnictwoMinisterstwaObronyNarodowej: Warszawa 1969

Pachoński, Jan. *Legiony Polskie: PrawdaiLegenda 1794 – 1807 – Tom IV, Z Ziemi Włoskiej Do Polski 1800 - 1807*. WydawnictwoMinisterstwaObronyNarodowej: Warszawa 1969

http://pl.wikipedia.org/wiki/Wojna_polsko-austriacka

Previato, Luciano. *Le legion polacche in italia 1797 – 1806.* Giorgio Migliavacca: Pavia 1980

Reddaway, W. F.; Penson, J.H. ;Halecki, Oscar; Dyboski, R. Editors. *The Cambridge History of Poland: From Augustus II to Pilsudski (1697 – 1935)*. Cambridge University Press: London 1941

Riehn, Richard K. *The French Imperial Army: The Campaigns of 1813-1814 and Waterloo*. New York: Imrie/ Risley 1972

Skowronek, Jerzy. *Książę Józef Poniatowski.* Wrocław: Zakład Narodowy imienia Ossolińskich – Wydawnictwo. 1984

Smith, Neil. *A Desperate Struggle for Survival.***Wargames Illustrated**. Issue 293. March 2012

Smoliński, Aleksander. *Mundur i Barwy: Artylerii Polskiej w XVIII i XIX wieku*. Wydawnictwo Naukowe Uniwersytetu Mikołaja Kopernika: Torun 2010

Von Pivka, Otto. *Napoleon's Polish Troops*. Hippocrane Books: New York 1974

INDEX

1809 Campaign, 35-38
1812 Campaign, 89-90
1813 Campaign, 94
1814 Campaign, 95
Axamitowski, Wincenty, 19, 29, 31, 100, 117
Cavalry Regiments
    1st, 40, 61-62
    2nd, 40, 68
    3rd, 40, 68-69
    4th, 41, 62-63
    5th, 41, 63
    6th, 41, 69
    7th, 44, 69-70
    8th, 45, 70-71
    9th, 45, 71
    9th Cheval Legers, 81, 90
    10th, 45, 65-66
    11th, 45, 72
    12th, 46
    13th, 46, 66
    14th, 45-46, 59-60
    15th, 46
    16th, 46
    17th, 72, 89
    18th, 90
    19th, 90
    20th, 90
    21st, 90
    Guides, 43-44, 59
    Krakus, 90-92
Chłopicki, Józef, 28, 30, 32, 77, 102
Danube Legion, 23, 26
Dąbrowski, Jan Henryk, 9, 11, 13, 17-19, 27, 30, 35, 38, 49, 88, 94, 102, 111, 113, 117, 119, 127, 133, 138, 141, 156,
Denisko, Joachim, 7, 103
Duchy of Warsaw, 34-37, 89, 120
Engineers, 56
Fisher, Stanisław, 104, 154
Foot Artillery, 41, 55
Grabinski, Józef, 10, 31-32, 104
Guard Infantry, 82-83
Guard Lancers, 82-86
Haiti Expedition, 13-17, 24
Horse Artillery, 41, 73-74, 94-95

Infantry Regiments
    1st, 38
    2nd, 38, 50, 51
    3rd, 38, 50
    4th, 38, 48-49, 51-52
    5th, 39, 52, 88
    6th, 39
    7th, 39, 48-49
    8th, 39, 52
    9th, 39, 48-49
    10th, 39, 52, 88
    11th, 40, 88, 154
    12th, 40
    13th, 42-43, 52
    14th, 43
    15th, 43
    16th, 44
    17th, 44, 50, 52
    18th, 89
    19th, 89
    20th, 89
    21th, 89
    22nd, 89
    Veteran Units, 58
Jabłonowski, Władysław, 13, 31, 106
Joselewicz, Berek, 106, 138
Kniaziewicz, Karol, 7, 10, 12, 28, 31, 107, 115
Konopka, Jan, 107, 128, 157, 161
Kościuszko, Thaddeus, 7, 10, 108
Kosinski, Amilkar, 18, 19, 108
Krasinski, Wincenty, 109
Legion of the North 18-19, 25
Lithuanian Infantry, 91-92
Lithuanian-Tartar Cavalry, 82-84
Lombardy Legion, 12, 23, 26
National Guard, 57
Pelletier, Jean, 35, 109
Polish-Italian Legion, 25, 26-29, 32
Polish Legion, 30-31
Poniatowski, Józef, 18, 35-38, 49, 109, 134, 136, 141, 149, 153-4, 161
Rożniecki, Alexander, 18, 109, 144
Rymkiewicz, Franciszek, 10, 109
Sokolnicki, Michael, 109, 136, 151
Strzyżewski, Piotr, 36, 110
Vistula Ułans, 78-80

Vistula Legion, 76-81
Wielhorski, Józef, 10, 110, 117
Wybicki, Józef, 111
Zajączek, Józef, 32, 34, 38, 112

Look for more books from Winged Hussar Publishing, LLC – E-books, paperbacks and Limited Edition hardcovers. The best in history, science fiction and fantasy at:

https://wingedhussarpublishing.com

or follow us on Facebook at:

Winged Hussar Publishing LLC

Or on twitter at:

WingHusPubLLC

For information and upcoming publications

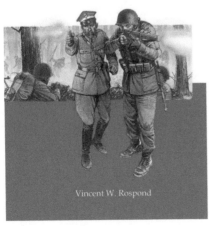

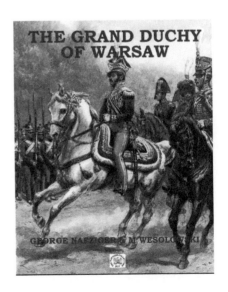

About the author

Vincent W. Rospond received his MA in history from the University of Illinois. He has written and edited many books on military history; specializing in Eastern Europe. His works includes books and articles on the Polish armies of the 18th, 19th and 20th centuries. Mr. Rospond has also written speculative fiction and SF&F for Zmok Books.

Printed in the USA